HELLBOY™

MASKS *and* MONSTERS

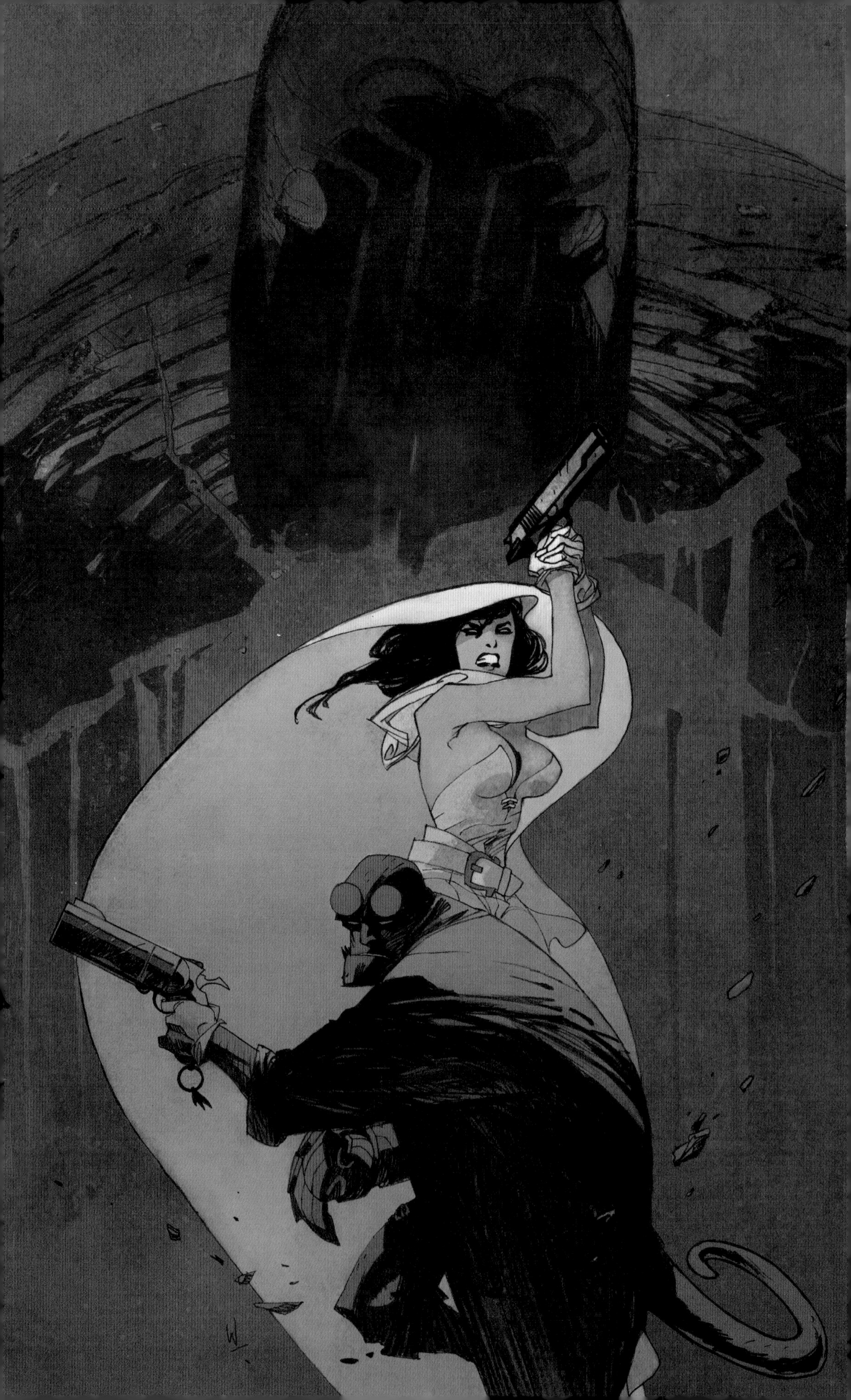

MASKS *and* MONSTERS

by

MIKE MIGNOLA

JAMES ROBINSON

SCOTT BENEFIEL

JASEN RODRIGUEZ

Colored by
MATT HOLLINGSWORTH & PAMELA RAMBO

Lettered by
WILLIE SCHUBERT & SEAN KONOT

Cover art by
MIKE MIGNOLA & DAVE STEWART

Hellboy logo designed by
KEVIN NOWLAN

Original series edited by
SCOTT ALLIE & PETER TOMASI

Collection edited by
SAMANTHA ROBERTSON

Collection designed by
MIKE MIGNOLA, CARY GRAZZINI & AMY ARENDTS

Facing page by
CLAIRE WENDLING for the French edition of *Ghost / Hellboy*

Publisher
MIKE RICHARDSON

DARK HORSE BOOKS®

"Batman / Hellboy / Starman" written by JAMES ROBINSON, *drawn by* MIKE MIGNOLA, colored by MATT HOLLINGSWORTH, *lettered by* WILLIE SCHUBERT.

"Ghost / Hellboy" written and laid out by MIKE MIGNOLA, *penciled by* SCOTT BENEFIEL, *inked by* JASEN RODRIGUEZ, colored by PAMELA RAMBO, *lettered by* SEAN KONOT.

Special thanks to Scott Allie, Thierry Mornet, and Glen Murakami.

NEIL HANKERSON ✠ *Executive Vice President*

TOM WEDDLE ✠ *Chief Financial Officer*

RANDY STRADLEY ✠ *Vice President of Publishing*

MICHAEL MARTENS ✠ *Vice President of Business Development*

ANITA NELSON ✠ *Vice President of Business Affairs*

MICHA HERSHMAN ✠ *Vice President of Marketing*

DAVID SCROGGY ✠ *Vice President of Product Development*

DALE LaFOUNTAIN ✠ *Vice President of Information Technology*

DARLENE VOGEL ✠ *Director of Purchasing*

KEN LIZZI ✠ *General Counsel*

DAVEY ESTRADA ✠ *Editorial Director*

SCOTT ALLIE ✠ *Senior Managing Editor*

CHRIS WARNER ✠ *Senior Books Editor*

DIANA SCHUTZ ✠ *Executive Editor*

CARY GRAZZINI ✠ *Director of Design and Production*

LIA RIBACCHI ✠ *Art Director*

CARA NIECE ✠ *Director of Scheduling*

Published by
Dark Horse Books
A division of Dark Horse Comics, Inc.
10956 SE Main Street
Milwaukie, OR 97222

First Edition
October 2010
ISBN 978-1-59582-567-4

This volume collects *Batman / Hellboy / Starman* #1–#2, originally published by DC Comics, and *Ghost / Hellboy*, originally published by Dark Horse Comics.

1 3 5 7 9 10 8 6 4 2

Printed at Midas Printing International, Ltd., Huizhou, China

For Archie Goodwin

BATMAN|HELLBOY|STARMAN

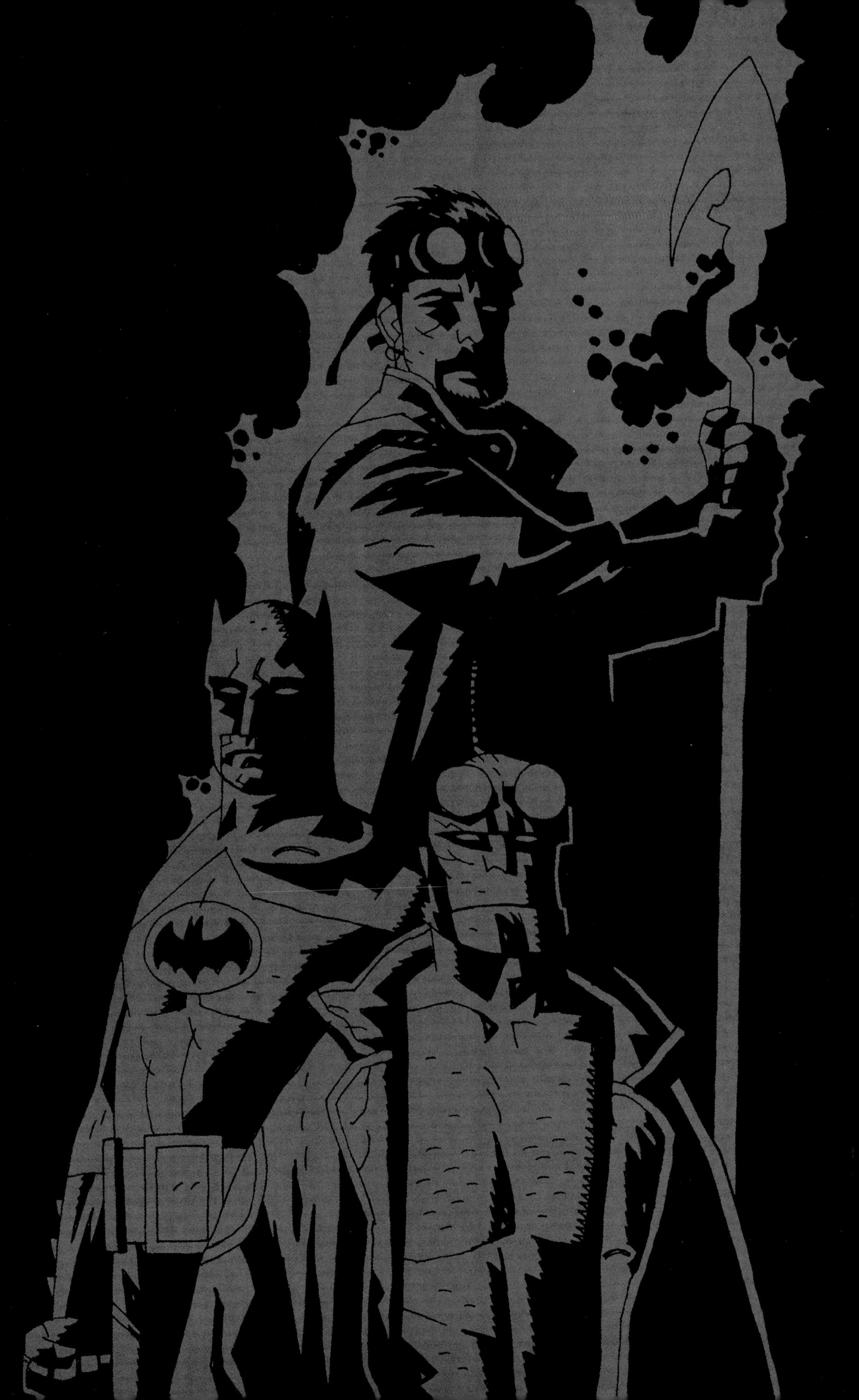

CHAPTER ONE

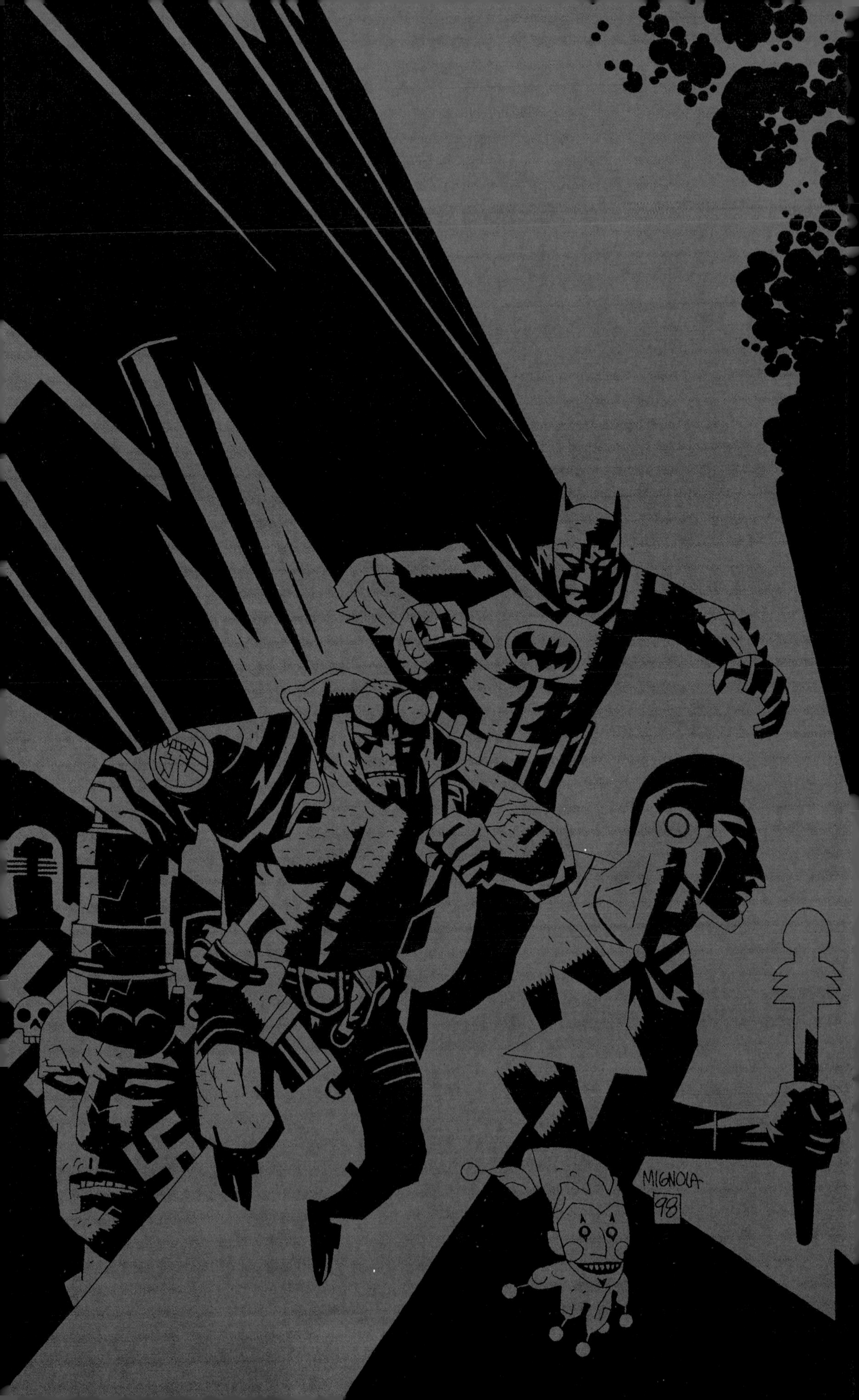
MIGNOLA
98

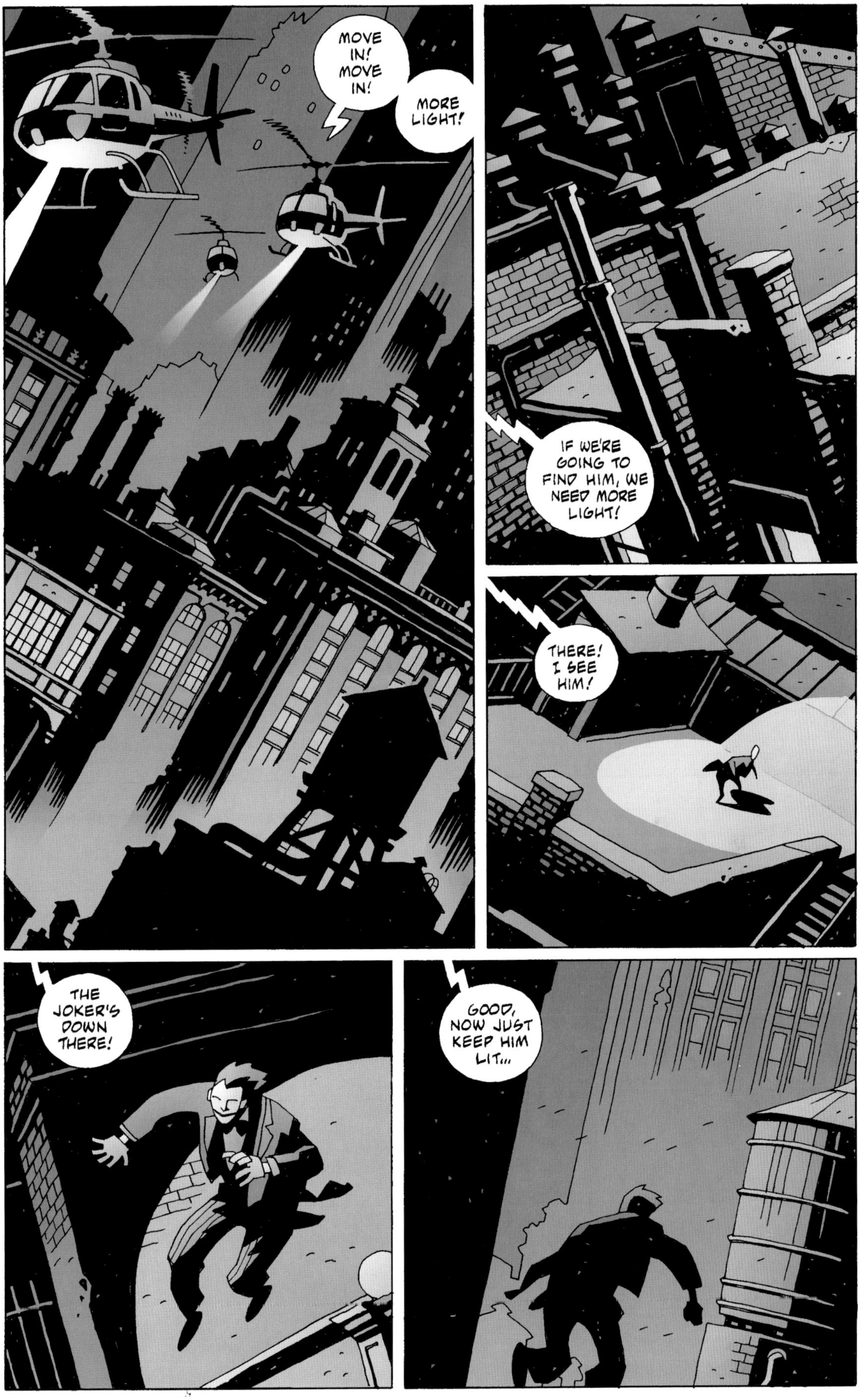
MOVE IN! MOVE IN!
MORE LIGHT!
IF WE'RE GOING TO FIND HIM, WE NEED MORE LIGHT!
THERE! I SEE HIM!
THE JOKER'S DOWN THERE!
GOOD, NOW JUST KEEP HIM LIT...

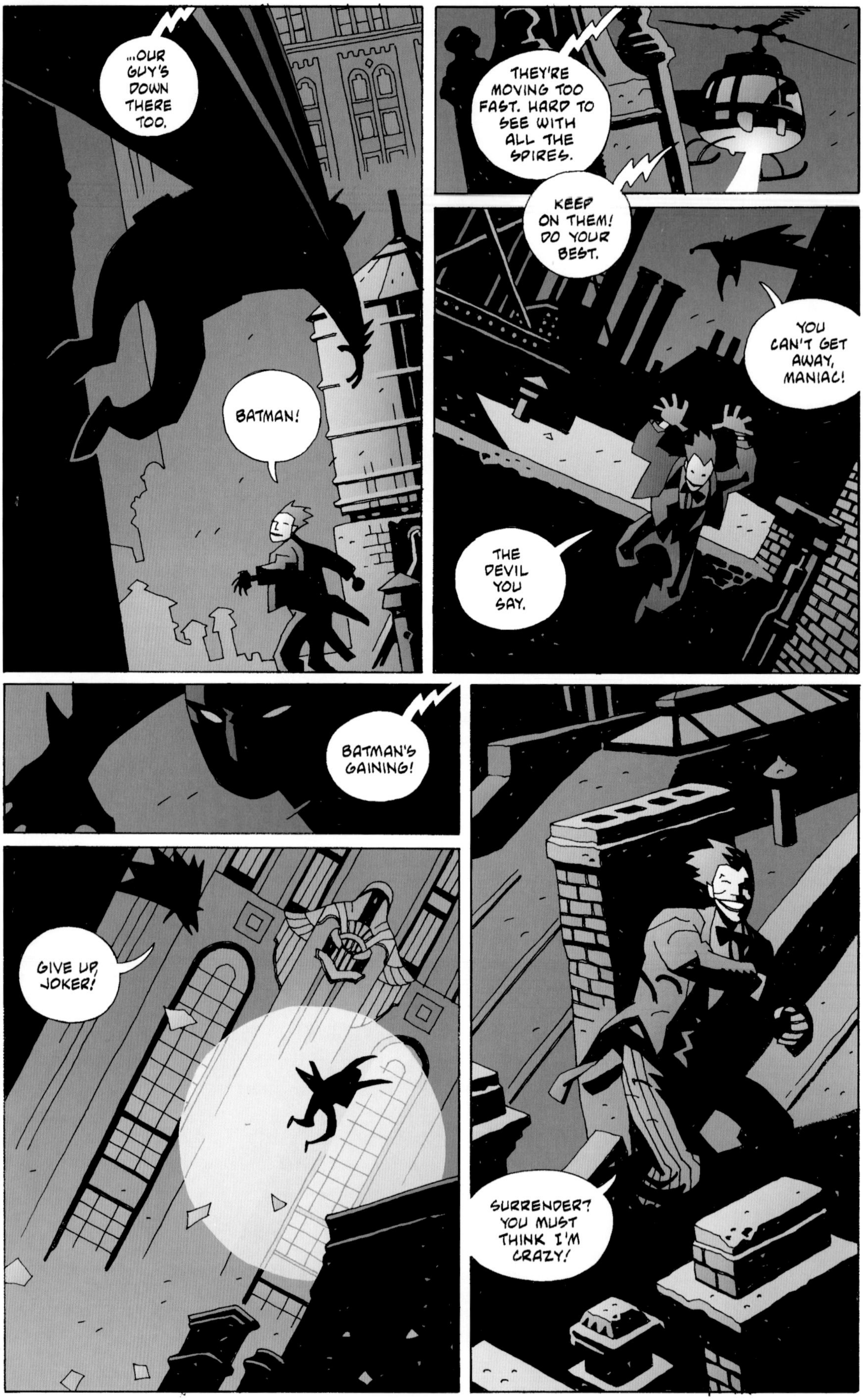
...OUR GUY'S DOWN THERE TOO.
BATMAN!
THEY'RE MOVING TOO FAST. HARD TO SEE WITH ALL THE SPIRES.
KEEP ON THEM! DO YOUR BEST.
YOU CAN'T GET AWAY, MANIAC!
THE DEVIL YOU SAY.
BATMAN'S GAINING!
GIVE UP, JOKER!
SURRENDER? YOU MUST THINK I'M CRAZY!

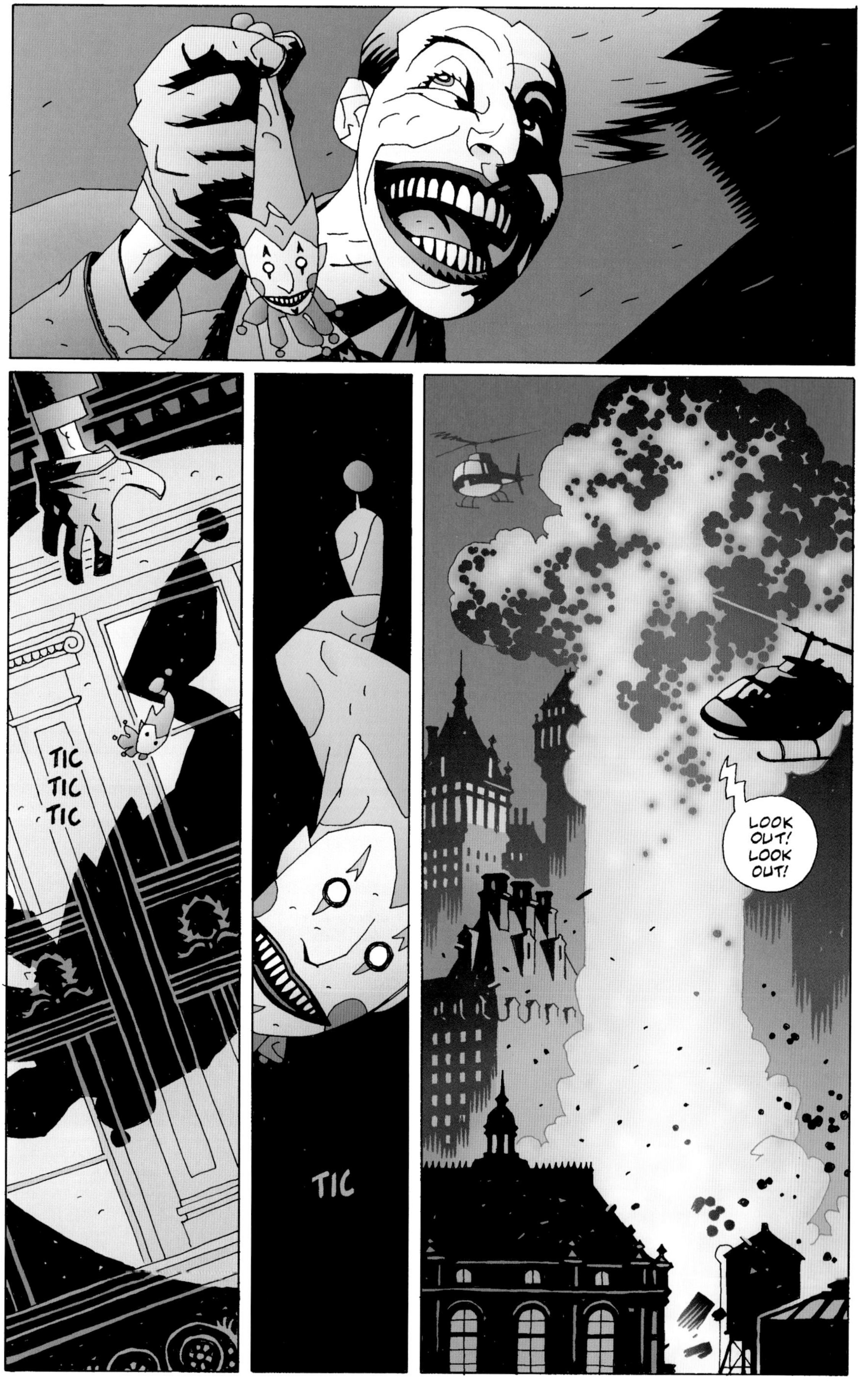
TIC
TIC
TIC
TIC
LOOK OUT! LOOK OUT!

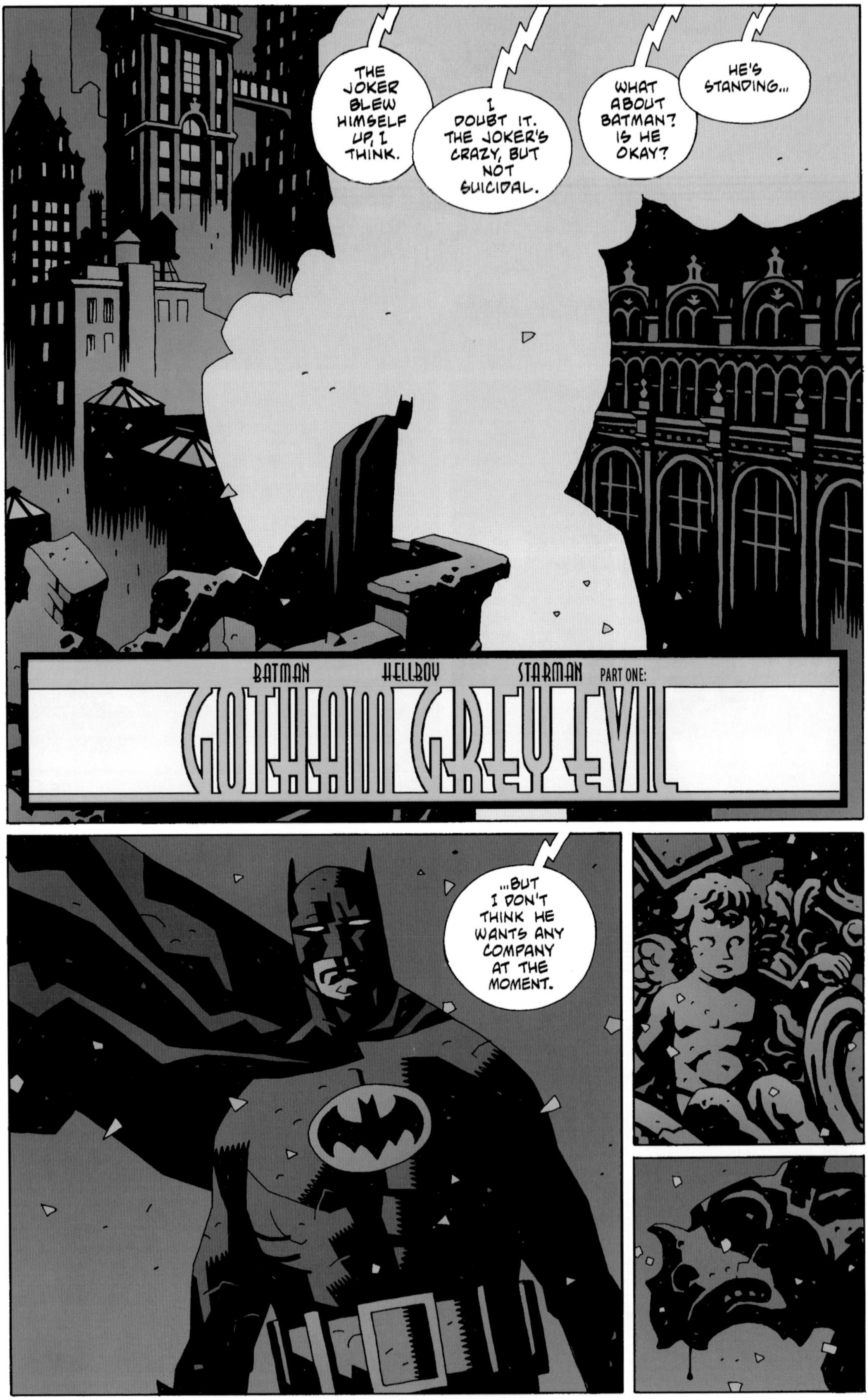
THE JOKER BLEW HIMSELF UP, I THINK.
I DOUBT IT. THE JOKER'S CRAZY, BUT NOT SUICIDAL.
WHAT ABOUT BATMAN? IS HE OKAY?
HE'S STANDING...
BATMAN HELLBOY STARMAN PART ONE:
GOTHAM GREY EVIL
...BUT I DON'T THINK HE WANTS ANY COMPANY AT THE MOMENT.

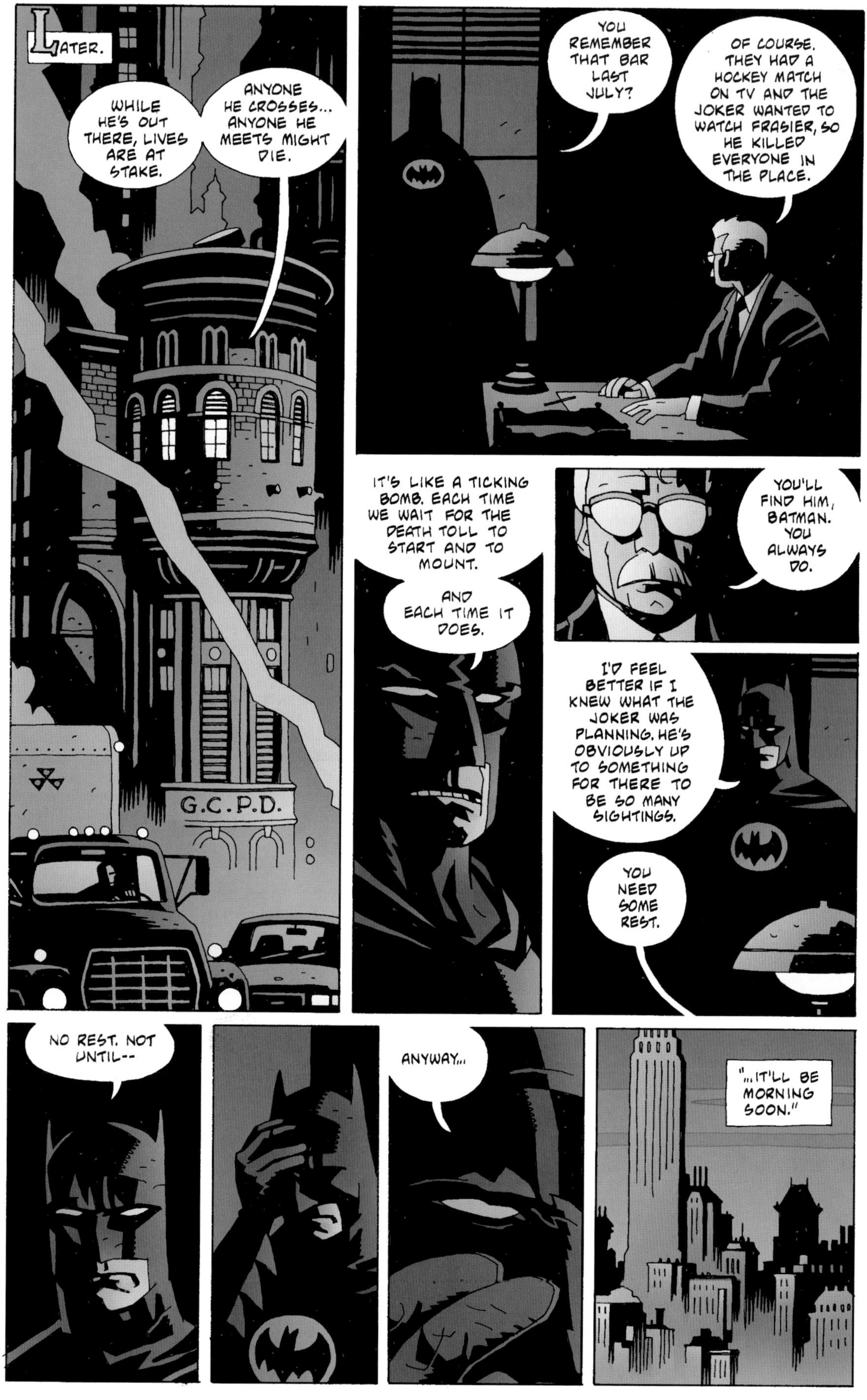
LATER.
WHILE HE'S OUT THERE, LIVES ARE AT STAKE.
ANYONE HE CROSSES... ANYONE HE MEETS MIGHT DIE.
G.C.P.D.
YOU REMEMBER THAT BAR LAST JULY?
OF COURSE. THEY HAD A HOCKEY MATCH ON TV AND THE JOKER WANTED TO WATCH FRASIER, SO HE KILLED EVERYONE IN THE PLACE.
IT'S LIKE A TICKING BOMB. EACH TIME WE WAIT FOR THE DEATH TOLL TO START AND TO MOUNT.
AND EACH TIME IT DOES.
YOU'LL FIND HIM, BATMAN. YOU ALWAYS DO.
I'D FEEL BETTER IF I KNEW WHAT THE JOKER WAS PLANNING. HE'S OBVIOUSLY UP TO SOMETHING FOR THERE TO BE SO MANY SIGHTINGS.
YOU NEED SOME REST.
NO REST. NOT UNTIL--
ANYWAY...
"...IT'LL BE MORNING SOON."

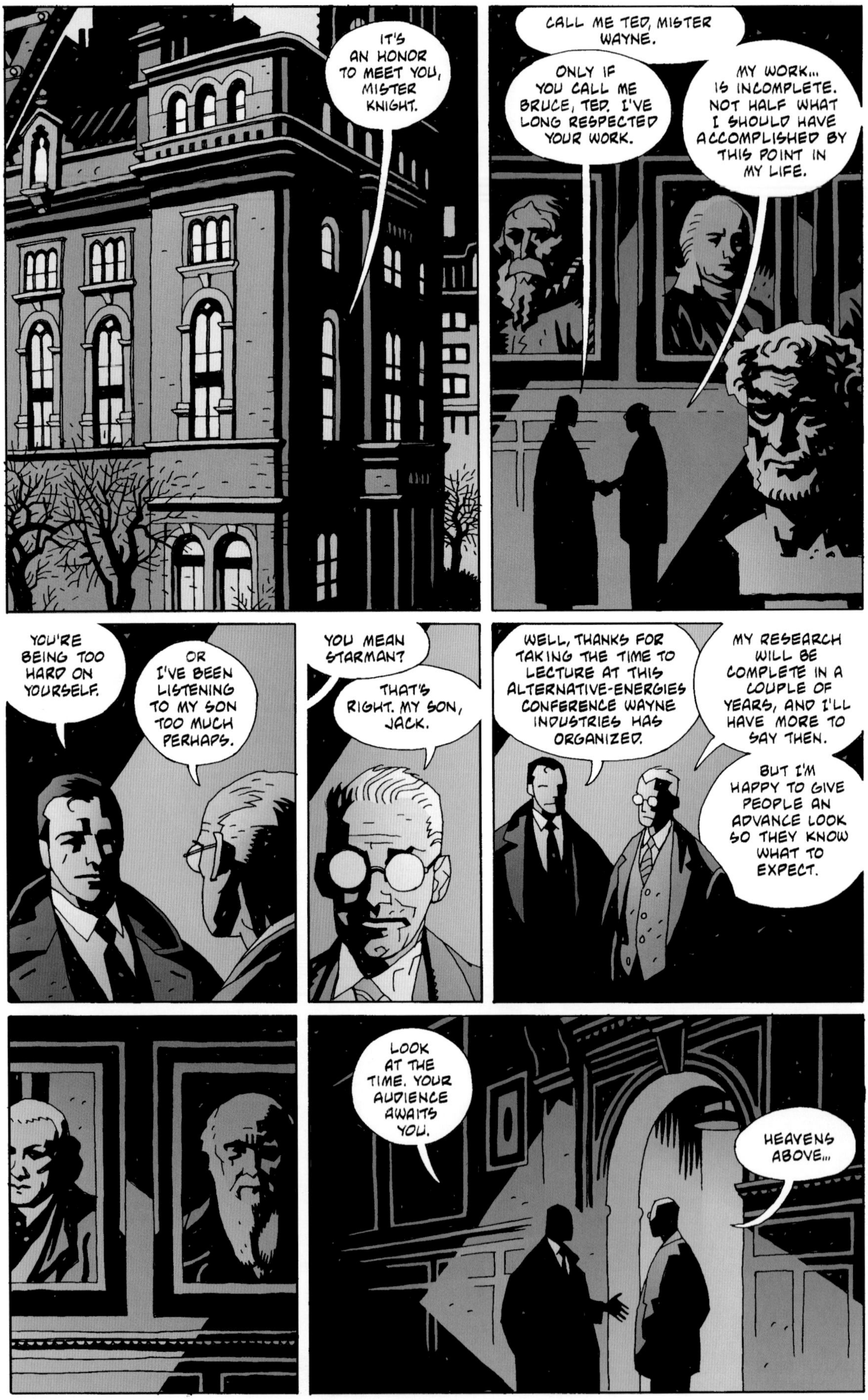
IT'S AN HONOR TO MEET YOU, MISTER KNIGHT.
CALL ME TED, MISTER WAYNE.
ONLY IF YOU CALL ME BRUCE, TED. I'VE LONG RESPECTED YOUR WORK.
MY WORK... IS INCOMPLETE. NOT HALF WHAT I SHOULD HAVE ACCOMPLISHED BY THIS POINT IN MY LIFE.
YOU'RE BEING TOO HARD ON YOURSELF.
OR I'VE BEEN LISTENING TO MY SON TOO MUCH PERHAPS.
YOU MEAN STARMAN?
THAT'S RIGHT. MY SON, JACK.
WELL, THANKS FOR TAKING THE TIME TO LECTURE AT THIS ALTERNATIVE-ENERGIES CONFERENCE WAYNE INDUSTRIES HAS ORGANIZED.
MY RESEARCH WILL BE COMPLETE IN A COUPLE OF YEARS, AND I'LL HAVE MORE TO SAY THEN.
BUT I'M HAPPY TO GIVE PEOPLE AN ADVANCE LOOK SO THEY KNOW WHAT TO EXPECT.
LOOK AT THE TIME. YOUR AUDIENCE AWAITS YOU.
HEAVENS ABOVE...

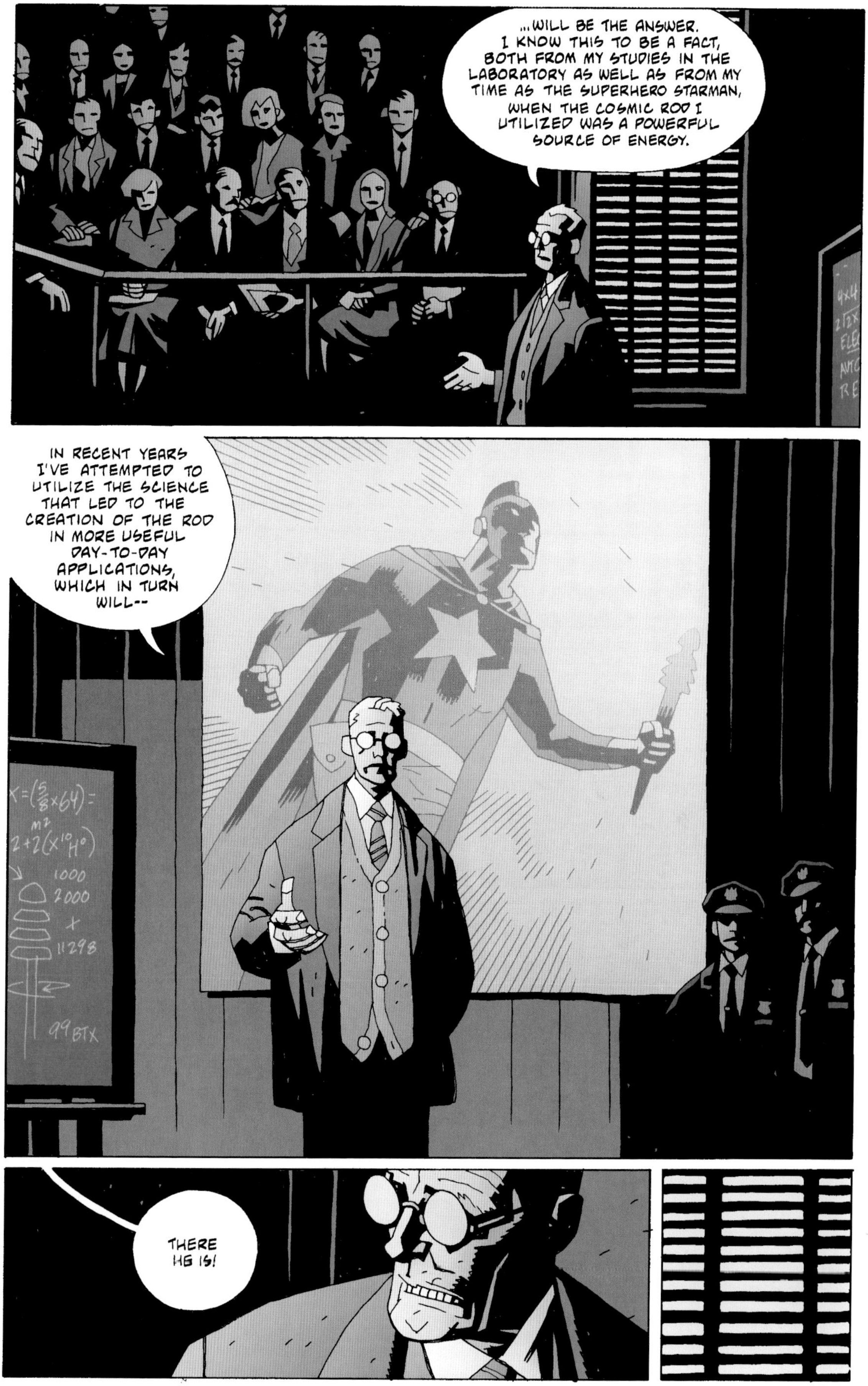
...WILL BE THE ANSWER. I KNOW THIS TO BE A FACT, BOTH FROM MY STUDIES IN THE LABORATORY AS WELL AS FROM MY TIME AS THE SUPERHERO STARMAN, WHEN THE COSMIC ROD I UTILIZED WAS A POWERFUL SOURCE OF ENERGY.
IN RECENT YEARS I'VE ATTEMPTED TO UTILIZE THE SCIENCE THAT LED TO THE CREATION OF THE ROD IN MORE USEFUL DAY-TO-DAY APPLICATIONS, WHICH IN TURN WILL--
THERE HE IS!

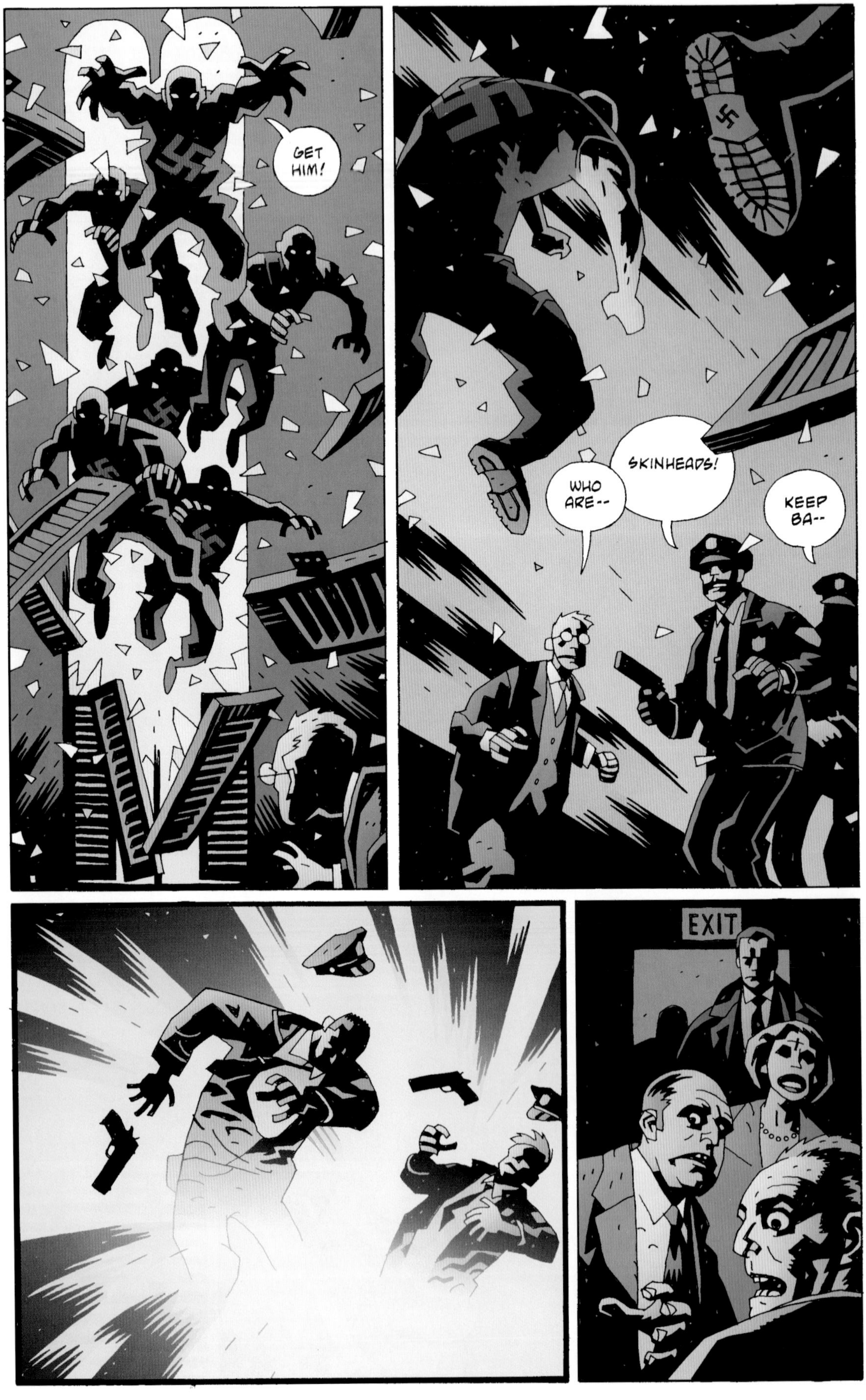
GET HIM!
WHO ARE--
SKINHEADS!
KEEP BA--
EXIT

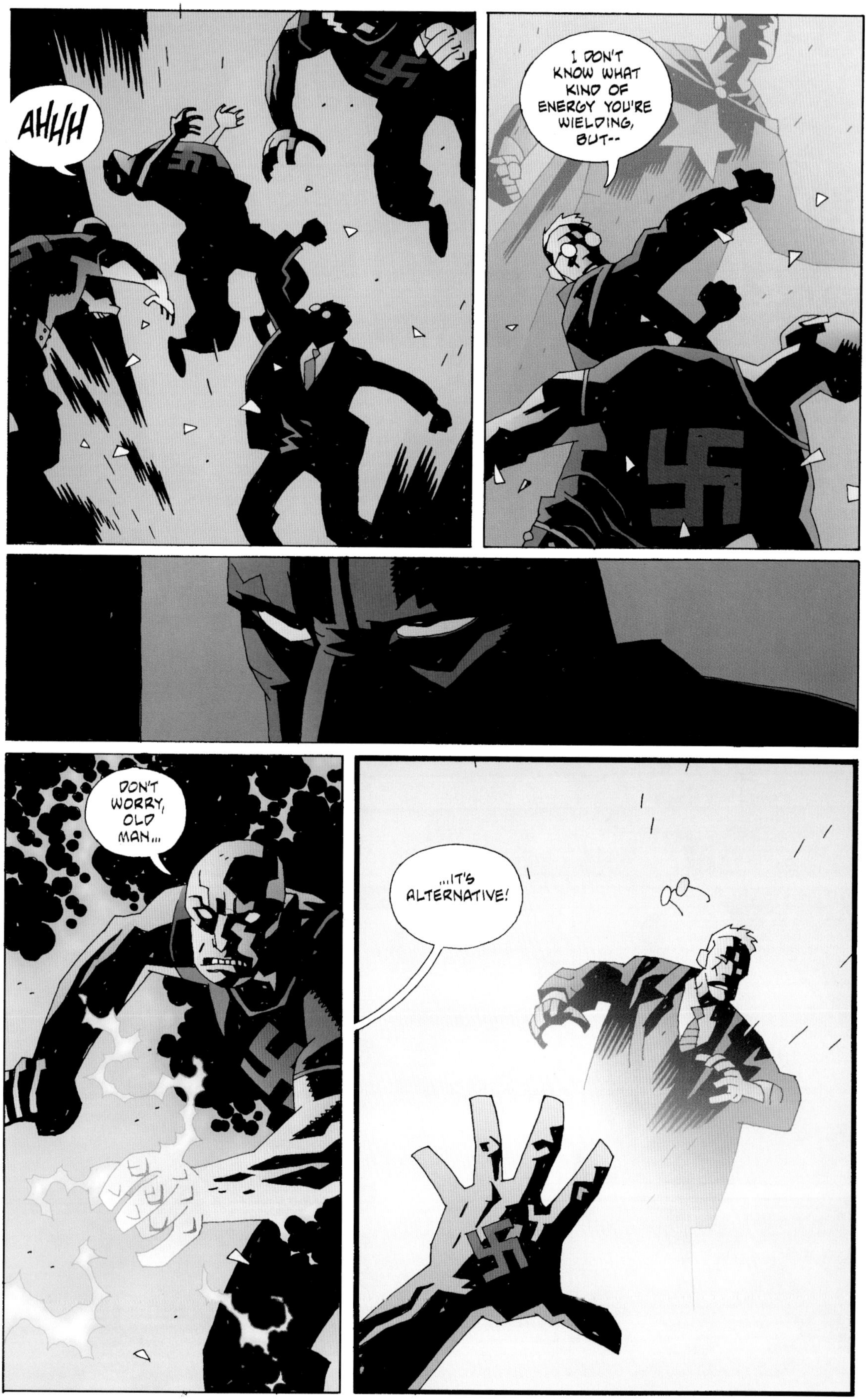
AHHH
I DON'T KNOW WHAT KIND OF ENERGY YOU'RE WIELDING, BUT--
DON'T WORRY, OLD MAN...
...IT'S ALTERNATIVE!

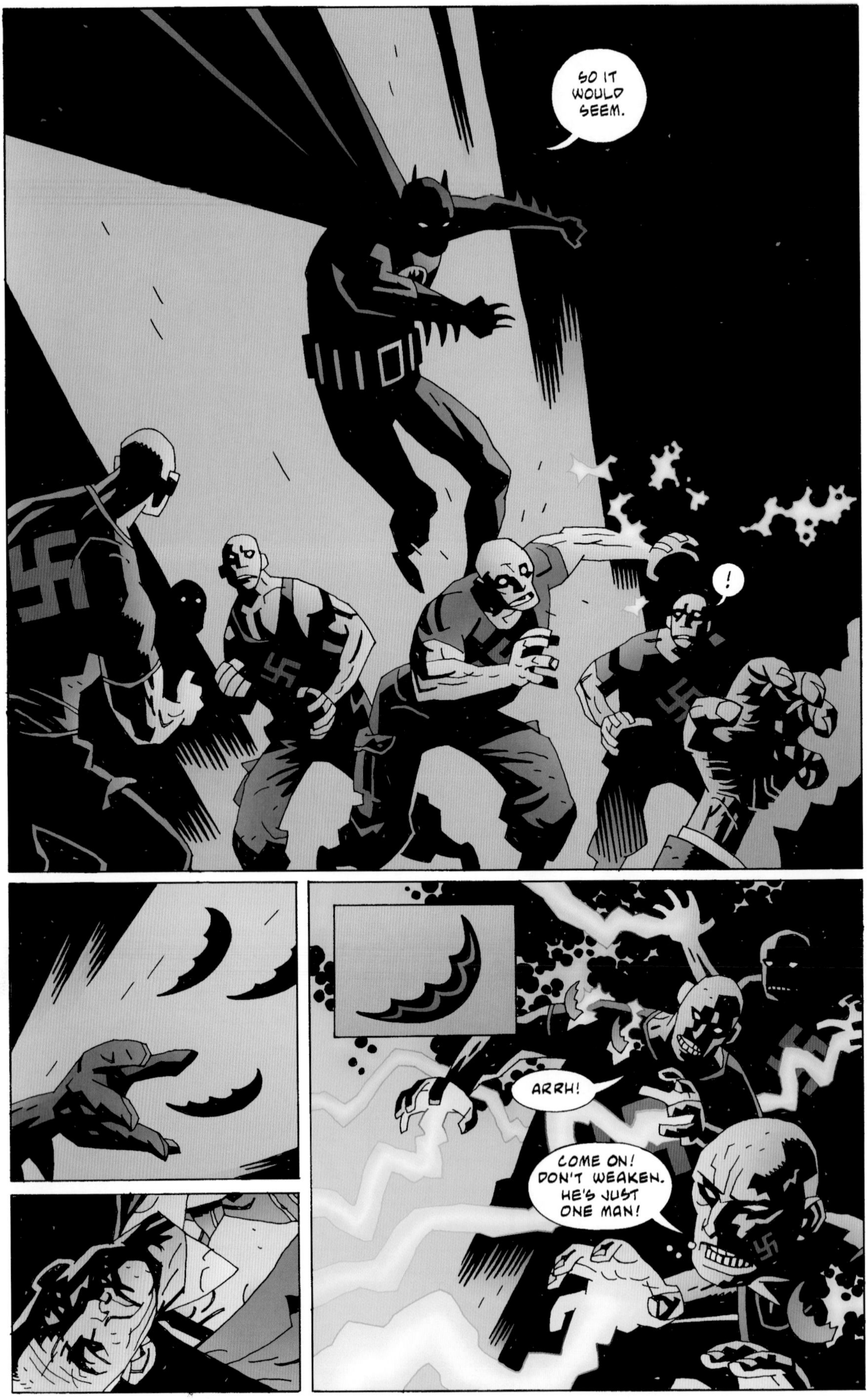
SO IT WOULD SEEM.
!
ARRH!
COME ON! DON'T WEAKEN. HE'S JUST ONE MAN!

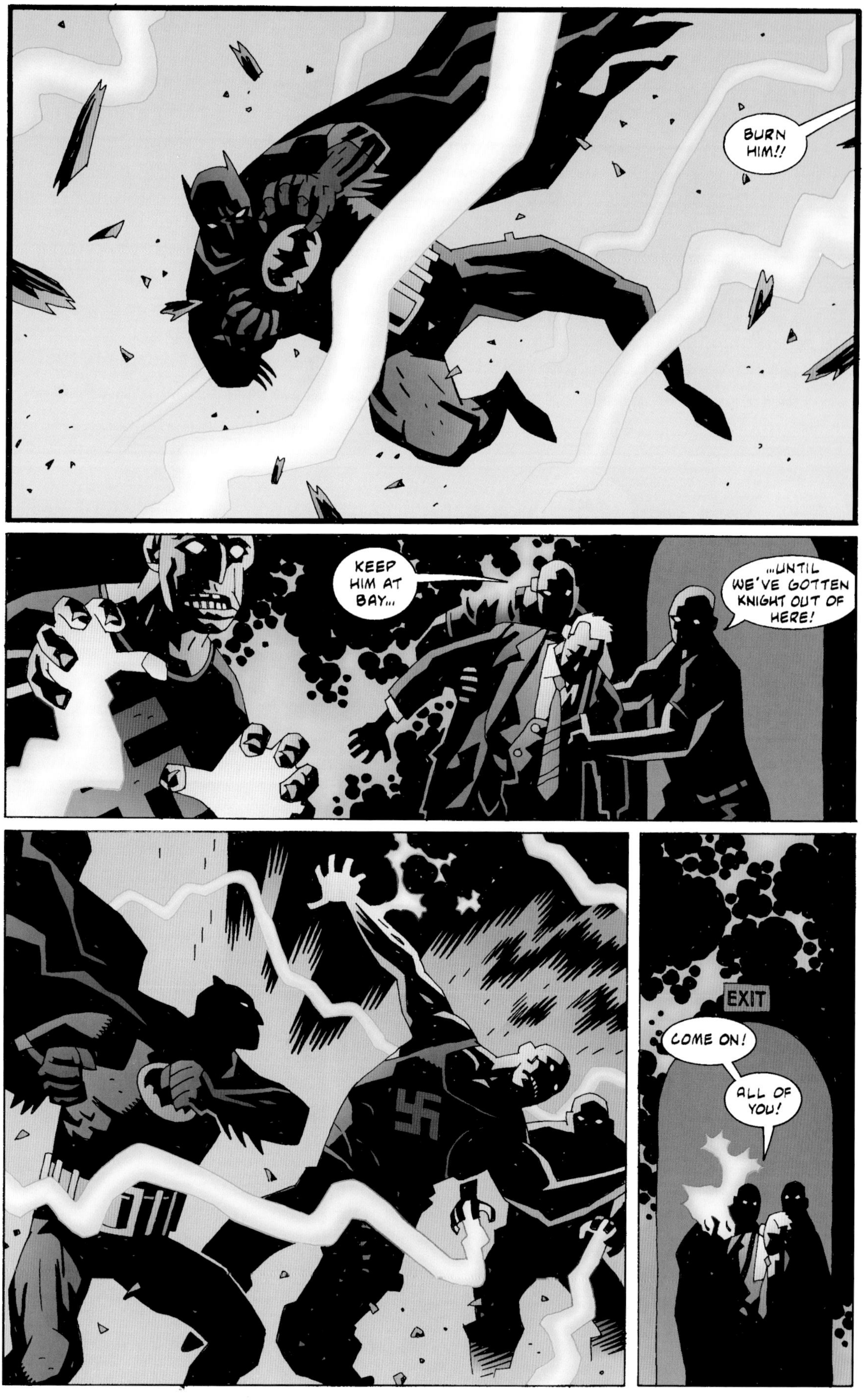
BURN HIM!!
KEEP HIM AT BAY...
...UNTIL WE'VE GOTTEN KNIGHT OUT OF HERE!
EXIT
COME ON!
ALL OF YOU!

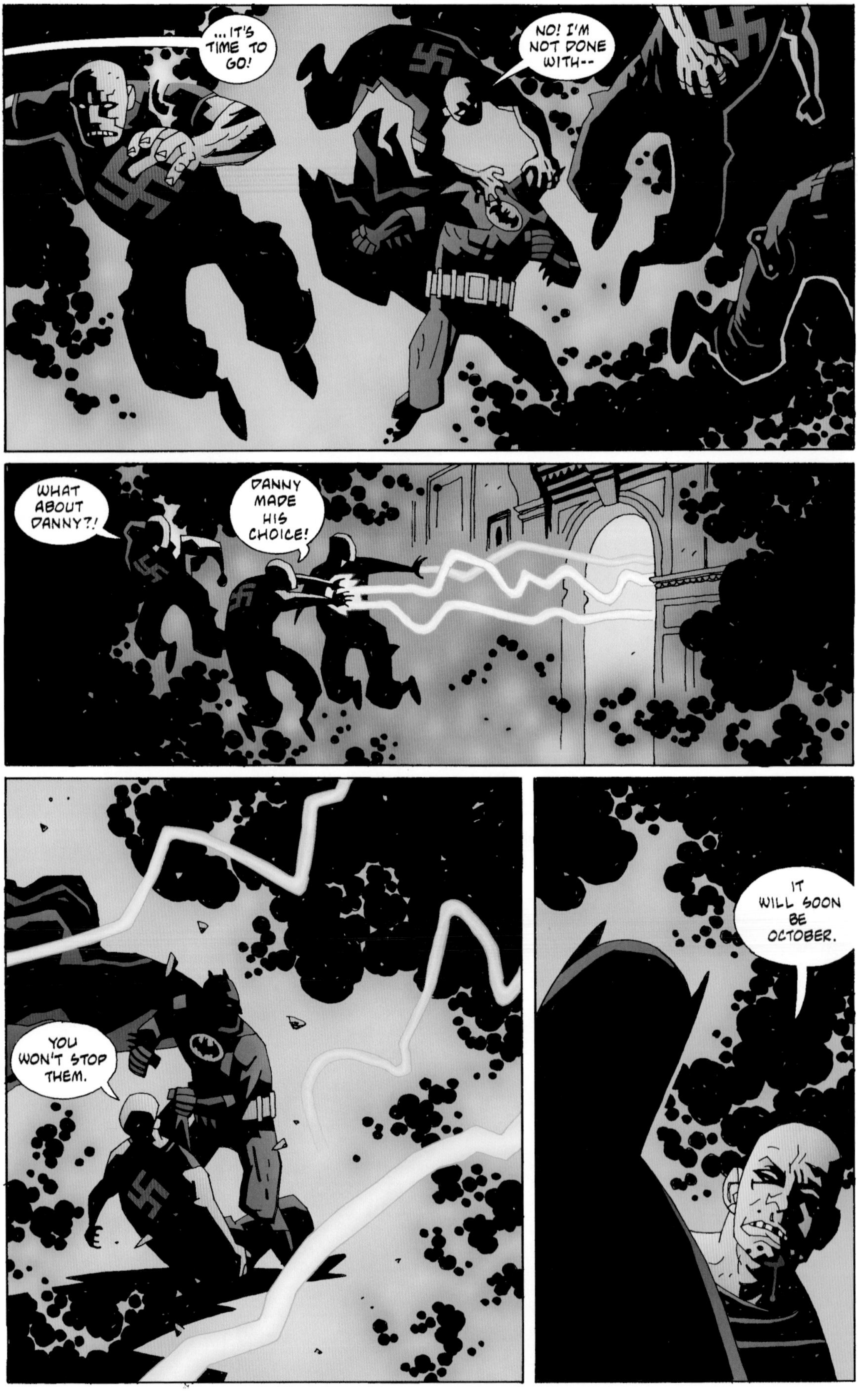
...IT'S TIME TO GO!
NO! I'M NOT DONE WITH--
WHAT ABOUT DANNY?!
DANNY MADE HIS CHOICE!
YOU WON'T STOP THEM.
IT WILL SOON BE OCTOBER.

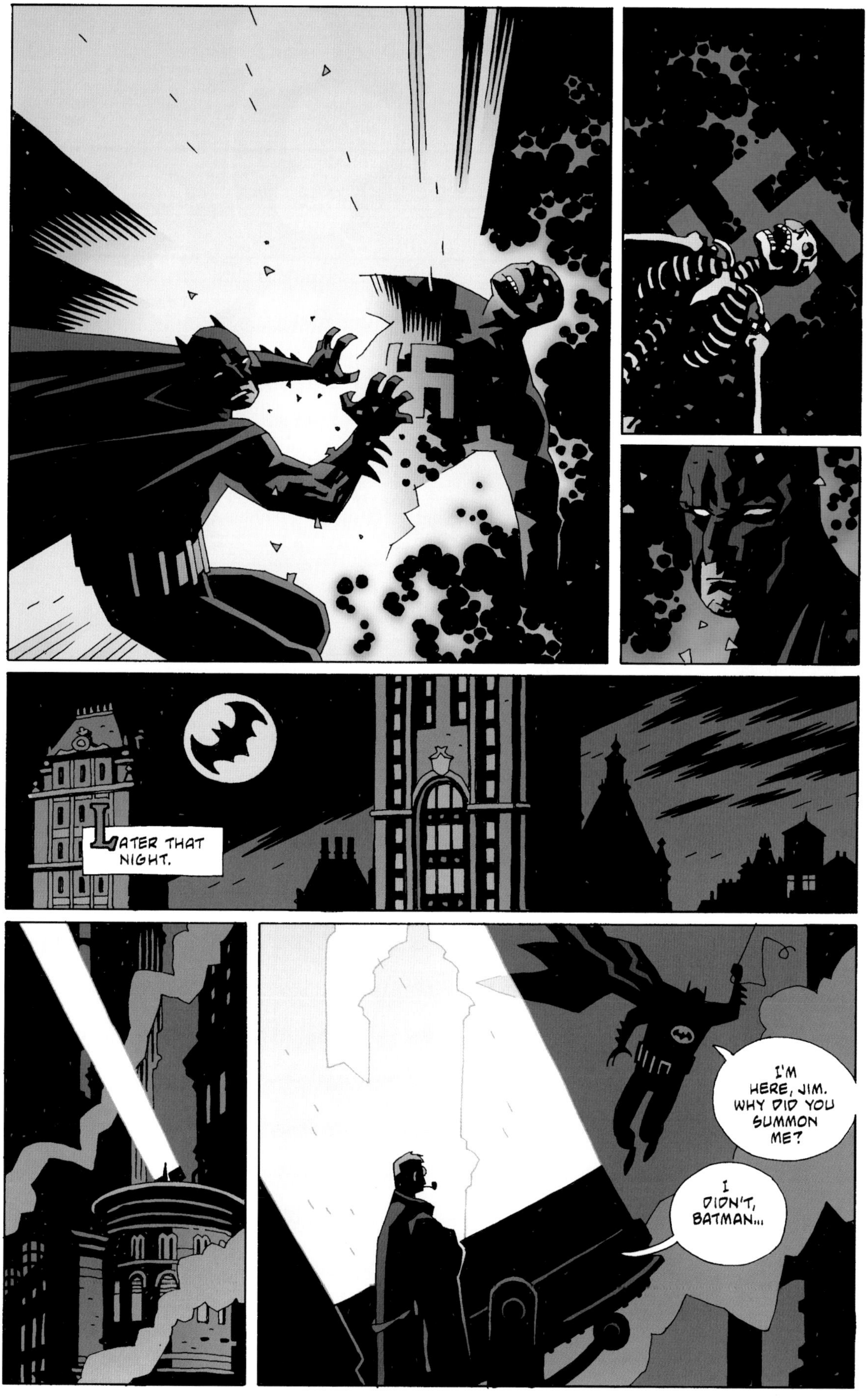
LATER THAT NIGHT.
I'M HERE, JIM. WHY DID YOU SUMMON ME?
I DIDN'T, BATMAN...

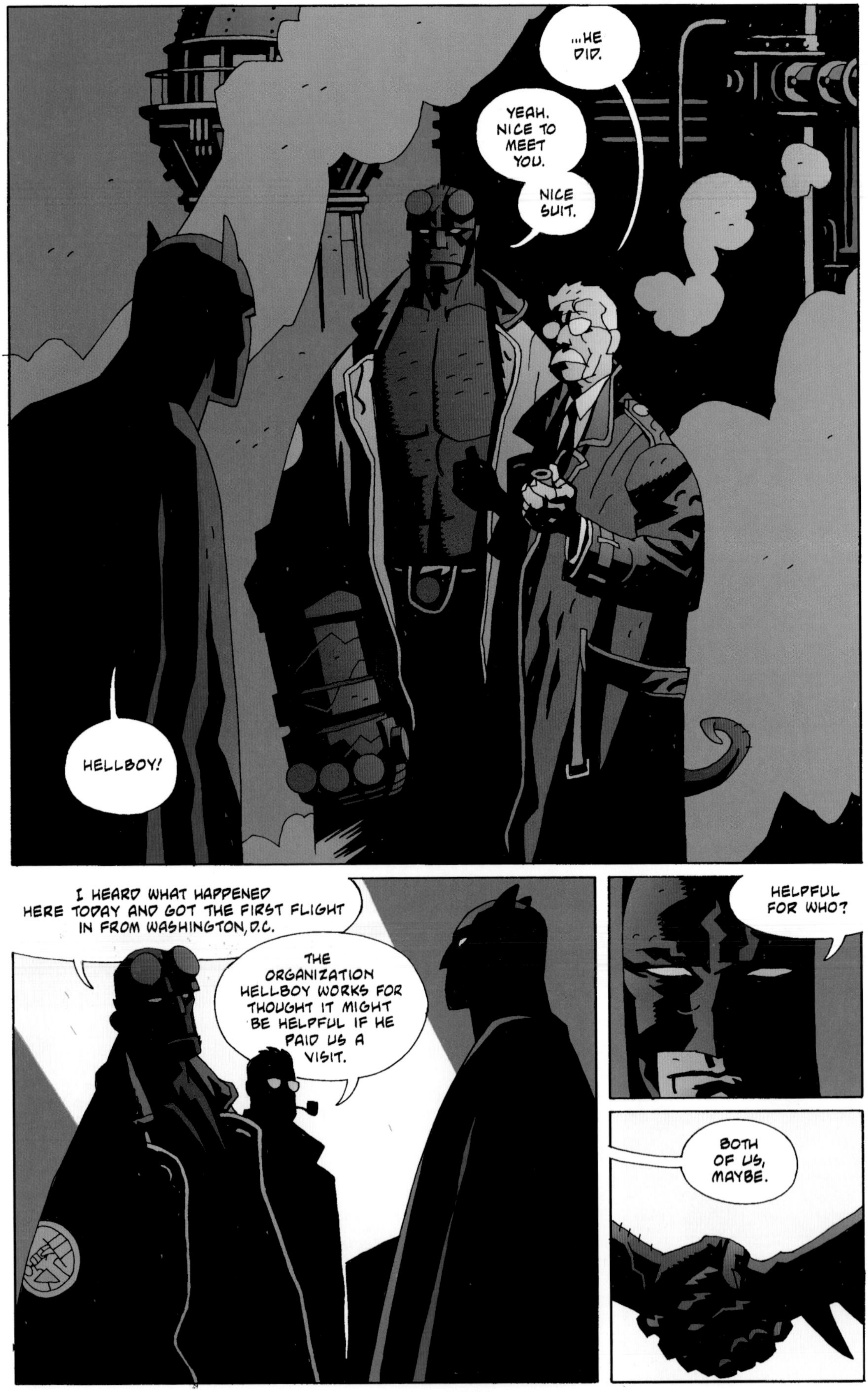
...HE DID.
YEAH. NICE TO MEET YOU.
NICE SUIT.
HELLBOY!
I HEARD WHAT HAPPENED HERE TODAY AND GOT THE FIRST FLIGHT IN FROM WASHINGTON, D.C.
THE ORGANIZATION HELLBOY WORKS FOR THOUGHT IT MIGHT BE HELPFUL IF HE PAID US A VISIT.
HELPFUL FOR WHO?
BOTH OF US, MAYBE.

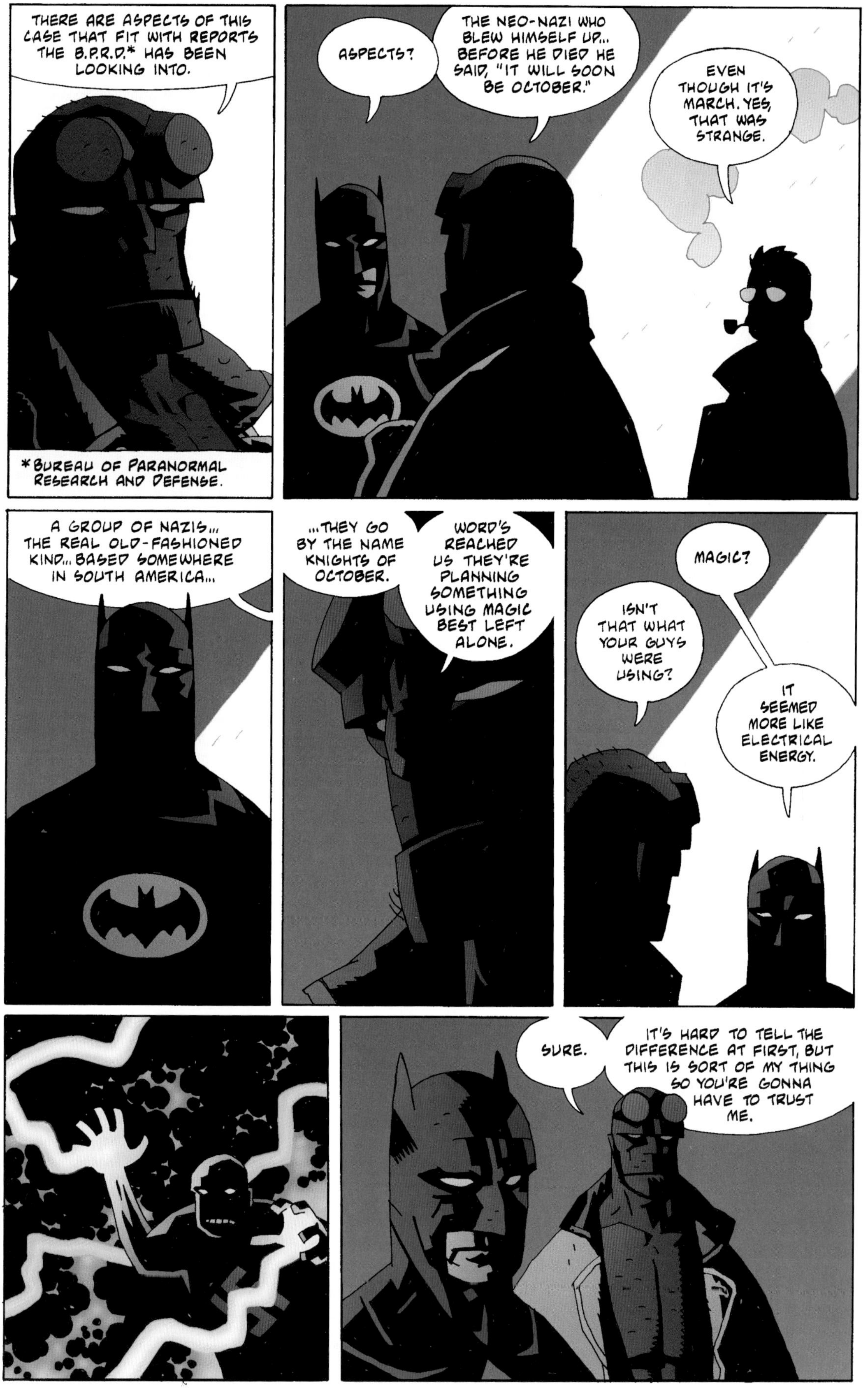
THERE ARE ASPECTS OF THIS CASE THAT FIT WITH REPORTS THE B.P.R.D.* HAS BEEN LOOKING INTO.
*BUREAU OF PARANORMAL RESEARCH AND DEFENSE.
ASPECTS?
THE NEO-NAZI WHO BLEW HIMSELF UP... BEFORE HE DIED HE SAID, "IT WILL SOON BE OCTOBER."
EVEN THOUGH IT'S MARCH. YES, THAT WAS STRANGE.
A GROUP OF NAZIS... THE REAL OLD-FASHIONED KIND... BASED SOMEWHERE IN SOUTH AMERICA...
...THEY GO BY THE NAME KNIGHTS OF OCTOBER.
WORD'S REACHED US THEY'RE PLANNING SOMETHING USING MAGIC BEST LEFT ALONE.
MAGIC?
ISN'T THAT WHAT YOUR GUYS WERE USING?
IT SEEMED MORE LIKE ELECTRICAL ENERGY.
SURE.
IT'S HARD TO TELL THE DIFFERENCE AT FIRST, BUT THIS IS SORT OF MY THING SO YOU'RE GONNA HAVE TO TRUST ME.

I'LL TAKE EVERYTHING YOU'VE SAID UNDER ADVISEMENT, HELLBOY, AS I CONTINUE MY INVESTIGATION.

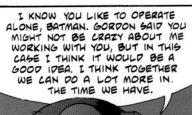

I KNOW YOU LIKE TO OPERATE ALONE, BATMAN. GORDON SAID YOU MIGHT NOT BE CRAZY ABOUT ME WORKING WITH YOU, BUT IN THIS CASE I THINK IT WOULD BE A GOOD IDEA. I THINK TOGETHER WE CAN DO A LOT MORE IN THE TIME WE HAVE.

AND HOW MUCH TIME IS THAT?

CLICK

I DON'T KNOW. BUT MAYBE WE SHOULD BE ASKING HOW MUCH TIME DOES TED KNIGHT HAVE.

WITH ALL DUE RESPECT, YOU MAY THINK YOU'RE EXPERIENCED WITH MAGIC, BATMAN. BUT REALLY, COMPARED TO ME...

...YOU HAVE NO IDEA.

HE CAN HELP YOU, BATMAN.

WHY DO YOU THINK THEY WANTED TED KNIGHT? A SCIENTIST.

I'M NOT SURE. BUT SPELLS AND RITES USE FORMULAS AND PHYSICS AS MUCH AS THEY USE CHARMS AND POTIONS. SCIENCE...THE ALIGNMENT OF PLANETS...THAT'S ALL STUFF MISTER KNIGHT MIGHT BE NEEDED TO HELP THEM WITH.

WELL, I SUPPOSE WE'LL KNOW WHEN KNIGHT'S LOCATED.

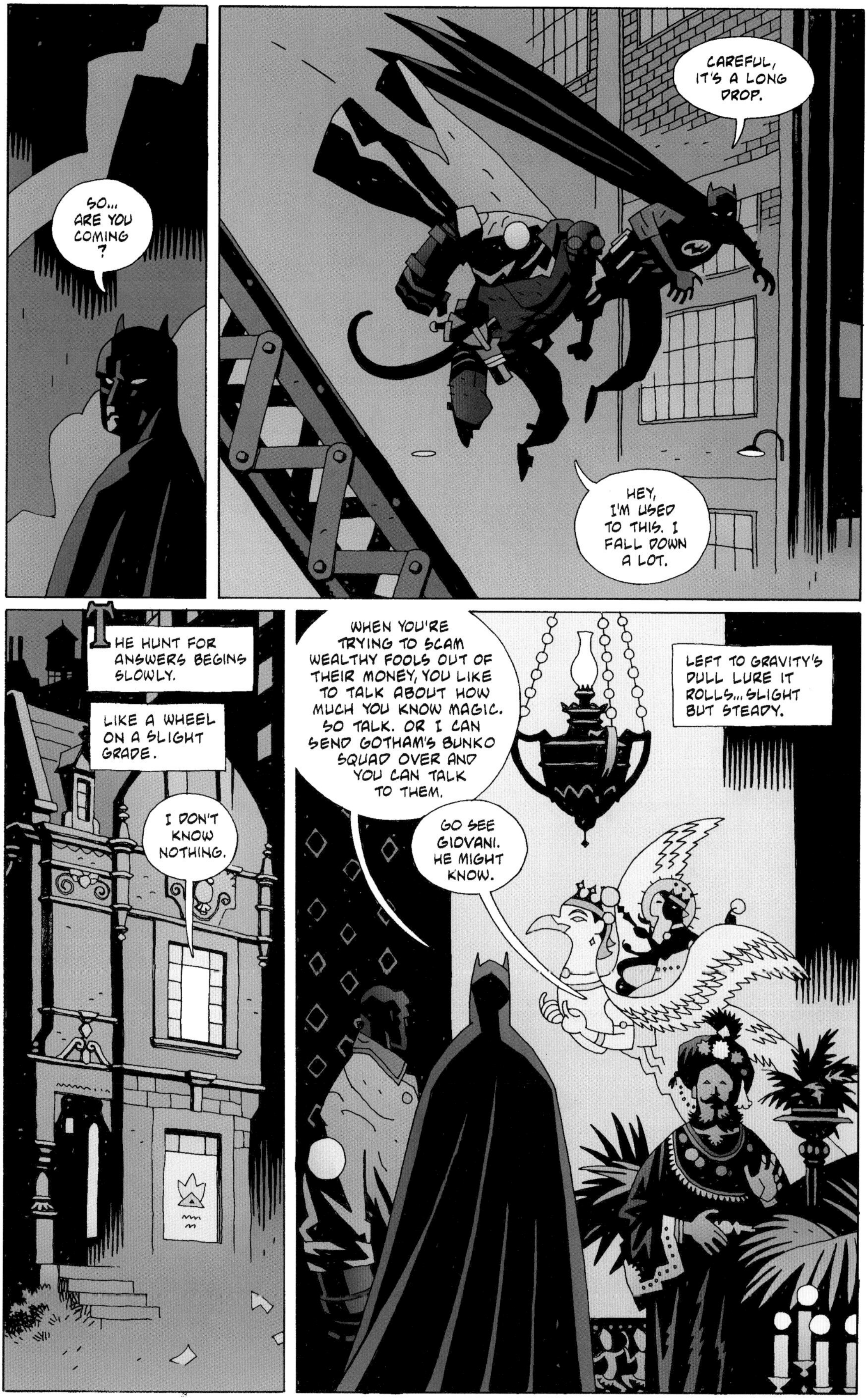
SO... ARE YOU COMING ?
CAREFUL, IT'S A LONG DROP.
HEY, I'M USED TO THIS. I FALL DOWN A LOT.
THE HUNT FOR ANSWERS BEGINS SLOWLY.
LIKE A WHEEL ON A SLIGHT GRADE.
I DON'T KNOW NOTHING.
WHEN YOU'RE TRYING TO SCAM WEALTHY FOOLS OUT OF THEIR MONEY, YOU LIKE TO TALK ABOUT HOW MUCH YOU KNOW MAGIC. SO TALK. OR I CAN SEND GOTHAM'S BUNKO SQUAD OVER AND YOU CAN TALK TO THEM.
GO SEE GIOVANI. HE MIGHT KNOW.
LEFT TO GRAVITY'S DULL LURE IT ROLLS... SLIGHT BUT STEADY.

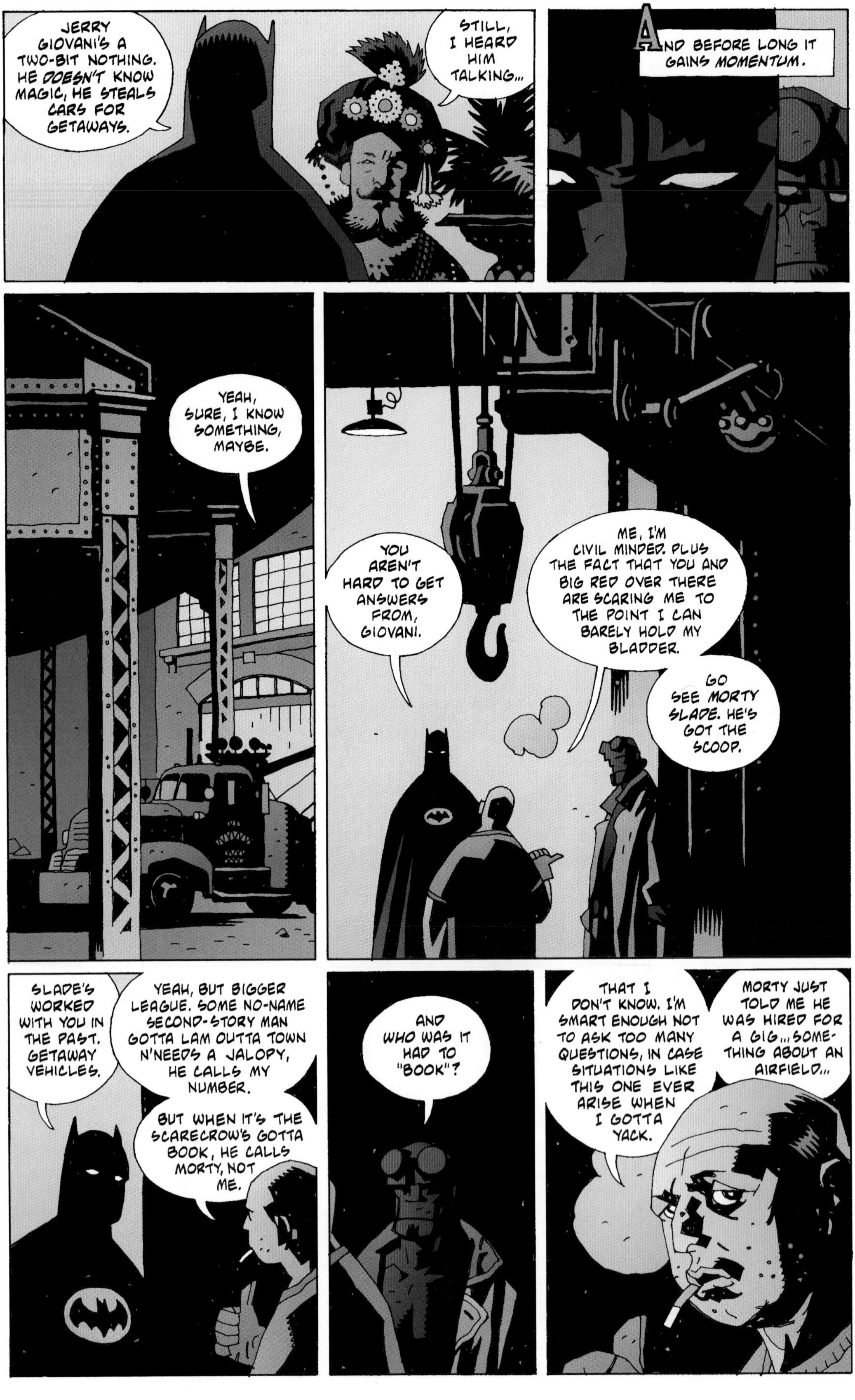
JERRY GIOVANI'S A TWO-BIT NOTHING. HE DOESN'T KNOW MAGIC, HE STEALS CARS FOR GETAWAYS.
STILL, I HEARD HIM TALKING...
AND BEFORE LONG IT GAINS MOMENTUM.
YEAH, SURE, I KNOW SOMETHING, MAYBE.
YOU AREN'T HARD TO GET ANSWERS FROM, GIOVANI.
ME, I'M CIVIL MINDED. PLUS THE FACT THAT YOU AND BIG RED OVER THERE ARE SCARING ME TO THE POINT I CAN BARELY HOLD MY BLADDER.
GO SEE MORTY SLADE. HE'S GOT THE SCOOP.
SLADE'S WORKED WITH YOU IN THE PAST. GETAWAY VEHICLES.
YEAH, BUT BIGGER LEAGUE. SOME NO-NAME SECOND-STORY MAN GOTTA LAM OUTTA TOWN N'NEEDS A JALOPY, HE CALLS MY NUMBER.
BUT WHEN IT'S THE SCARECROW'S GOTTA BOOK, HE CALLS MORTY, NOT ME.
AND WHO WAS IT HAD TO "BOOK"?
THAT I DON'T KNOW. I'M SMART ENOUGH NOT TO ASK TOO MANY QUESTIONS, IN CASE SITUATIONS LIKE THIS ONE EVER ARISE WHEN I GOTTA YACK.
MORTY JUST TOLD ME HE WAS HIRED FOR A GIG... SOME-THING ABOUT AN AIRFIELD...

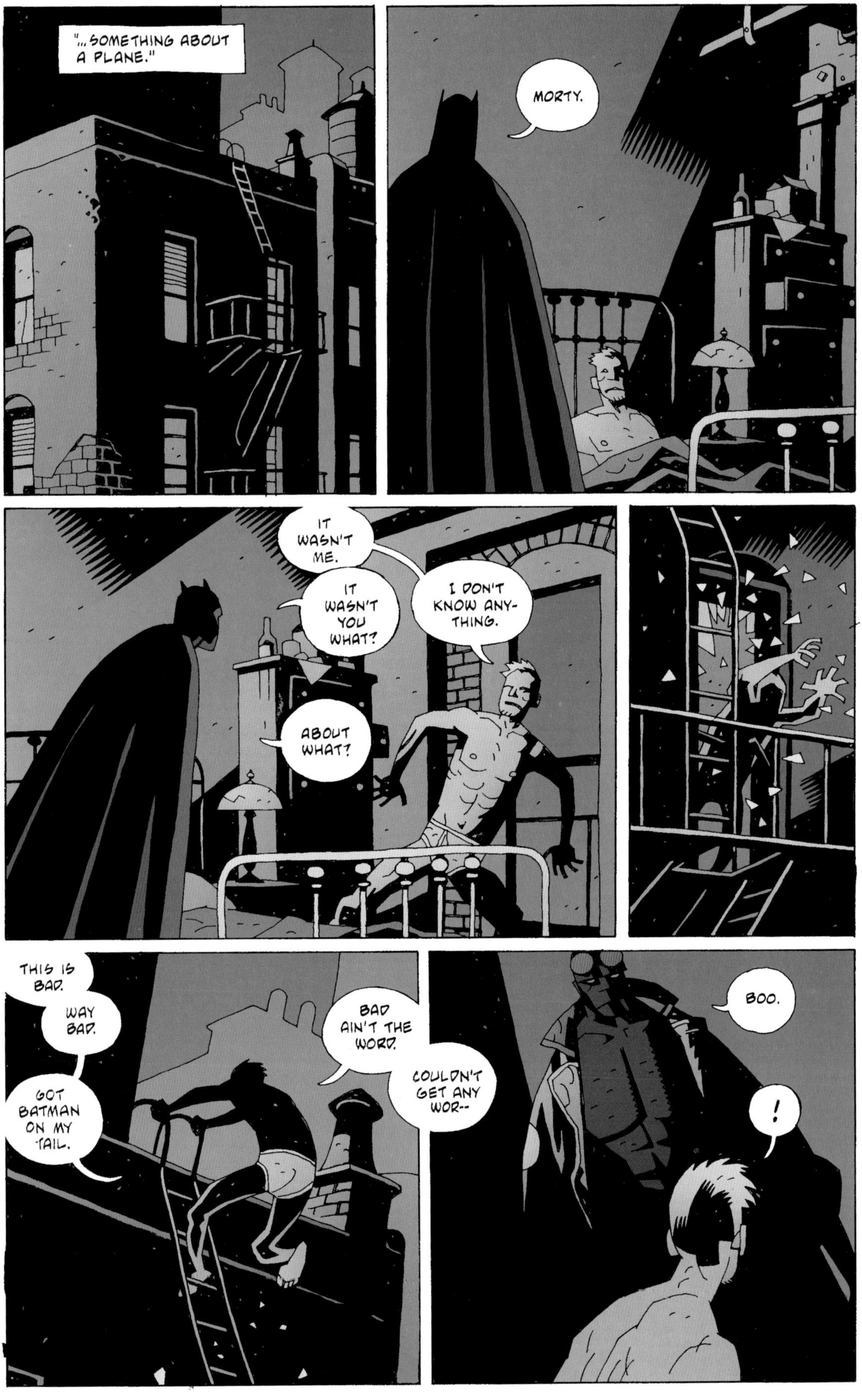
"... SOMETHING ABOUT A PLANE."
MORTY.
IT WASN'T ME.
IT WASN'T YOU WHAT?
I DON'T KNOW ANY-THING.
ABOUT WHAT?
THIS IS BAD.
WAY BAD.
GOT BATMAN ON MY TAIL.
BAD AIN'T THE WORD.
COULDN'T GET ANY WOR--
BOO.
!

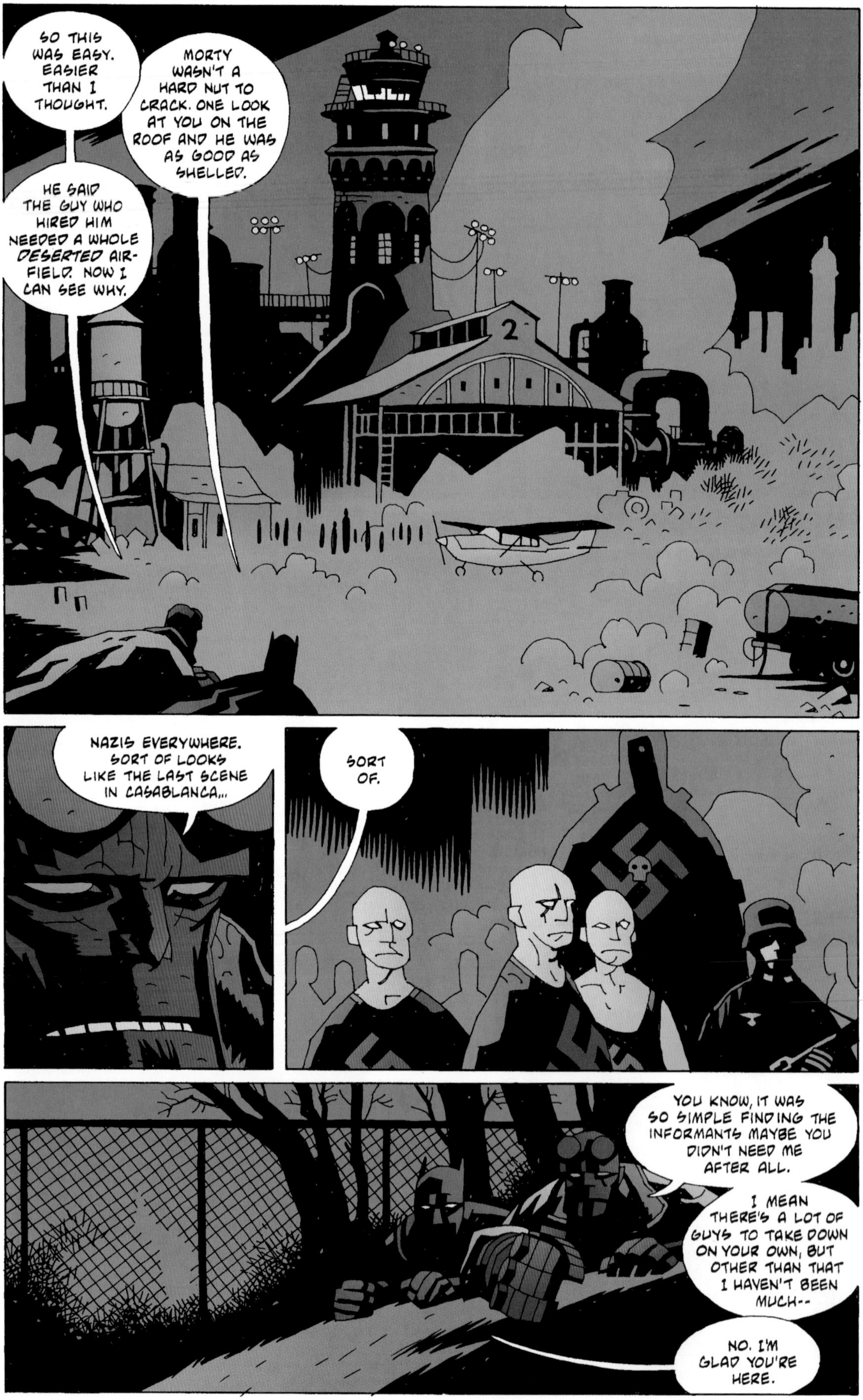
SO THIS WAS EASY. EASIER THAN I THOUGHT.
HE SAID THE GUY WHO HIRED HIM NEEDED A WHOLE DESERTED AIR-FIELD. NOW I CAN SEE WHY.
MORTY WASN'T A HARD NUT TO CRACK. ONE LOOK AT YOU ON THE ROOF AND HE WAS AS GOOD AS SHELLED.
2
NAZIS EVERYWHERE. SORT OF LOOKS LIKE THE LAST SCENE IN CASABLANCA...
SORT OF.
YOU KNOW, IT WAS SO SIMPLE FINDING THE INFORMANTS MAYBE YOU DIDN'T NEED ME AFTER ALL.
I MEAN THERE'S A LOT OF GUYS TO TAKE DOWN ON YOUR OWN, BUT OTHER THAN THAT I HAVEN'T BEEN MUCH--
NO. I'M GLAD YOU'RE HERE.

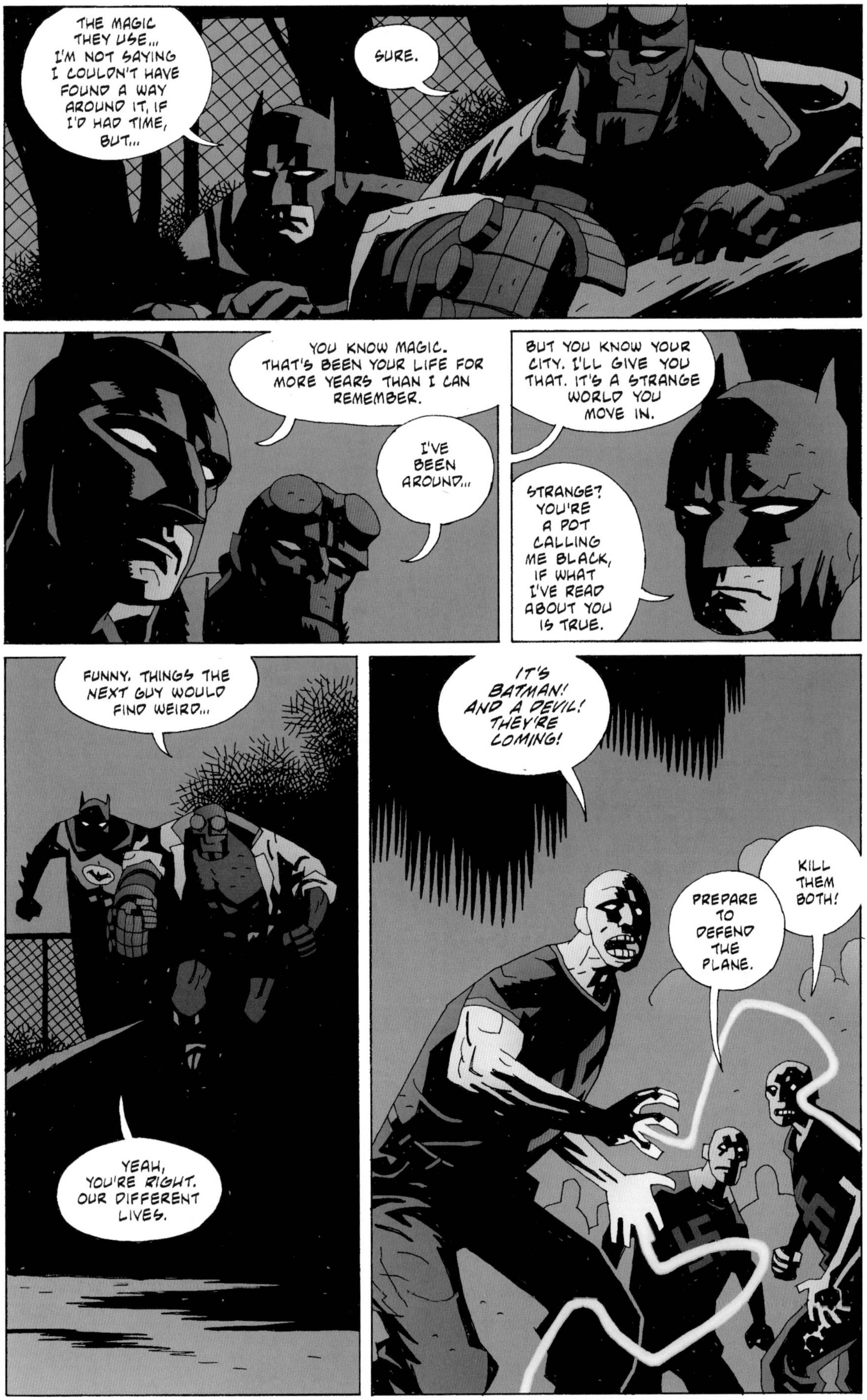
THE MAGIC THEY USE... I'M NOT SAYING I COULDN'T HAVE FOUND A WAY AROUND IT, IF I'D HAD TIME, BUT...
SURE.
YOU KNOW MAGIC. THAT'S BEEN YOUR LIFE FOR MORE YEARS THAN I CAN REMEMBER.
I'VE BEEN AROUND...
BUT YOU KNOW YOUR CITY. I'LL GIVE YOU THAT. IT'S A STRANGE WORLD YOU MOVE IN.
STRANGE? YOU'RE A POT CALLING ME BLACK, IF WHAT I'VE READ ABOUT YOU IS TRUE.
FUNNY. THINGS THE NEXT GUY WOULD FIND WEIRD...
YEAH, YOU'RE RIGHT. OUR DIFFERENT LIVES.
IT'S BATMAN! AND A DEVIL! THEY'RE COMING!
KILL THEM BOTH!
PREPARE TO DEFEND THE PLANE.

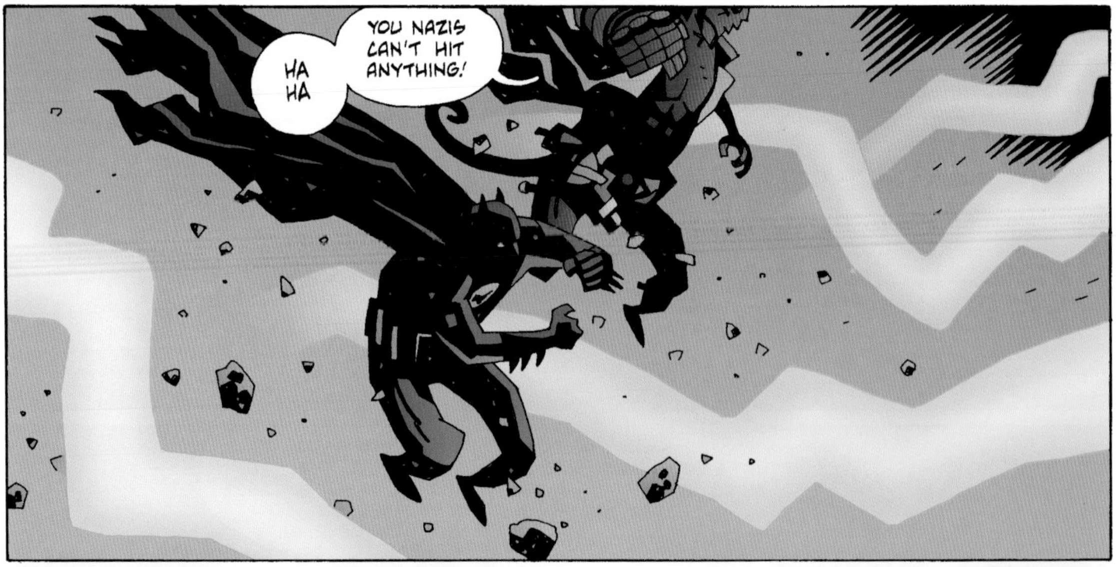
HA HA
YOU NAZIS CAN'T HIT ANYTHING!

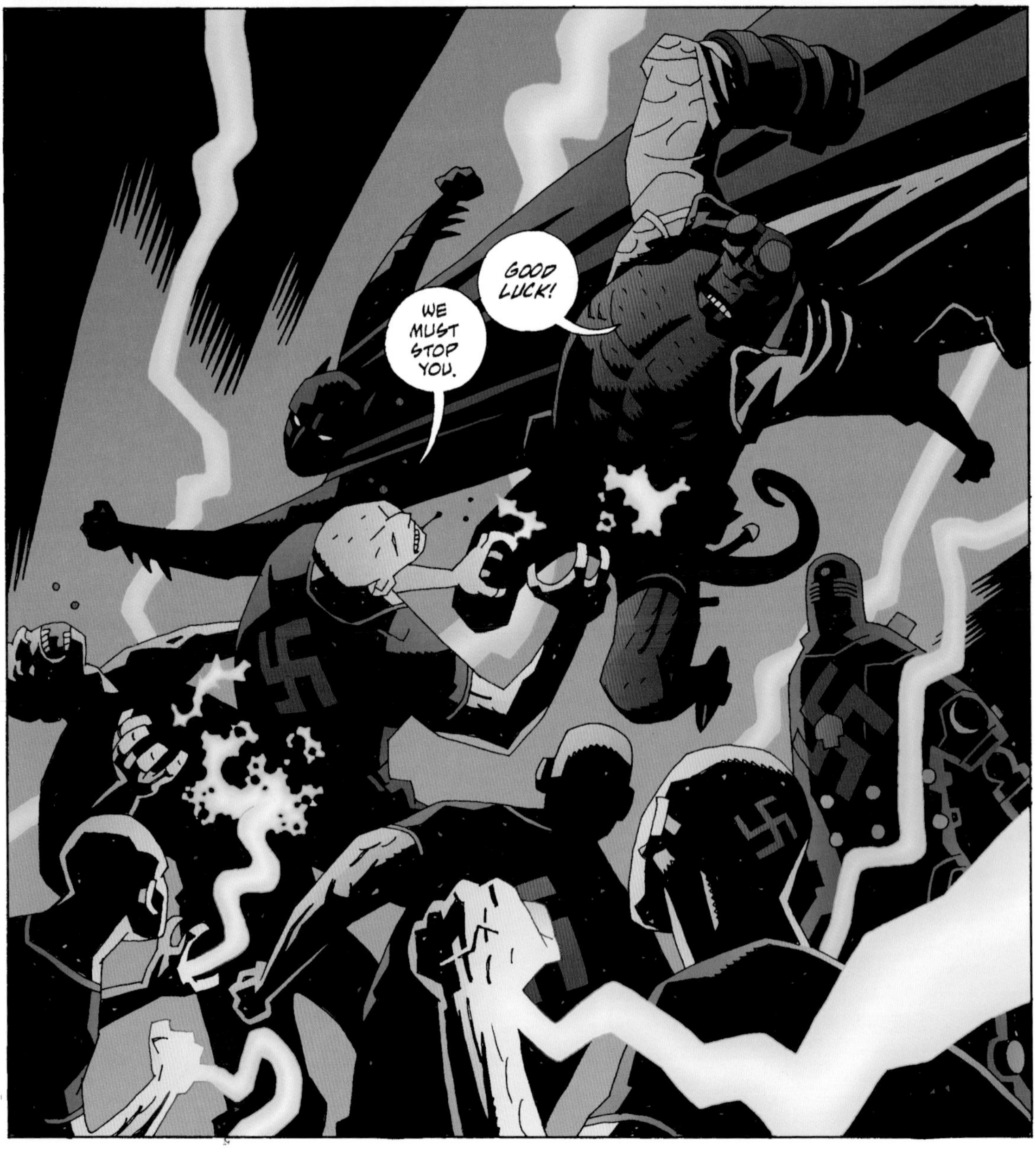
GOOD LUCK!
WE MUST STOP YOU.

PANG

HERR DANTZ, WHAT SHOULD WE DO?

DO? WHY, KEEP FIGHTING, YOU FOOL.

STOP THEM, DELAY THEM.

WE MUST GET THIS OLD MAN TO SAN DIABLO. DIE STOPPING THEM IF YOU MUST. USE THE SPELL OF PASSAGE.

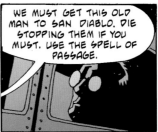

SPELL OF PASSAGE...

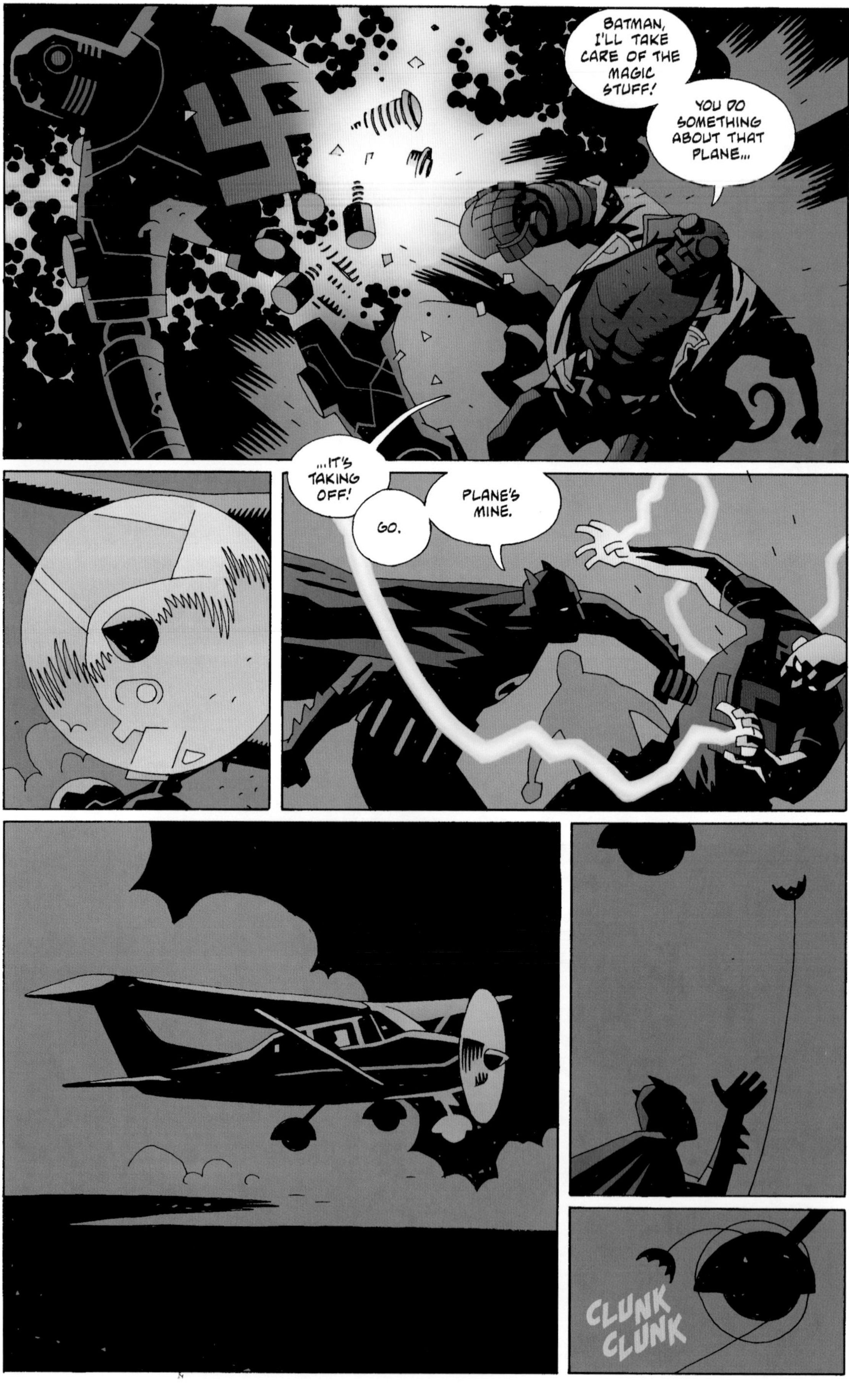
BATMAN, I'LL TAKE CARE OF THE MAGIC STUFF!
YOU DO SOMETHING ABOUT THAT PLANE...
...IT'S TAKING OFF!
GO.
PLANE'S MINE.
CLUNK CLUNK

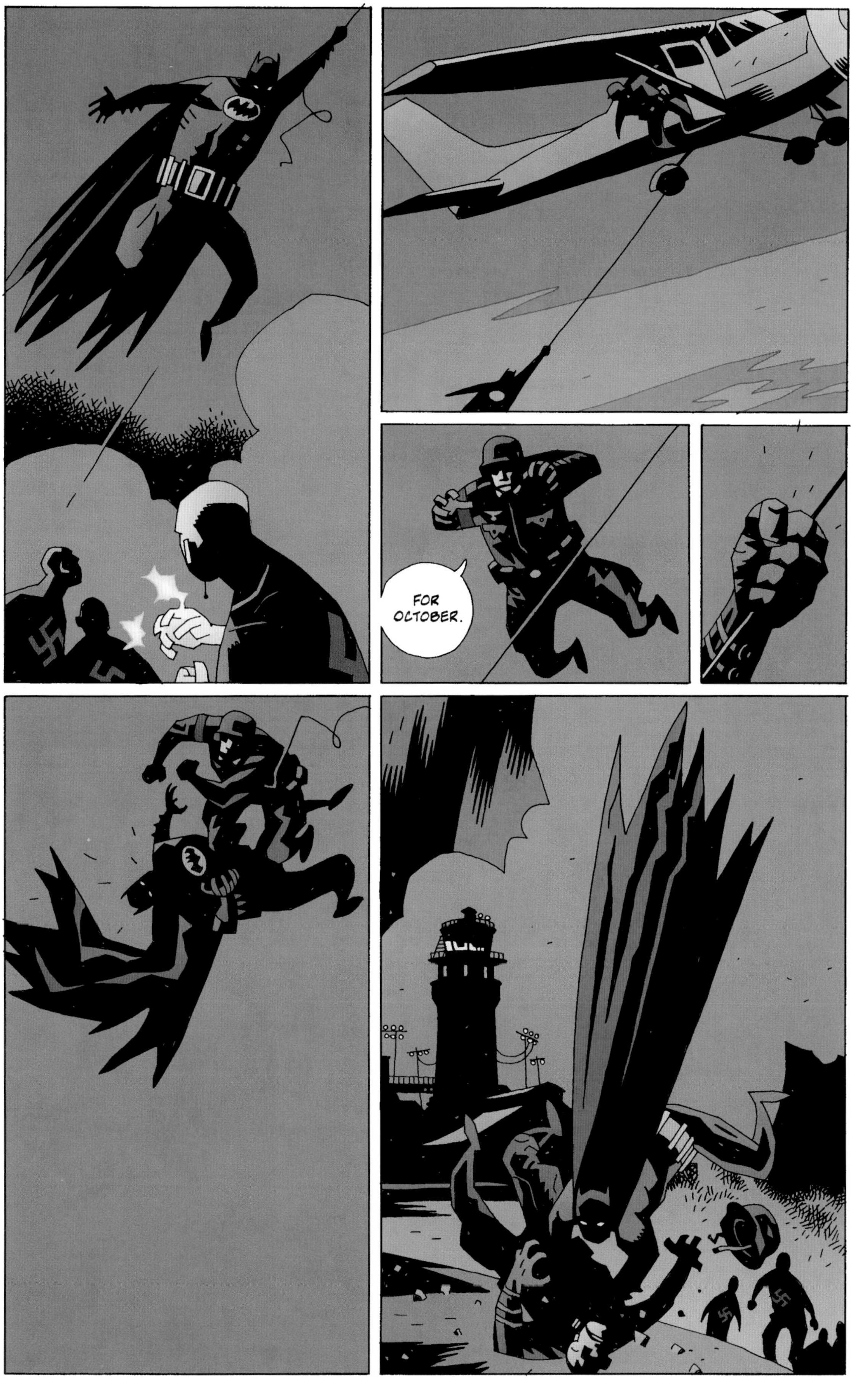
FOR OCTOBER.

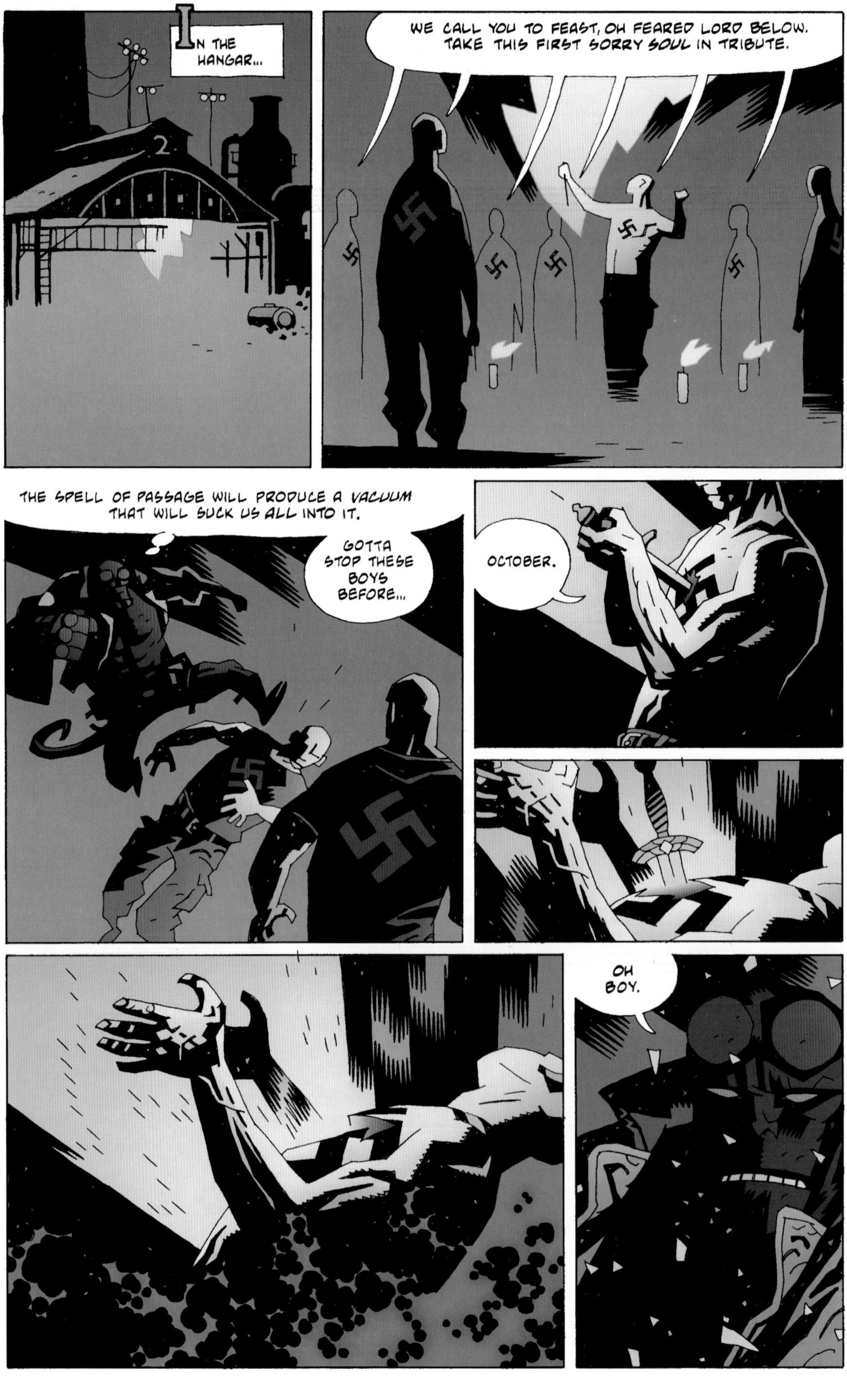
IN THE HANGAR...
WE CALL YOU TO FEAST, OH FEARED LORD BELOW. TAKE THIS FIRST SORRY SOUL IN TRIBUTE.
THE SPELL OF PASSAGE WILL PRODUCE A VACUUM THAT WILL SUCK US ALL INTO IT.
GOTTA STOP THESE BOYS BEFORE...
OCTOBER.
OH BOY.

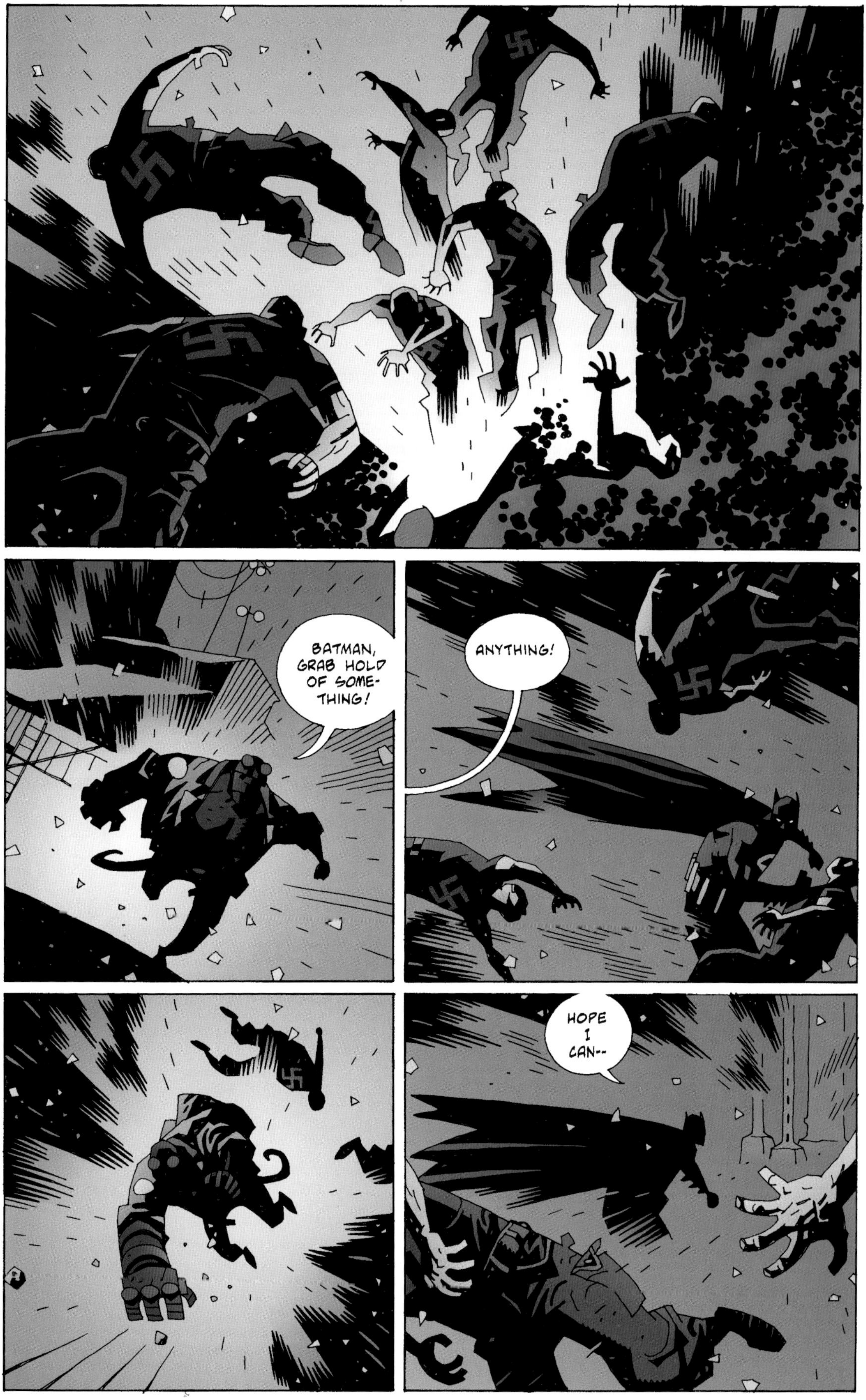
BATMAN, GRAB HOLD OF SOME-THING!
ANYTHING!
HOPE I CAN--

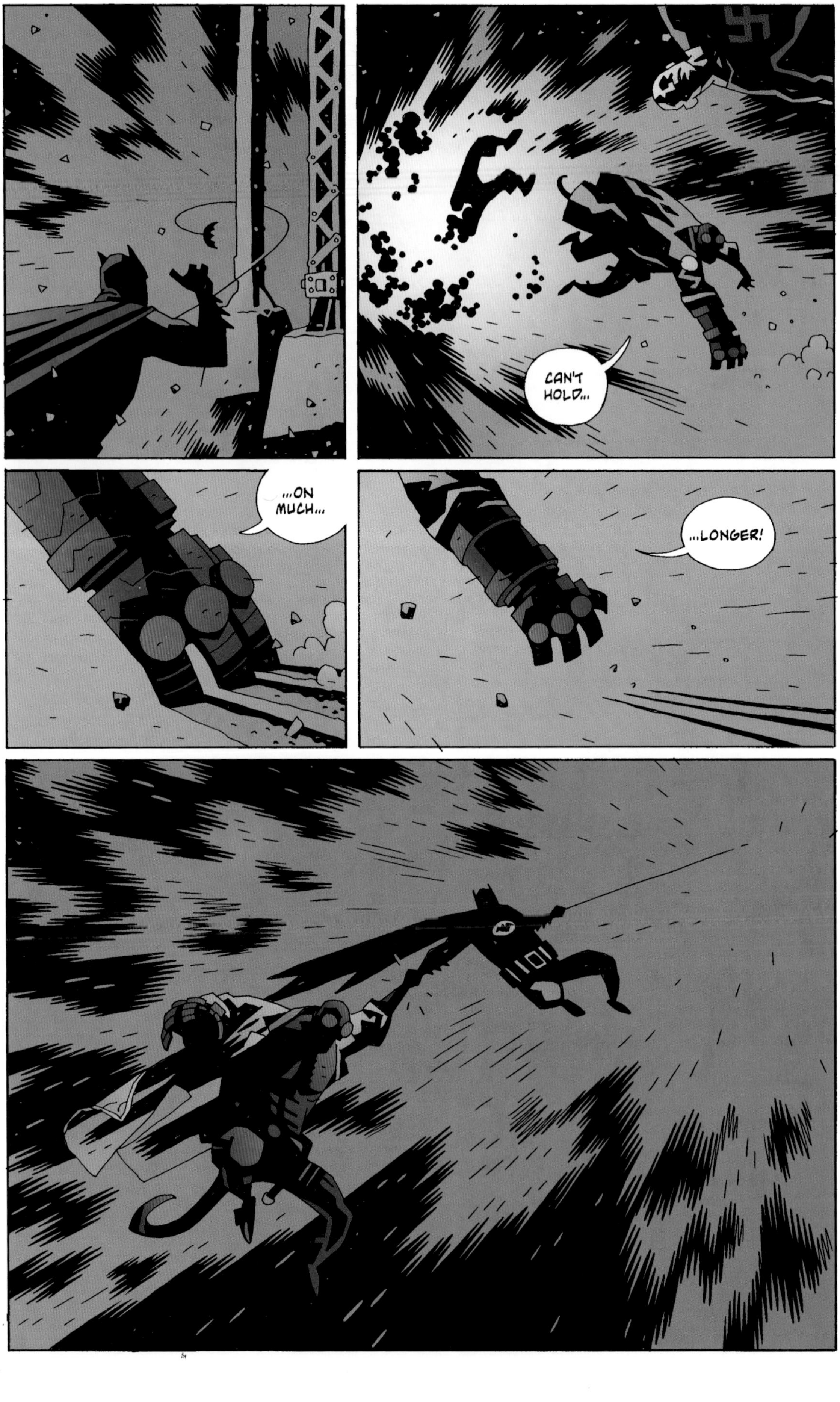
CAN'T HOLD...
...ON MUCH...
...LONGER!

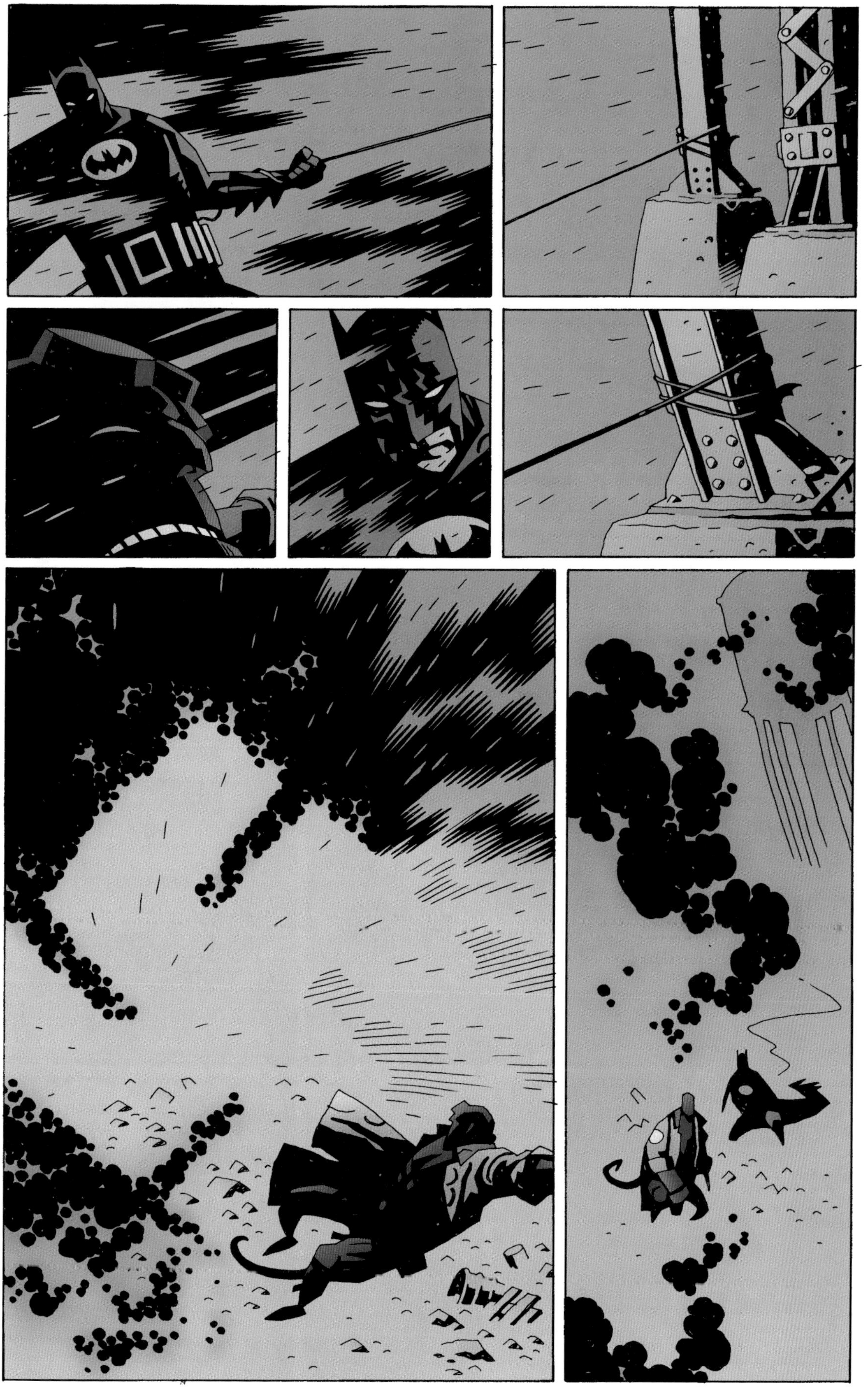

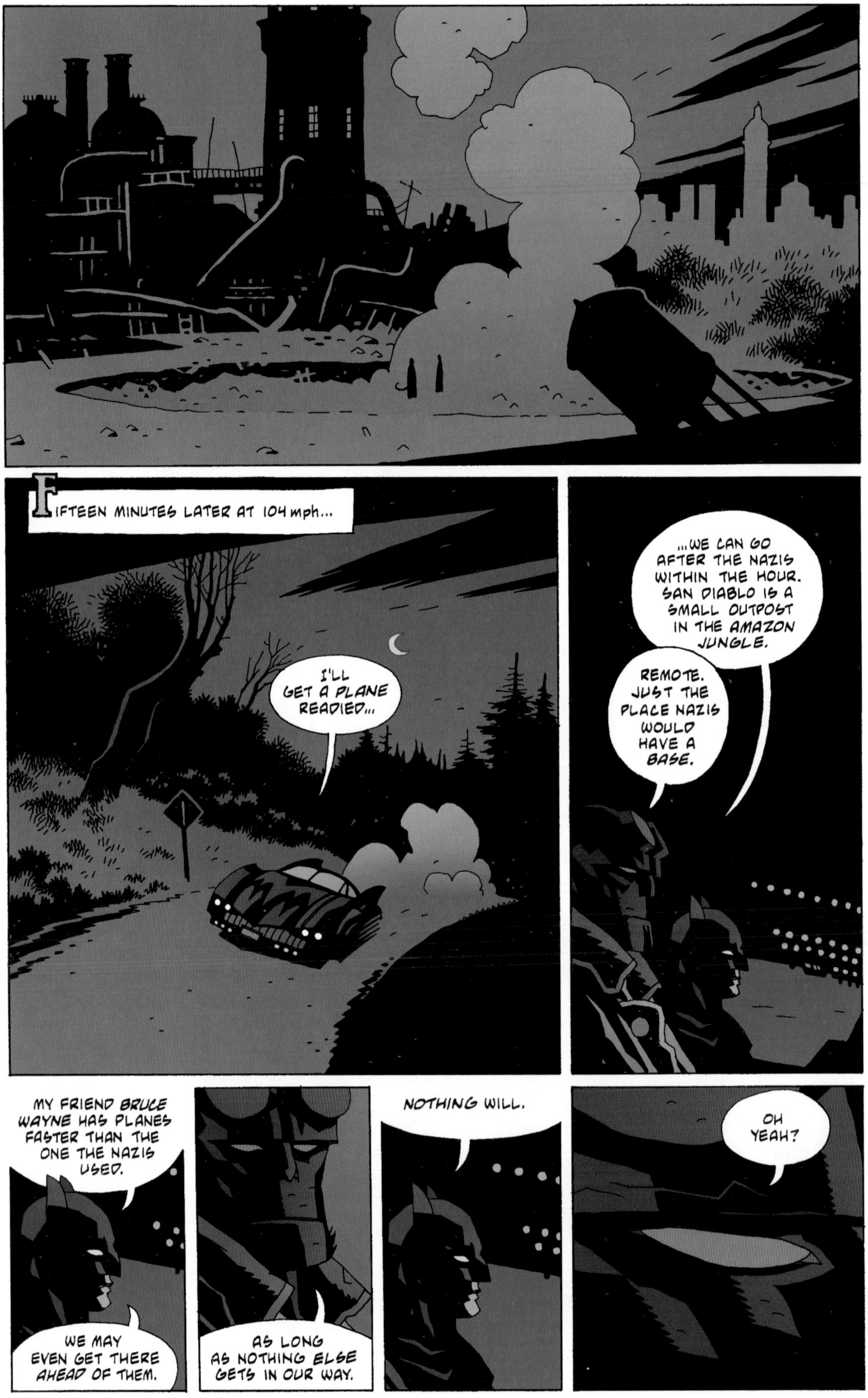
FIFTEEN MINUTES LATER AT 104 mph...
I'LL GET A PLANE READIED...
...WE CAN GO AFTER THE NAZIS WITHIN THE HOUR. SAN DIABLO IS A SMALL OUTPOST IN THE AMAZON JUNGLE.
REMOTE. JUST THE PLACE NAZIS WOULD HAVE A BASE.
MY FRIEND BRUCE WAYNE HAS PLANES FASTER THAN THE ONE THE NAZIS USED.
WE MAY EVEN GET THERE AHEAD OF THEM.
AS LONG AS NOTHING ELSE GETS IN OUR WAY.
NOTHING WILL.
OH YEAH?

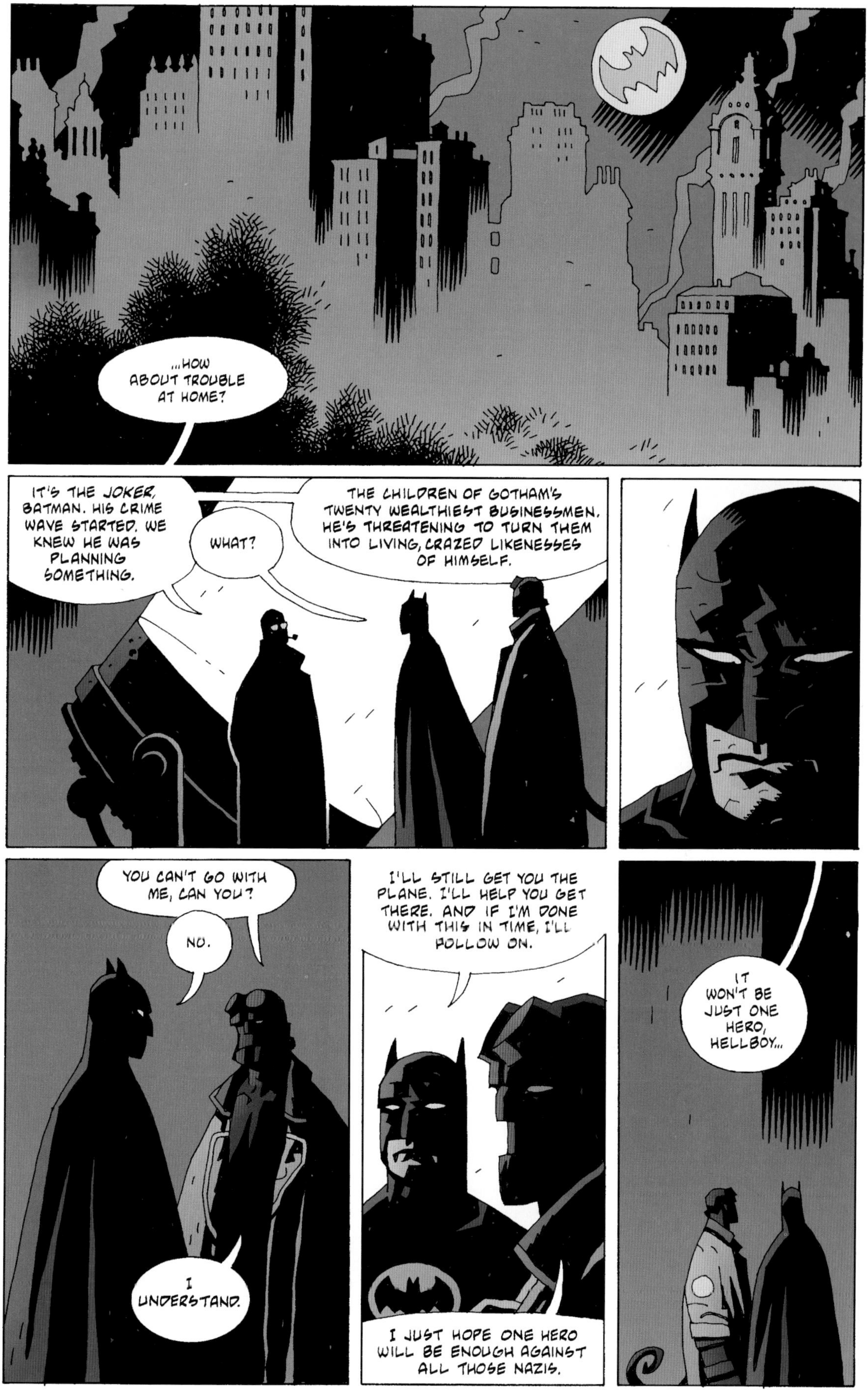
...HOW ABOUT TROUBLE AT HOME?
IT'S THE JOKER, BATMAN. HIS CRIME WAVE STARTED. WE KNEW HE WAS PLANNING SOMETHING.
WHAT?
THE CHILDREN OF GOTHAM'S TWENTY WEALTHIEST BUSINESSMEN. HE'S THREATENING TO TURN THEM INTO LIVING, CRAZED LIKENESSES OF HIMSELF.
YOU CAN'T GO WITH ME, CAN YOU?
NO.
I UNDERSTAND.
I'LL STILL GET YOU THE PLANE. I'LL HELP YOU GET THERE. AND IF I'M DONE WITH THIS IN TIME, I'LL FOLLOW ON.
I JUST HOPE ONE HERO WILL BE ENOUGH AGAINST ALL THOSE NAZIS.
IT WON'T BE JUST ONE HERO, HELLBOY...

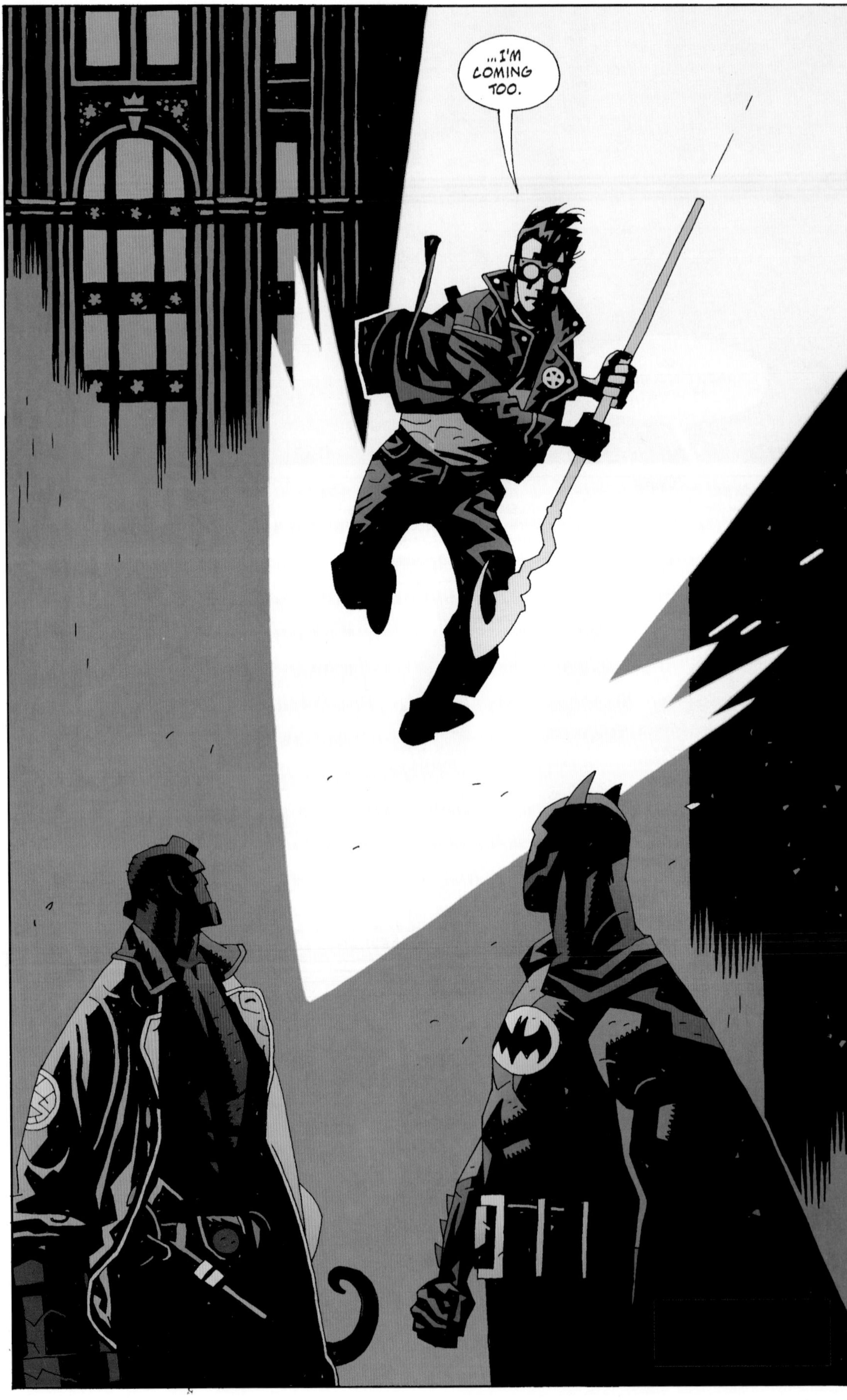
...I'M COMING TOO.

CHAPTER TWO

HARRIS
98

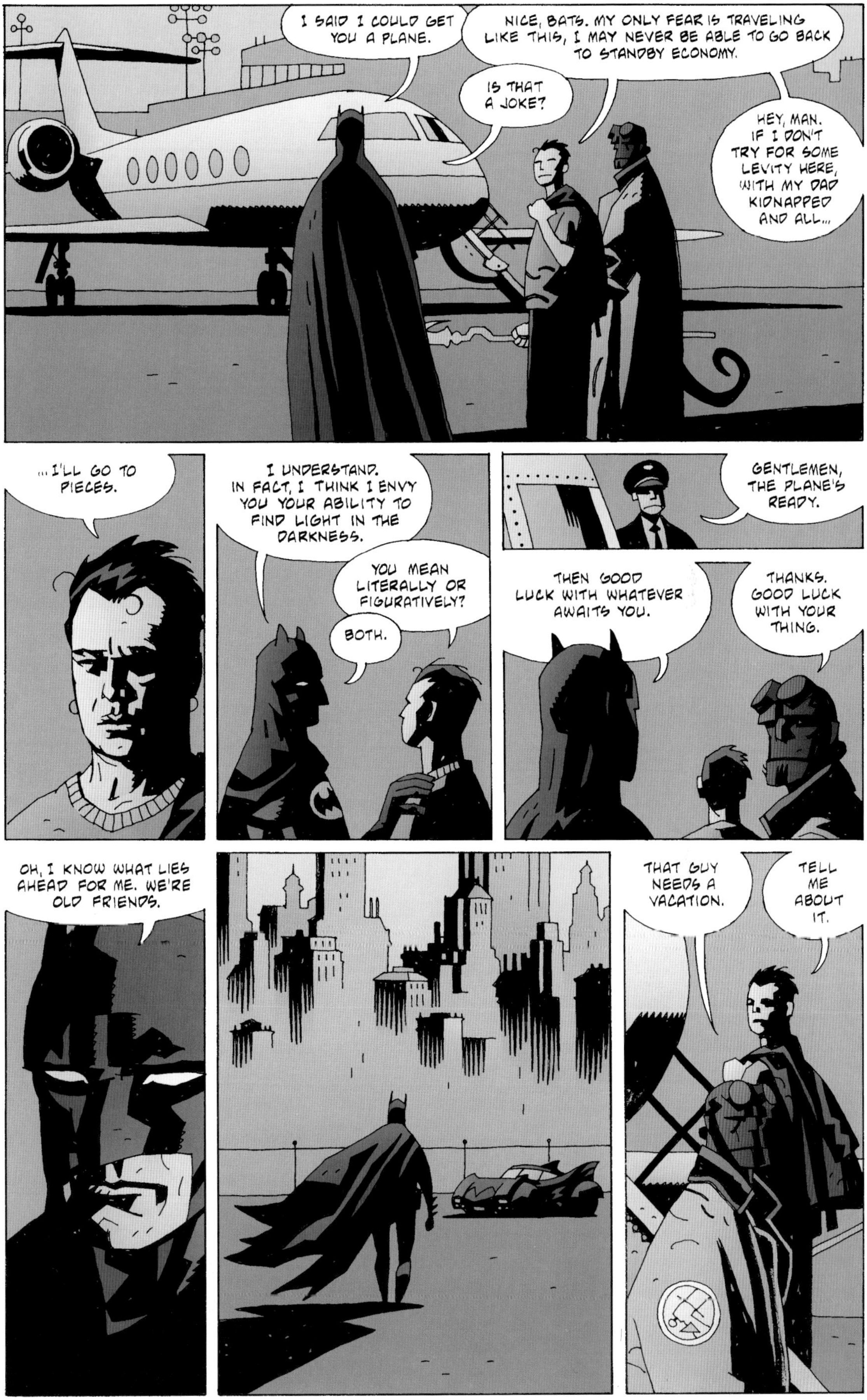
I SAID I COULD GET YOU A PLANE.
NICE, BATS. MY ONLY FEAR IS TRAVELING LIKE THIS, I MAY NEVER BE ABLE TO GO BACK TO STANDBY ECONOMY.
IS THAT A JOKE?
HEY, MAN. IF I DON'T TRY FOR SOME LEVITY HERE, WITH MY DAD KIDNAPPED AND ALL...
...I'LL GO TO PIECES.
I UNDERSTAND. IN FACT, I THINK I ENVY YOU YOUR ABILITY TO FIND LIGHT IN THE DARKNESS.
YOU MEAN LITERALLY OR FIGURATIVELY?
BOTH.
GENTLEMEN, THE PLANE'S READY.
THEN GOOD LUCK WITH WHATEVER AWAITS YOU.
THANKS. GOOD LUCK WITH YOUR THING.
OH, I KNOW WHAT LIES AHEAD FOR ME. WE'RE OLD FRIENDS.
THAT GUY NEEDS A VACATION.
TELL ME ABOUT IT.

AND YOU'RE SURE YOU HAVE NO IDEA WHY THE KNIGHTS OF OCTOBER WOULD KIDNAP YOUR FATHER?

HE FOUGHT FIFTH COLUMNISTS AND NAZIS DURING THE WAR. HE SERVED IN THE ARMY FOR LIKE A WEEK UNTIL HIS DUTIES AS STARMAN BROUGHT HIM BACK TO AMERICA FOR THE DURATION.

MAYBE IT'S SOME OLD NAZI KOOK WHO WANTS REVENGE.

THEN WHY NOT KILL YOUR FATHER BACK IN GOTHAM? IT WOULD HAVE BEEN A LOT EASIER THAN ALL THEY WENT THROUGH WITH ME AND BATMAN.

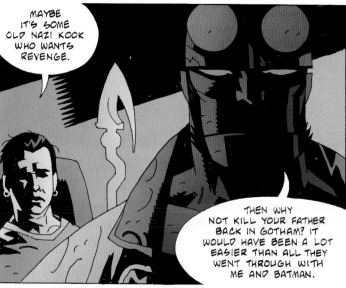

FROM WHAT I HEARD BEING SAID BY THE NAZI IN CHARGE, IT SEEMED LIKE THEY WANTED MISTER KNIGHT FOR A REASON.

CAN YOU THINK OF ANY METAPHYSICAL ANGLE TO YOUR FATHER'S WORK?

METAPHYSICAL? MY DAD FOUGHT CRIME ALONGSIDE THE SPECTRE AND DOCTOR FATE, YET STILL DENIES THE EXISTENCE OF AN AFTERLIFE.

PLUS HE MET A DEMON, ONCE. AND THERE ARE BEINGS LIKE YOU RUNNING AROUND.

NO OFFENSE.

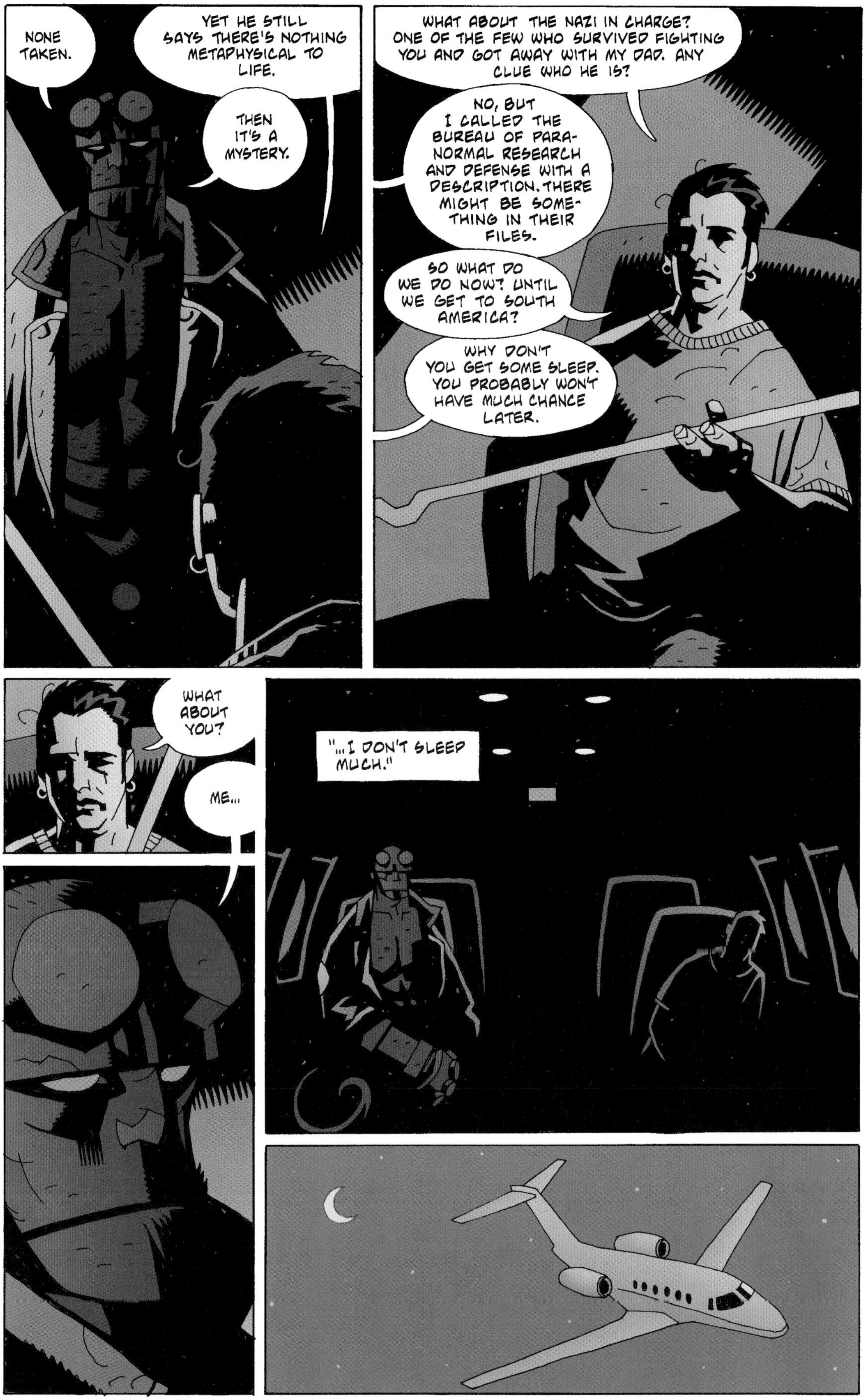
NONE TAKEN.
YET HE STILL SAYS THERE'S NOTHING METAPHYSICAL TO LIFE.
THEN IT'S A MYSTERY.
WHAT ABOUT THE NAZI IN CHARGE? ONE OF THE FEW WHO SURVIVED FIGHTING YOU AND GOT AWAY WITH MY DAD. ANY CLUE WHO HE IS?
NO, BUT I CALLED THE BUREAU OF PARA-NORMAL RESEARCH AND DEFENSE WITH A DESCRIPTION. THERE MIGHT BE SOME-THING IN THEIR FILES.
SO WHAT DO WE DO NOW? UNTIL WE GET TO SOUTH AMERICA?
WHY DON'T YOU GET SOME SLEEP. YOU PROBABLY WON'T HAVE MUCH CHANCE LATER.
WHAT ABOUT YOU?
ME...
"...I DON'T SLEEP MUCH."

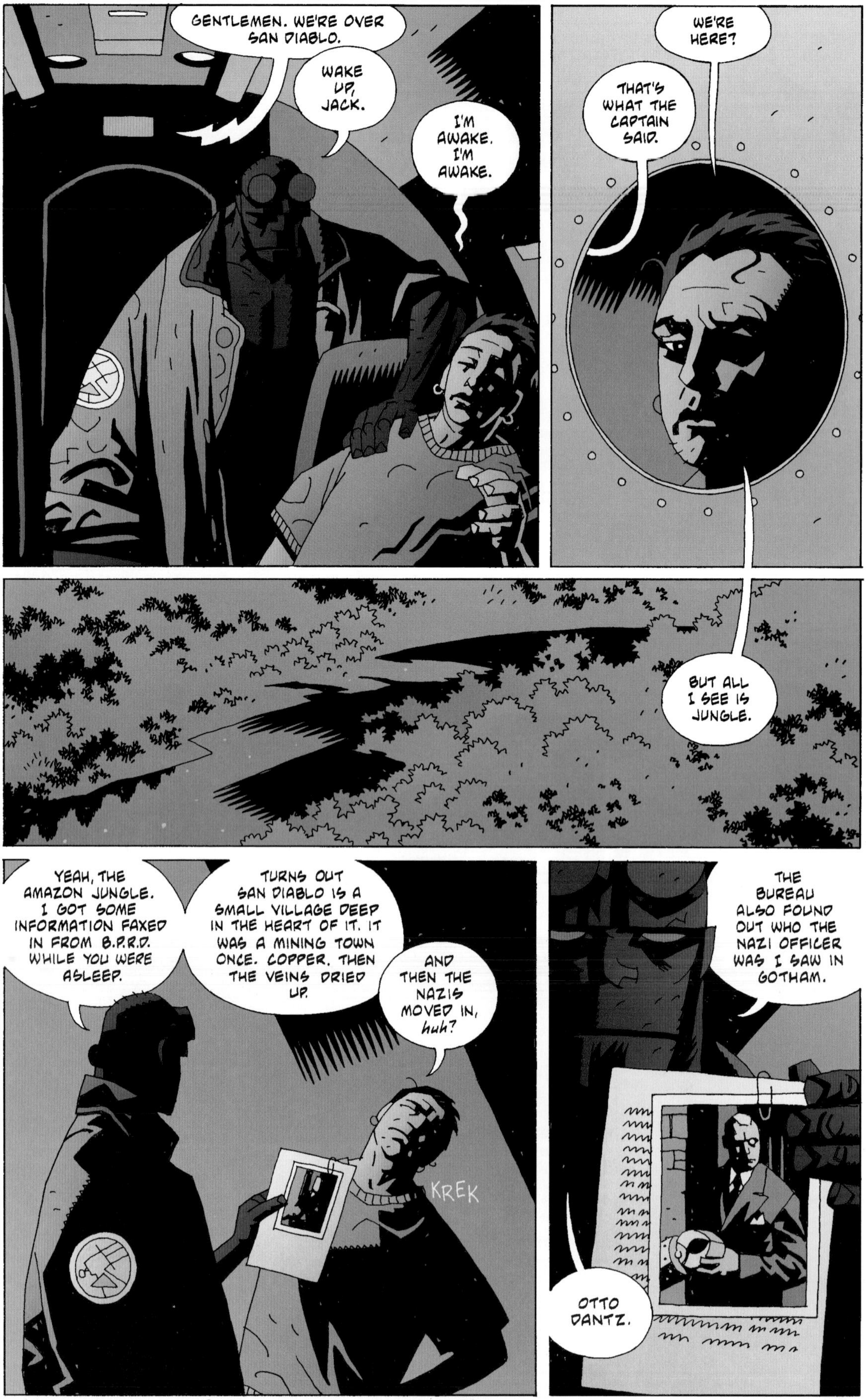
GENTLEMEN. WE'RE OVER SAN DIABLO.
WAKE UP, JACK.
I'M AWAKE. I'M AWAKE.
WE'RE HERE?
THAT'S WHAT THE CAPTAIN SAID.
BUT ALL I SEE IS JUNGLE.
YEAH, THE AMAZON JUNGLE. I GOT SOME INFORMATION FAXED IN FROM B.P.R.D. WHILE YOU WERE ASLEEP.
TURNS OUT SAN DIABLO IS A SMALL VILLAGE DEEP IN THE HEART OF IT. IT WAS A MINING TOWN ONCE. COPPER. THEN THE VEINS DRIED UP.
AND THEN THE NAZIS MOVED IN, huh?
KREK
THE BUREAU ALSO FOUND OUT WHO THE NAZI OFFICER WAS I SAW IN GOTHAM.
OTTO DANTZ.

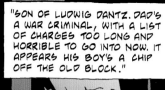

"SON OF LUDWIG DANTZ. DAD'S A WAR CRIMINAL, WITH A LIST OF CHARGES TOO LONG AND HORRIBLE TO GO INTO NOW. IT APPEARS HIS BOY'S A CHIP OFF THE OLD BLOCK."

I'D LIKE TO CHIP HIS BLOCK. AND WHO EXACTLY ARE THE KNIGHTS OF OCTOBER?

YOU'VE HEARD OF THE KNIGHTS TEMPLAR?

YEAH.

WELL, THE KNIGHTS OF OCTOBER WERE--

WE'RE OVER THE DROP ZONE, GENTLE-MEN.

LOOKS LIKE I'LL HAVE TO TELL YOU LATER. YOU KNOW HOW TO USE A PARACHUTE?

I DON'T NEED ONE. NEITHER WILL YOU. MY COSMIC ROD CAN GET US BOTH DOWN SAFELY.

YOU SURE?

I'M SICK OF JUMPING OUT OF PLANES AND THINGS NOT GOING RIGHT AND ME FALLING ALL THE WAY DOWN.

THAT WON'T HAPPEN BUDDY, PROMISE...

...NOT TONIGHT.

BATMAN   HELLBOY   STARMAN   PART TWO:

JUNGLE GREEN HORROR

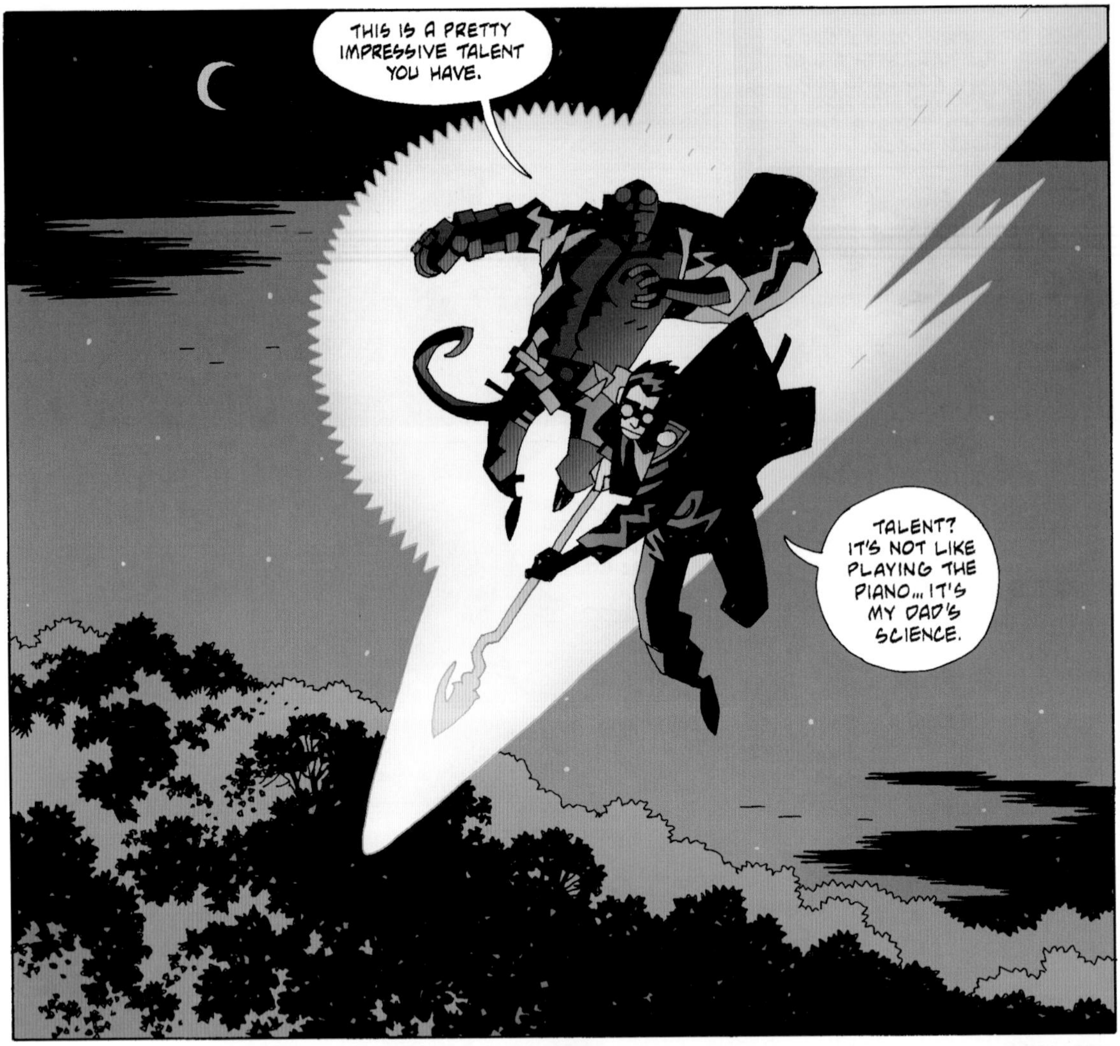
THIS IS A PRETTY IMPRESSIVE TALENT YOU HAVE.
TALENT? IT'S NOT LIKE PLAYING THE PIANO... IT'S MY DAD'S SCIENCE.

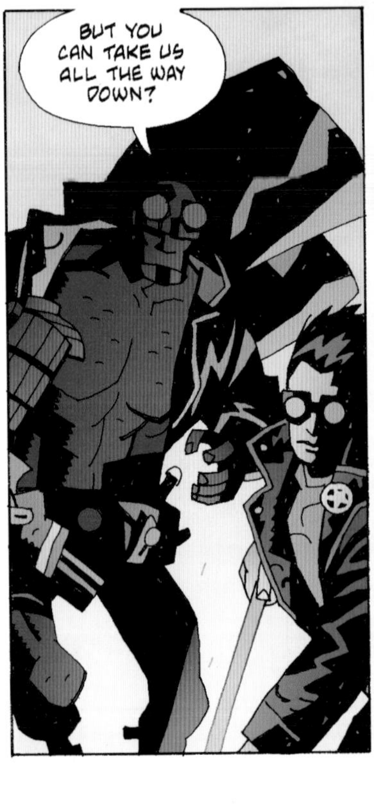
BUT YOU CAN TAKE US ALL THE WAY DOWN?

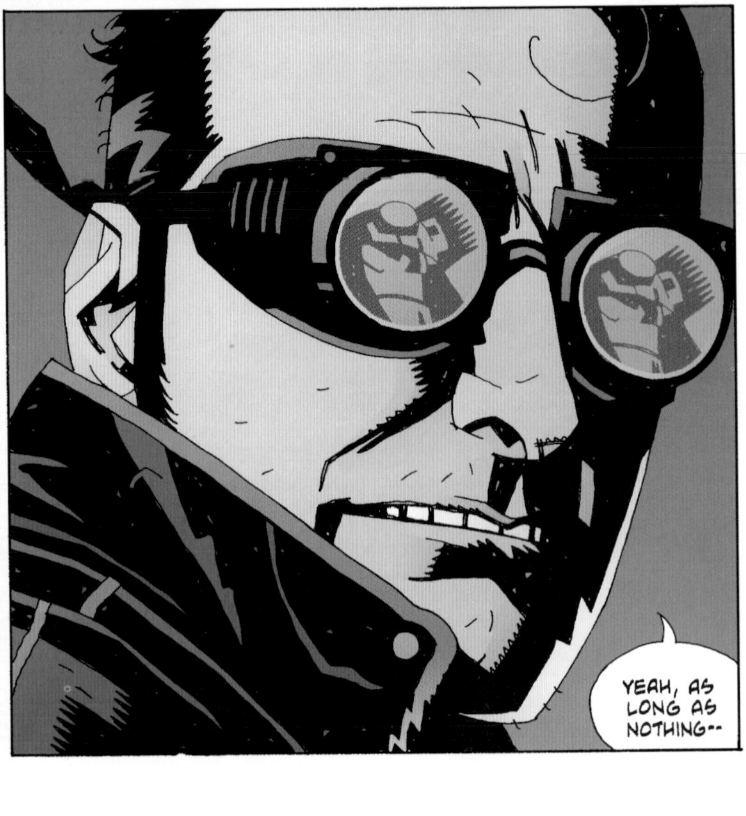
YEAH, AS LONG AS NOTHING--

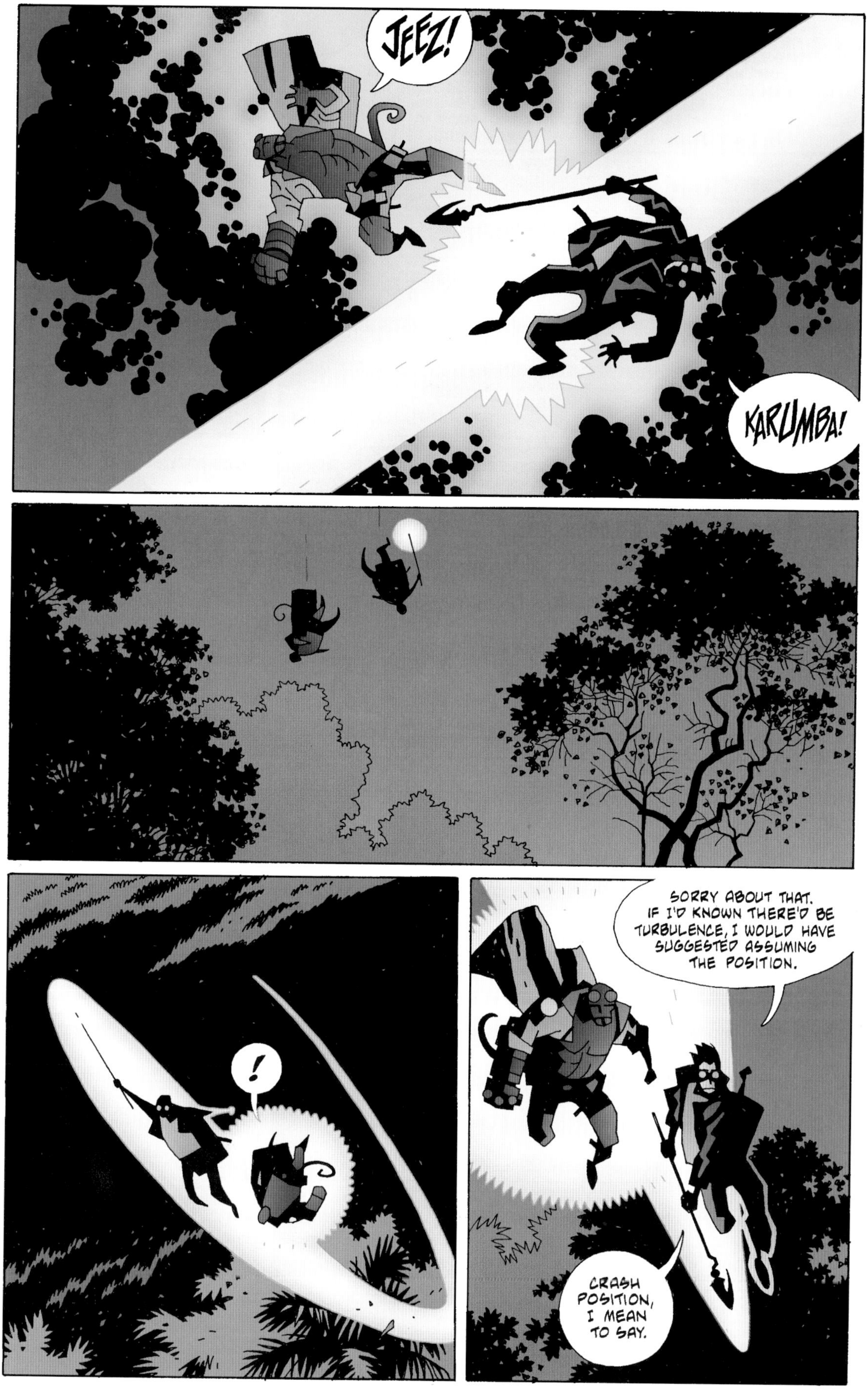
JEEZ!
KARUMBA!
!
SORRY ABOUT THAT. IF I'D KNOWN THERE'D BE TURBULENCE, I WOULD HAVE SUGGESTED ASSUMING THE POSITION.
CRASH POSITION, I MEAN TO SAY.

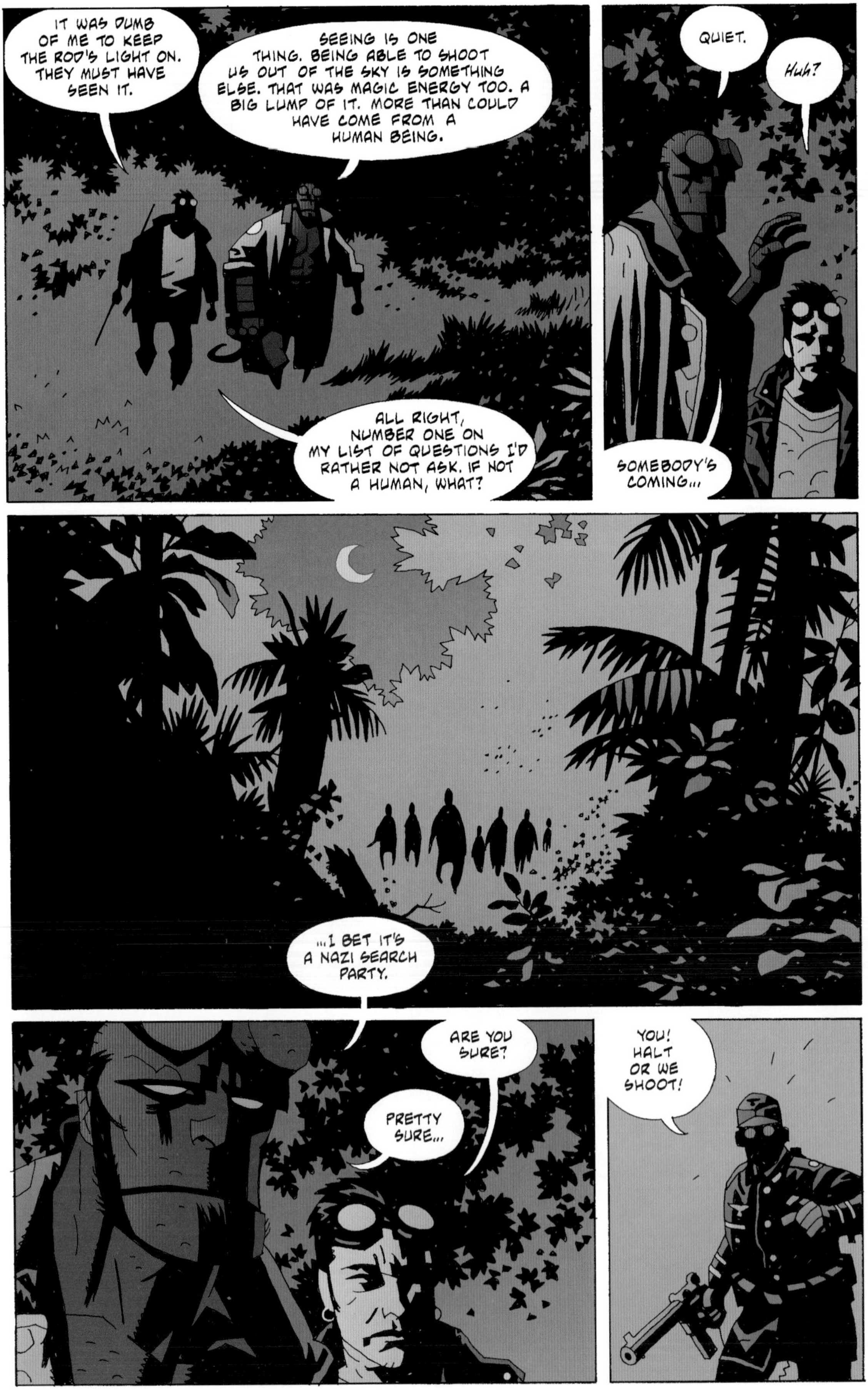
IT WAS DUMB OF ME TO KEEP THE ROD'S LIGHT ON. THEY MUST HAVE SEEN IT.
SEEING IS ONE THING. BEING ABLE TO SHOOT US OUT OF THE SKY IS SOMETHING ELSE. THAT WAS MAGIC ENERGY TOO. A BIG LUMP OF IT. MORE THAN COULD HAVE COME FROM A HUMAN BEING.
ALL RIGHT, NUMBER ONE ON MY LIST OF QUESTIONS I'D RATHER NOT ASK. IF NOT A HUMAN, WHAT?
QUIET.
Huh?
SOMEBODY'S COMING...
...I BET IT'S A NAZI SEARCH PARTY.
ARE YOU SURE?
PRETTY SURE...
YOU! HALT OR WE SHOOT!

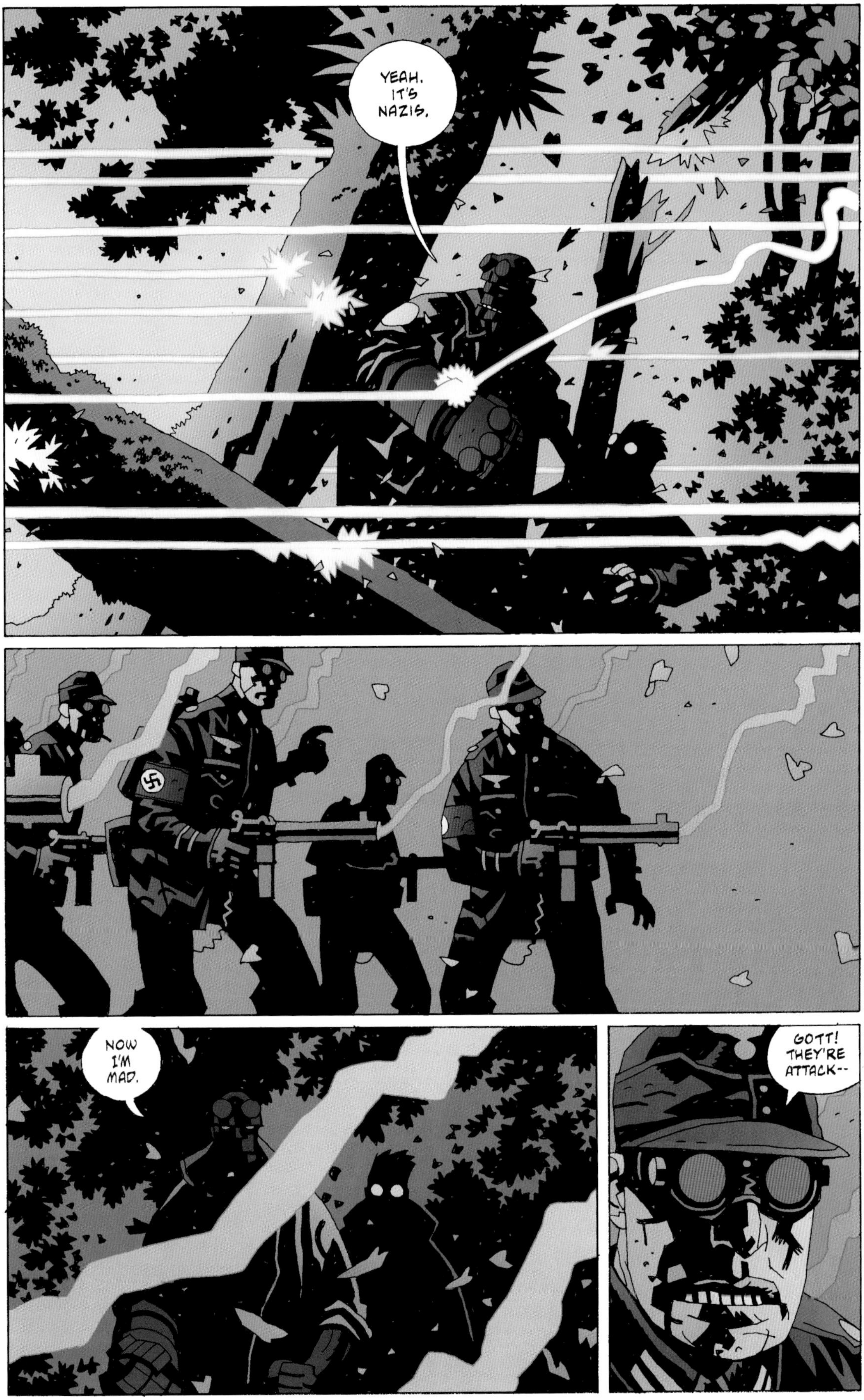
YEAH. IT'S NAZIS.
NOW I'M MAD.
GOTT! THEY'RE ATTACK--

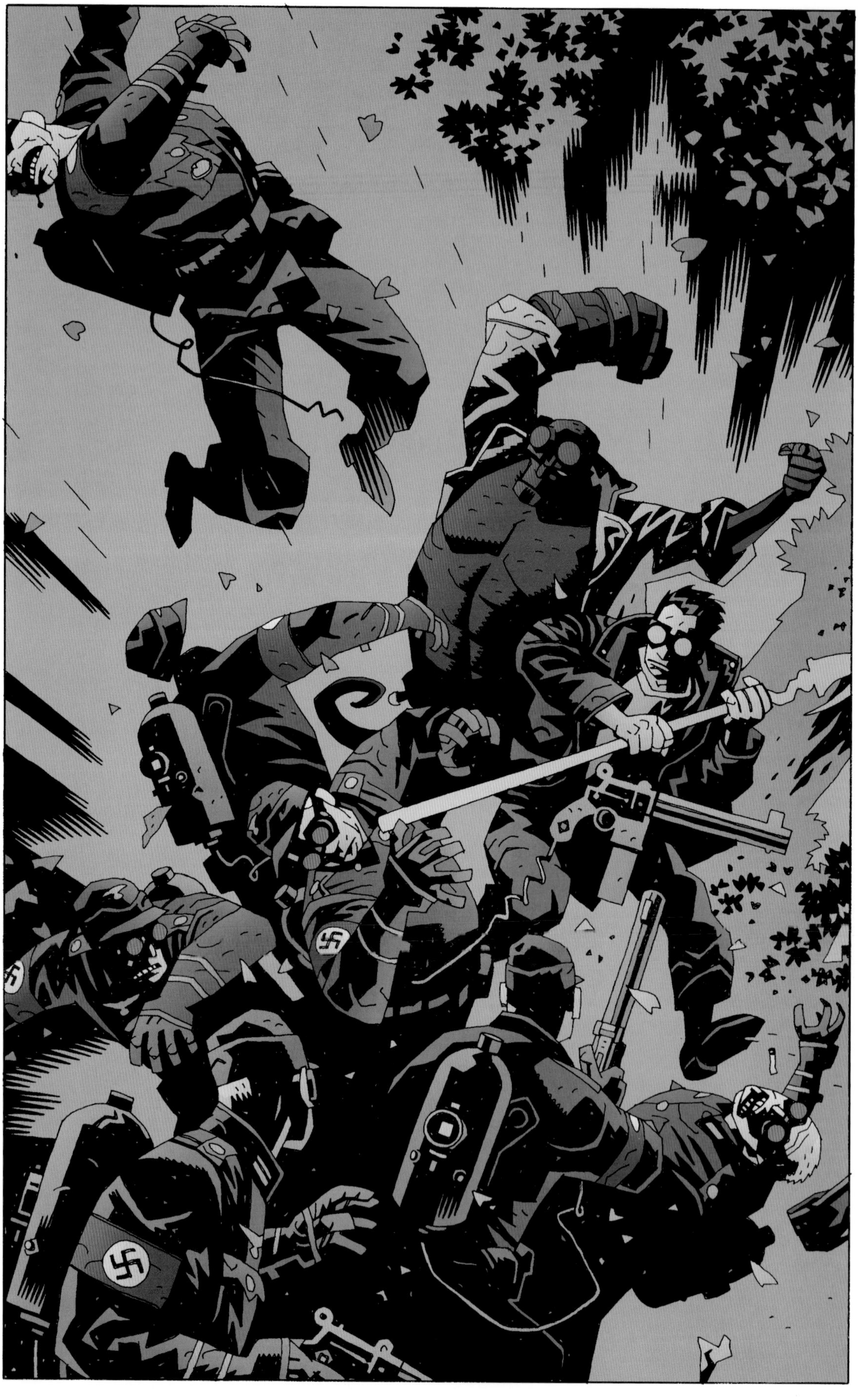

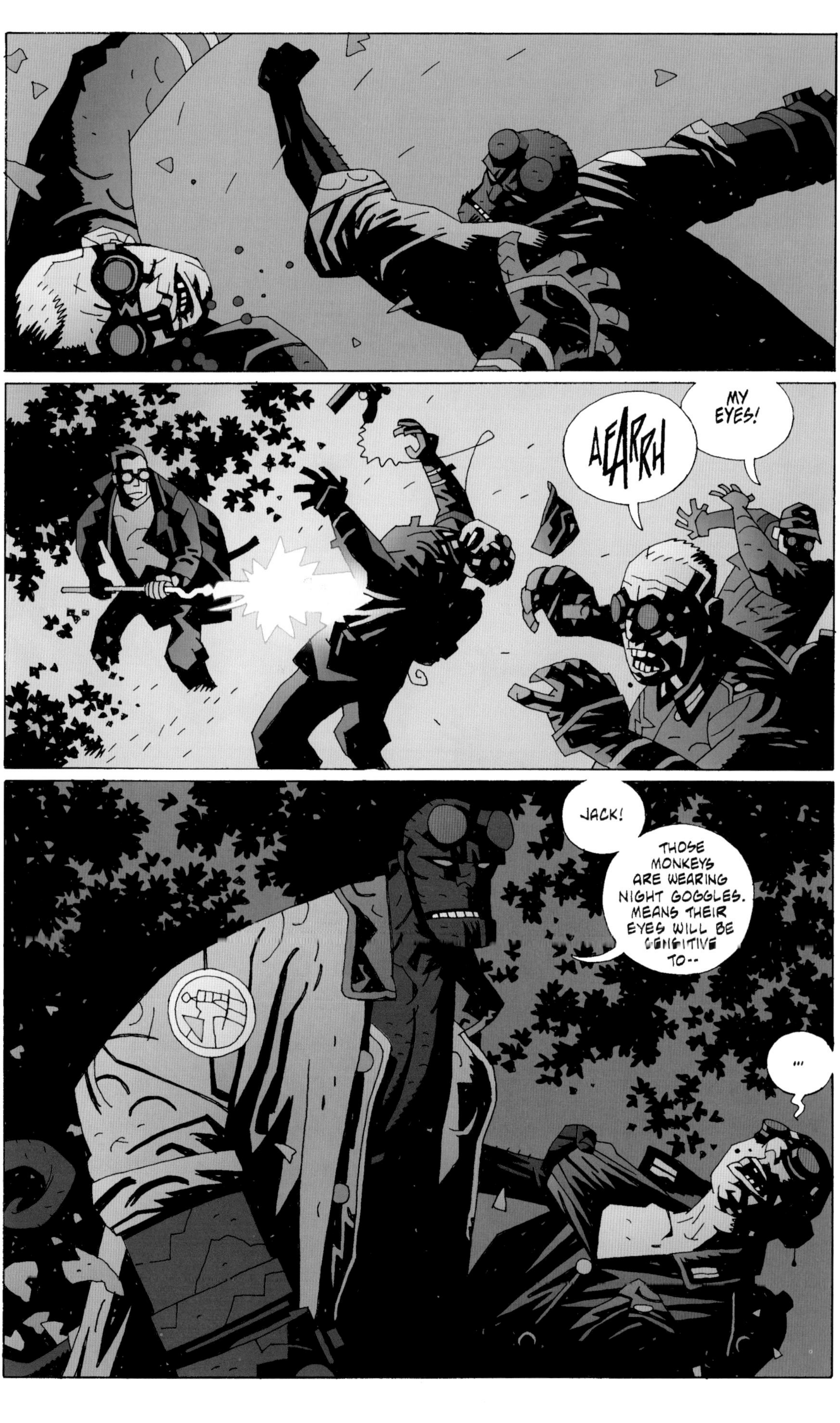
AEARRH
MY EYES!
JACK!
THOSE MONKEYS ARE WEARING NIGHT GOGGLES. MEANS THEIR EYES WILL BE SENSITIVE TO--
...

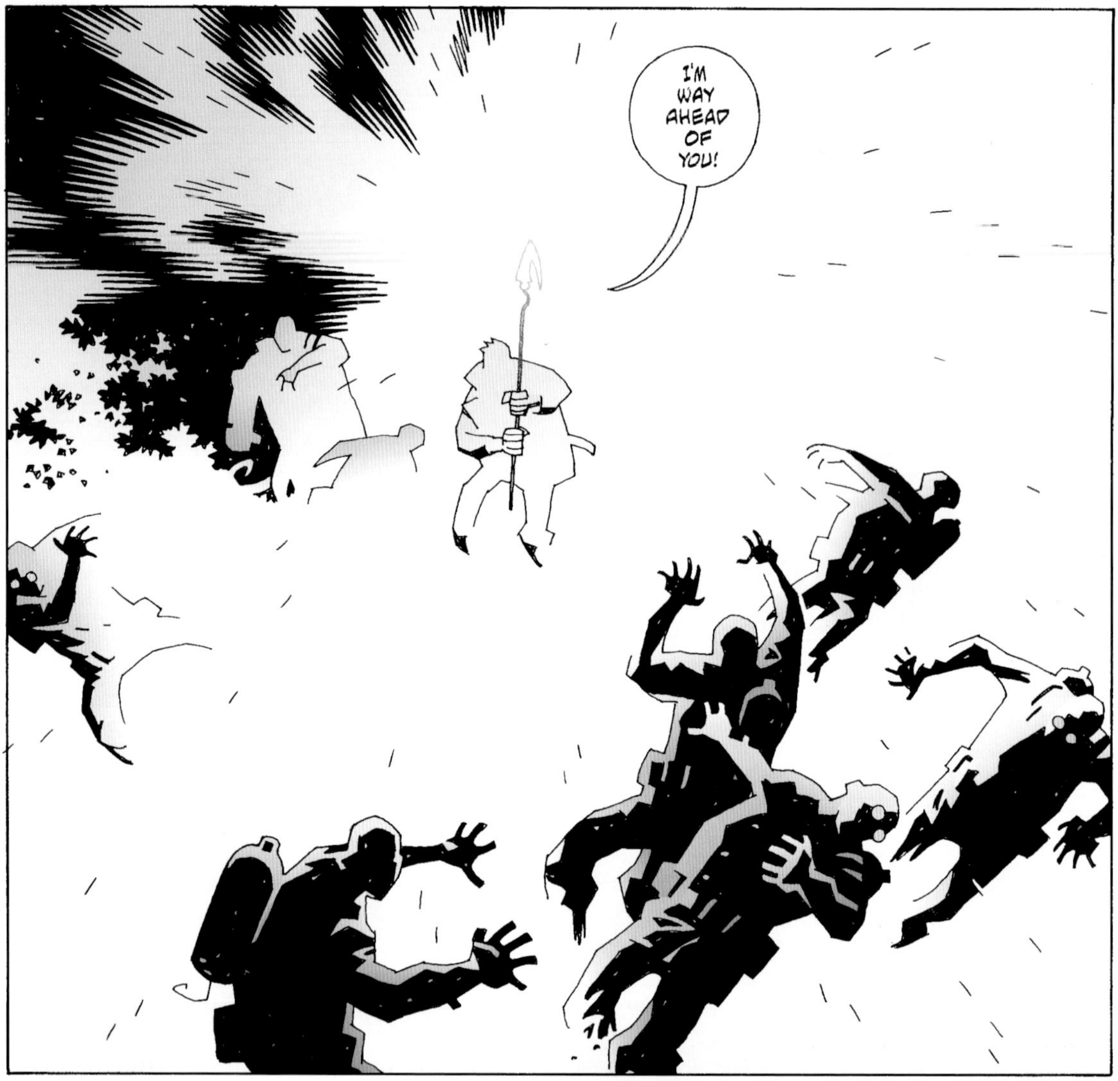
I'M WAY AHEAD OF YOU!

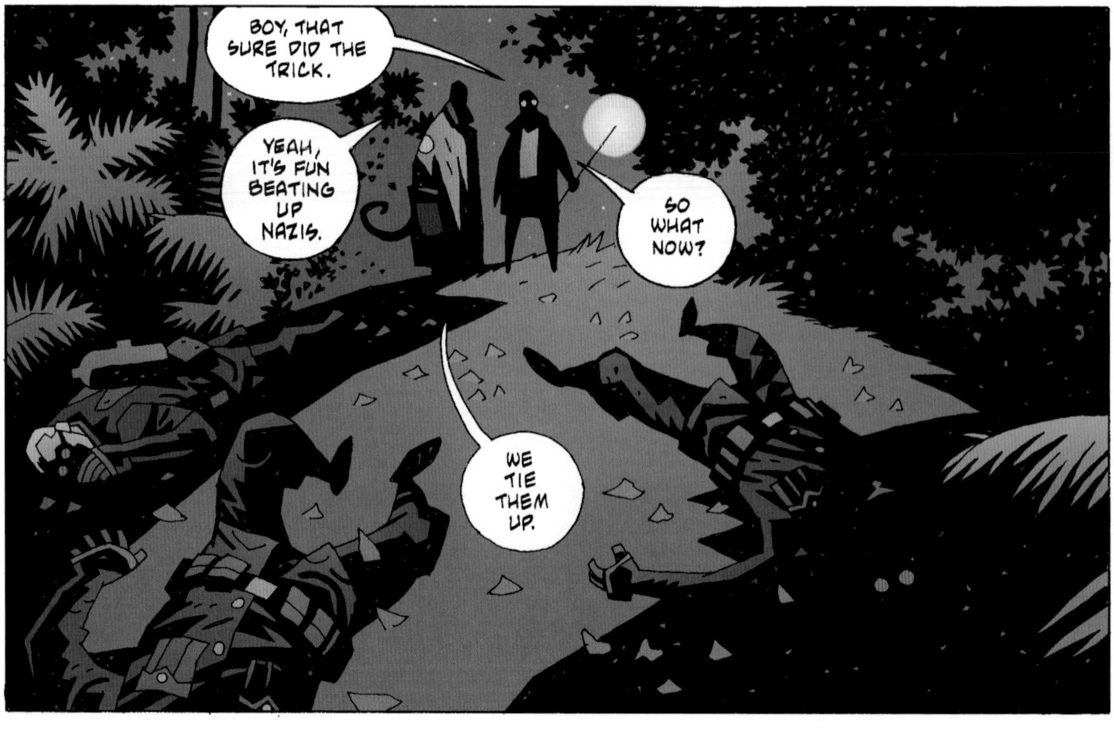
BOY, THAT SURE DID THE TRICK.
YEAH, IT'S FUN BEATING UP NAZIS.
SO WHAT NOW?
WE TIE THEM UP.

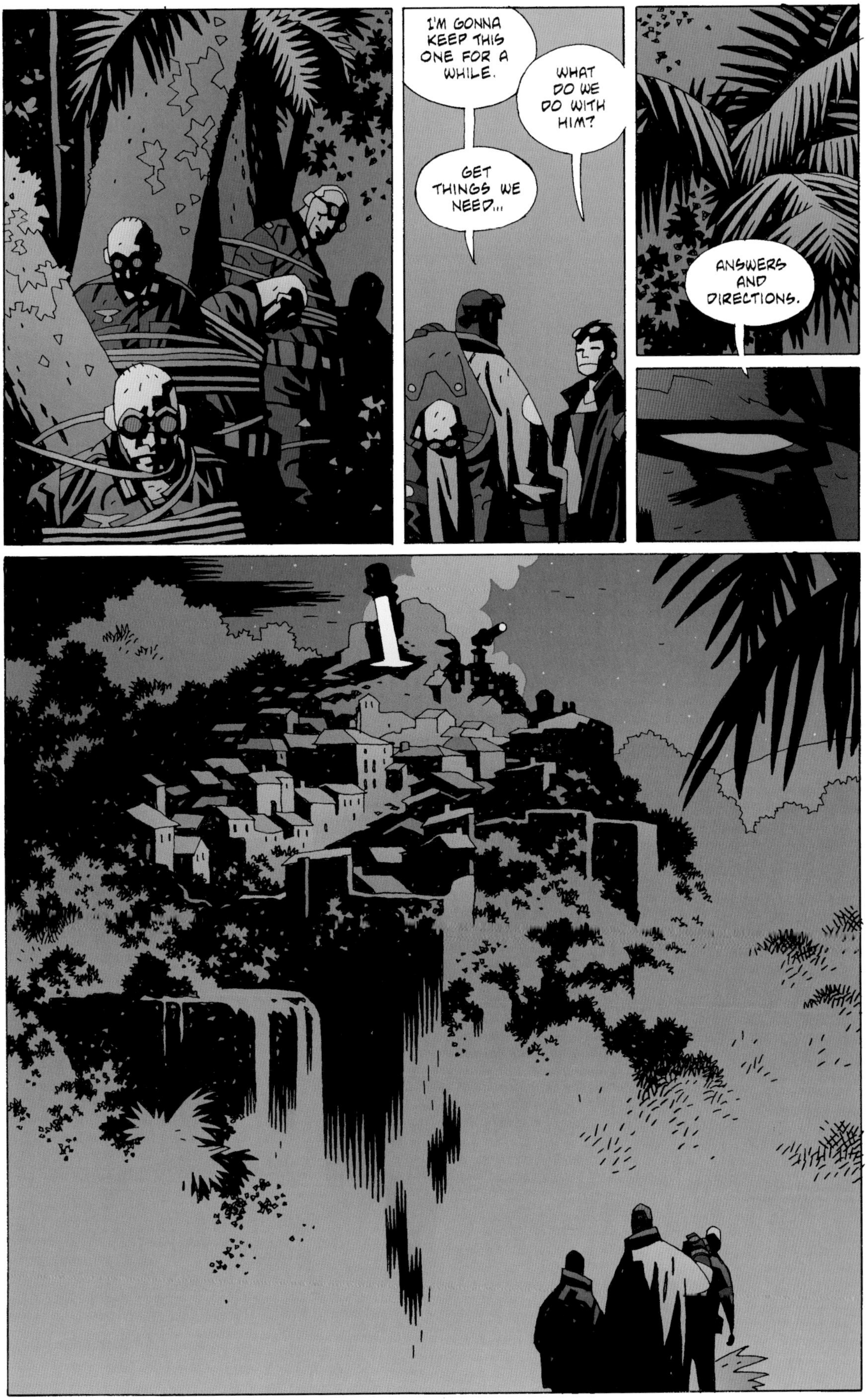
I'M GONNA KEEP THIS ONE FOR A WHILE.
WHAT DO WE DO WITH HIM?
GET THINGS WE NEED...
ANSWERS AND DIRECTIONS.

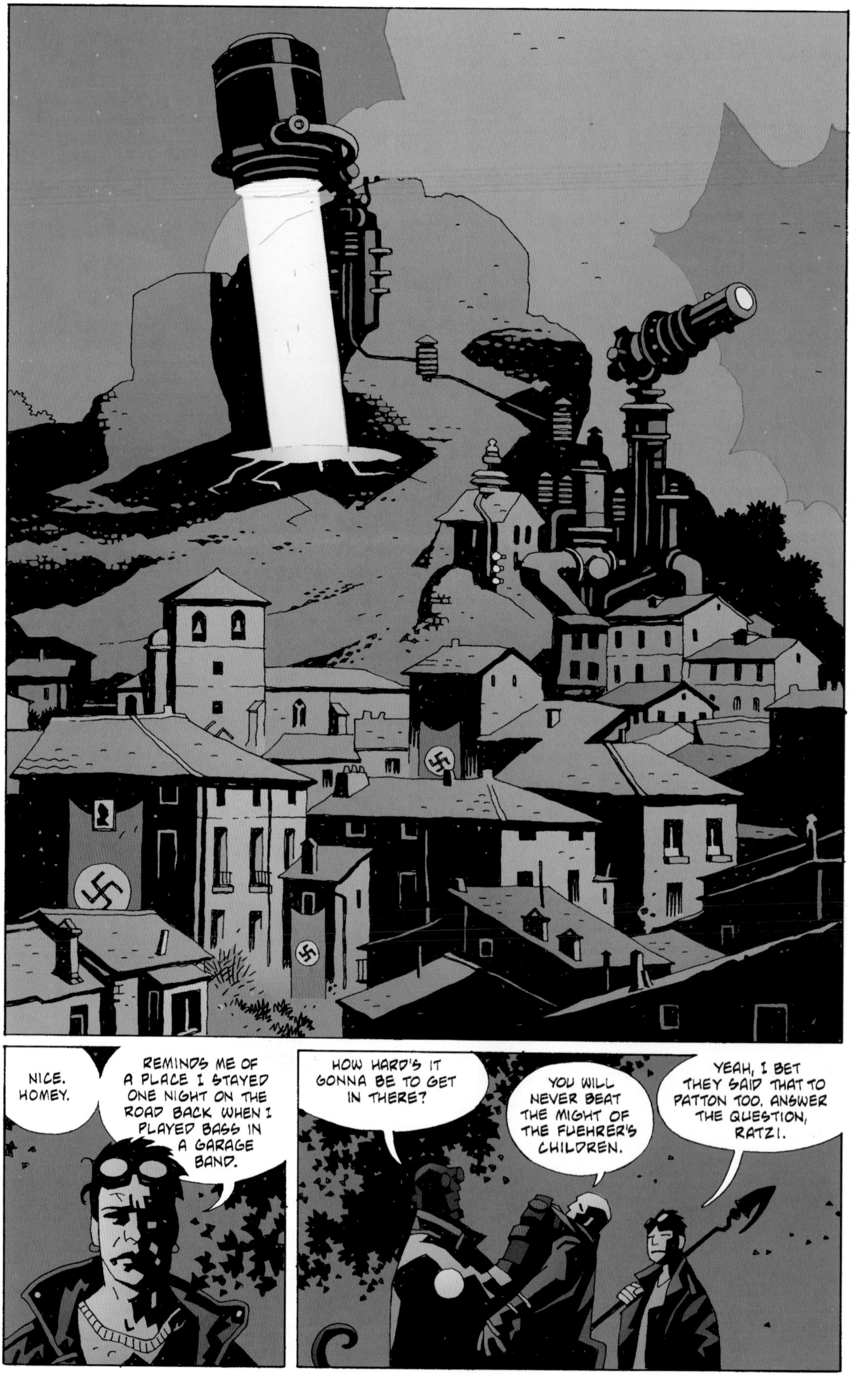
NICE. HOMEY.
REMINDS ME OF A PLACE I STAYED ONE NIGHT ON THE ROAD BACK WHEN I PLAYED BASS IN A GARAGE BAND.
HOW HARD'S IT GONNA BE TO GET IN THERE?
YOU WILL NEVER BEAT THE MIGHT OF THE FUEHRER'S CHILDREN.
YEAH, I BET THEY SAID THAT TO PATTON TOO. ANSWER THE QUESTION, RATZI.

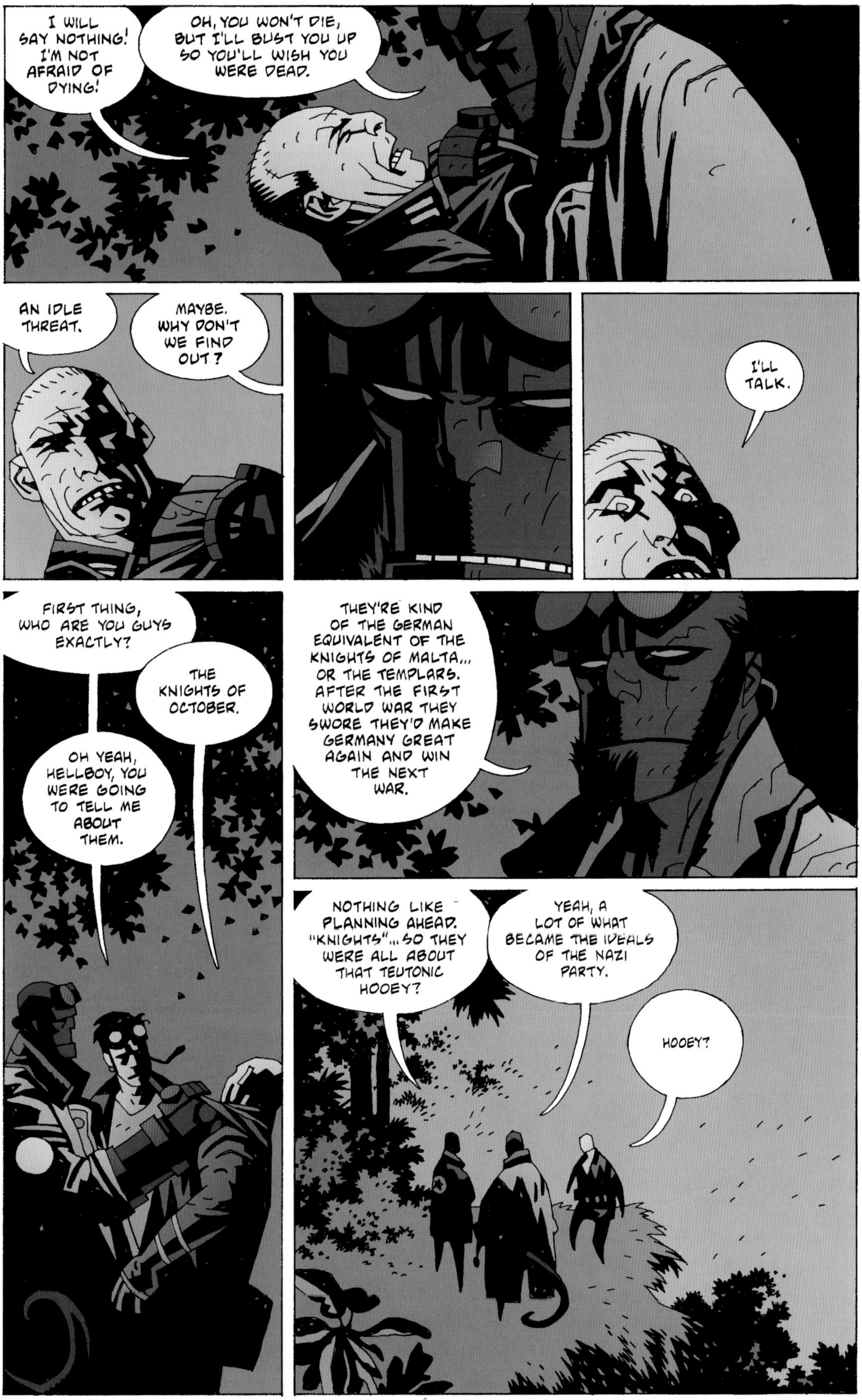

I WILL SAY NOTHING! I'M NOT AFRAID OF DYING!
OH, YOU WON'T DIE, BUT I'LL BUST YOU UP SO YOU'LL WISH YOU WERE DEAD.
AN IDLE THREAT.
MAYBE. WHY DON'T WE FIND OUT?
I'LL TALK.
FIRST THING, WHO ARE YOU GUYS EXACTLY?
THE KNIGHTS OF OCTOBER.
OH YEAH, HELLBOY, YOU WERE GOING TO TELL ME ABOUT THEM.
THEY'RE KIND OF THE GERMAN EQUIVALENT OF THE KNIGHTS OF MALTA... OR THE TEMPLARS. AFTER THE FIRST WORLD WAR THEY SWORE THEY'D MAKE GERMANY GREAT AGAIN AND WIN THE NEXT WAR.
NOTHING LIKE PLANNING AHEAD. "KNIGHTS"... SO THEY WERE ALL ABOUT THAT TEUTONIC HOOEY?
YEAH, A LOT OF WHAT BECAME THE IDEALS OF THE NAZI PARTY.
HOOEY?

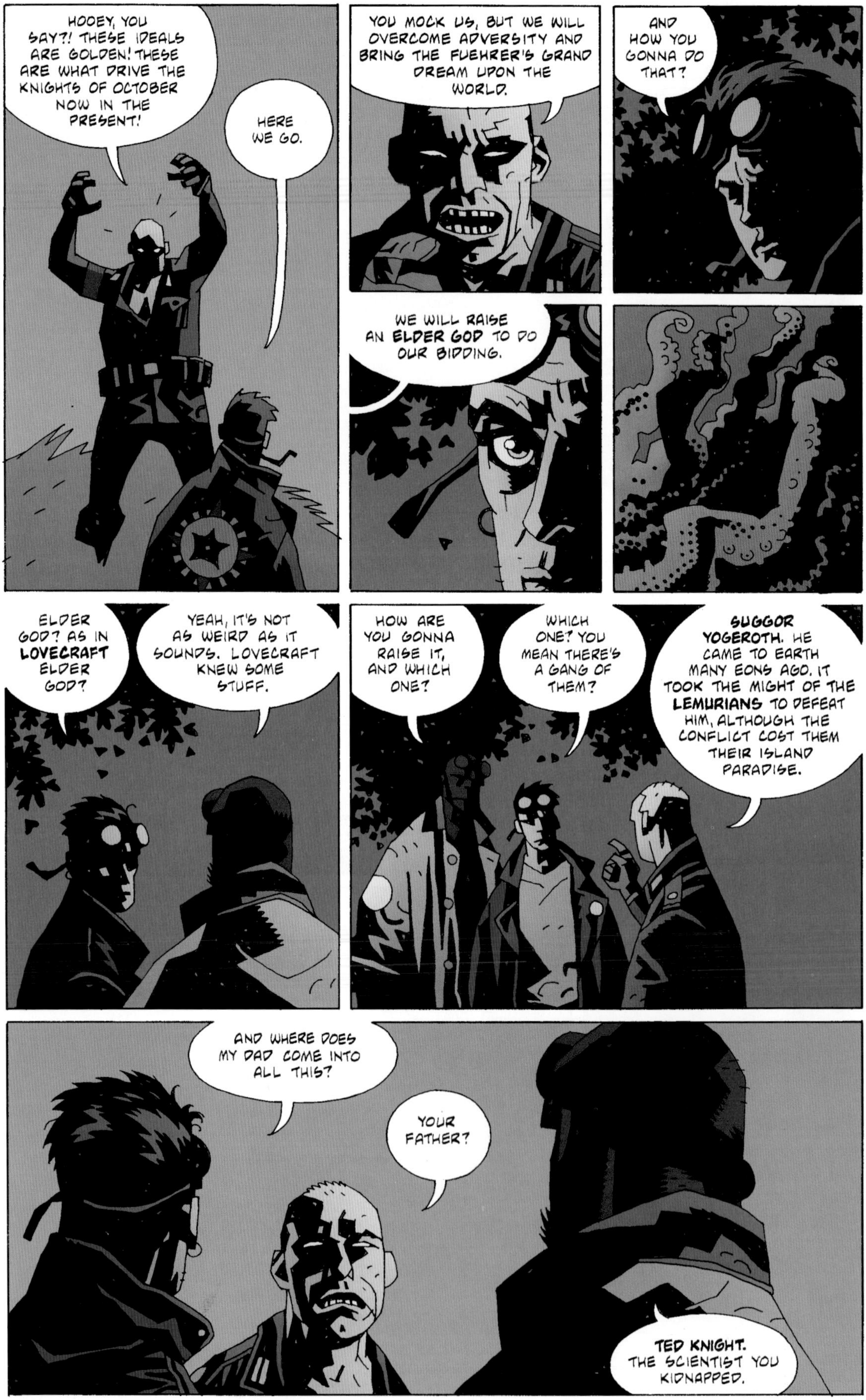
HOOEY, YOU SAY?! THESE IDEALS ARE GOLDEN! THESE ARE WHAT DRIVE THE KNIGHTS OF OCTOBER NOW IN THE PRESENT!
HERE WE GO.
YOU MOCK US, BUT WE WILL OVERCOME ADVERSITY AND BRING THE FUEHRER'S GRAND DREAM UPON THE WORLD.
AND HOW YOU GONNA DO THAT?
WE WILL RAISE AN ELDER GOD TO DO OUR BIDDING.
ELDER GOD? AS IN LOVECRAFT ELDER GOD?
YEAH, IT'S NOT AS WEIRD AS IT SOUNDS. LOVECRAFT KNEW SOME STUFF.
HOW ARE YOU GONNA RAISE IT, AND WHICH ONE?
WHICH ONE? YOU MEAN THERE'S A GANG OF THEM?
SUGGOR YOGEROTH. HE CAME TO EARTH MANY EONS AGO. IT TOOK THE MIGHT OF THE LEMURIANS TO DEFEAT HIM, ALTHOUGH THE CONFLICT COST THEM THEIR ISLAND PARADISE.
AND WHERE DOES MY DAD COME INTO ALL THIS?
YOUR FATHER?
TED KNIGHT. THE SCIENTIST YOU KIDNAPPED.

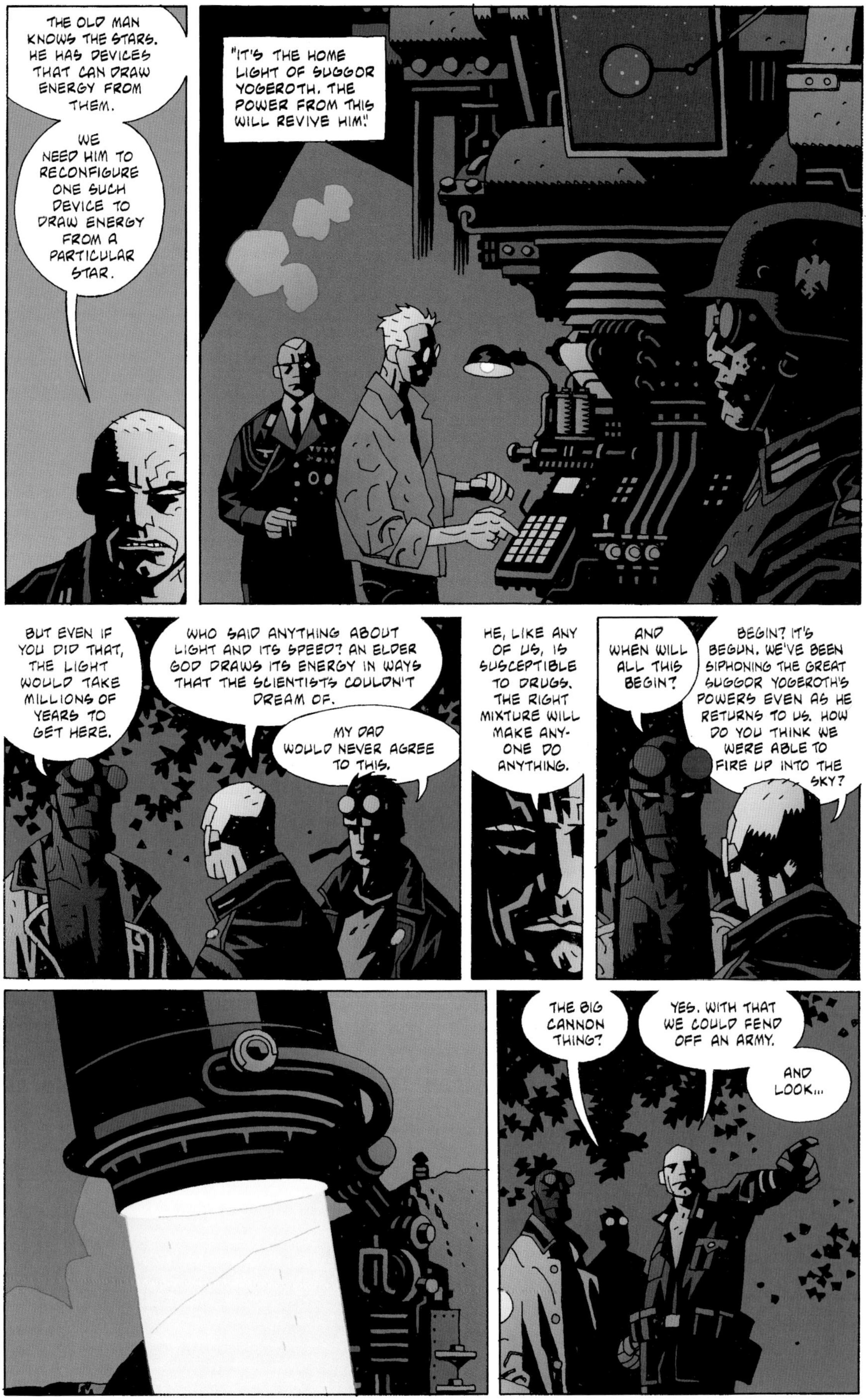
THE OLD MAN KNOWS THE STARS. HE HAS DEVICES THAT CAN DRAW ENERGY FROM THEM.
WE NEED HIM TO RECONFIGURE ONE SUCH DEVICE TO DRAW ENERGY FROM A PARTICULAR STAR.
"IT'S THE HOME LIGHT OF SUGGOR YOGEROTH. THE POWER FROM THIS WILL REVIVE HIM."
BUT EVEN IF YOU DID THAT, THE LIGHT WOULD TAKE MILLIONS OF YEARS TO GET HERE.
WHO SAID ANYTHING ABOUT LIGHT AND ITS SPEED? AN ELDER GOD DRAWS ITS ENERGY IN WAYS THAT THE SCIENTISTS COULDN'T DREAM OF.
MY DAD WOULD NEVER AGREE TO THIS.
HE, LIKE ANY OF US, IS SUSCEPTIBLE TO DRUGS. THE RIGHT MIXTURE WILL MAKE ANY-ONE DO ANYTHING.
AND WHEN WILL ALL THIS BEGIN?
BEGIN? IT'S BEGUN. WE'VE BEEN SIPHONING THE GREAT SUGGOR YOGEROTH'S POWERS EVEN AS HE RETURNS TO US. HOW DO YOU THINK WE WERE ABLE TO FIRE UP INTO THE SKY?
THE BIG CANNON THING?
YES. WITH THAT WE COULD FEND OFF AN ARMY.
AND LOOK...

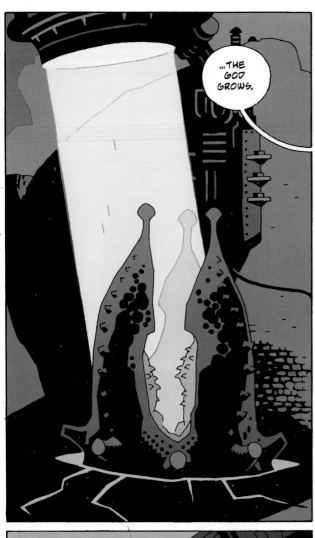

...THE GOD GROWS.

WHOA, HE'S A BIG BOY.

AND MANY-SIDED.

NOW THAT WAS FROM LOVECRAFT. DON'T BE TRYING TO IMPRESS ME WITH WATERED-DOWN H.P.

YEAH, YOU'RE GIVING ME A HEADACHE.

KLONK

NOW WHAT?

WE ATTACK AND GET YOUR FATHER OUT. THEN WE STOP THAT THING FROM GETTING ANY BIGGER.

ATTACK? YOU GOT A PLAN?

NOPE.

JUST ASKING.

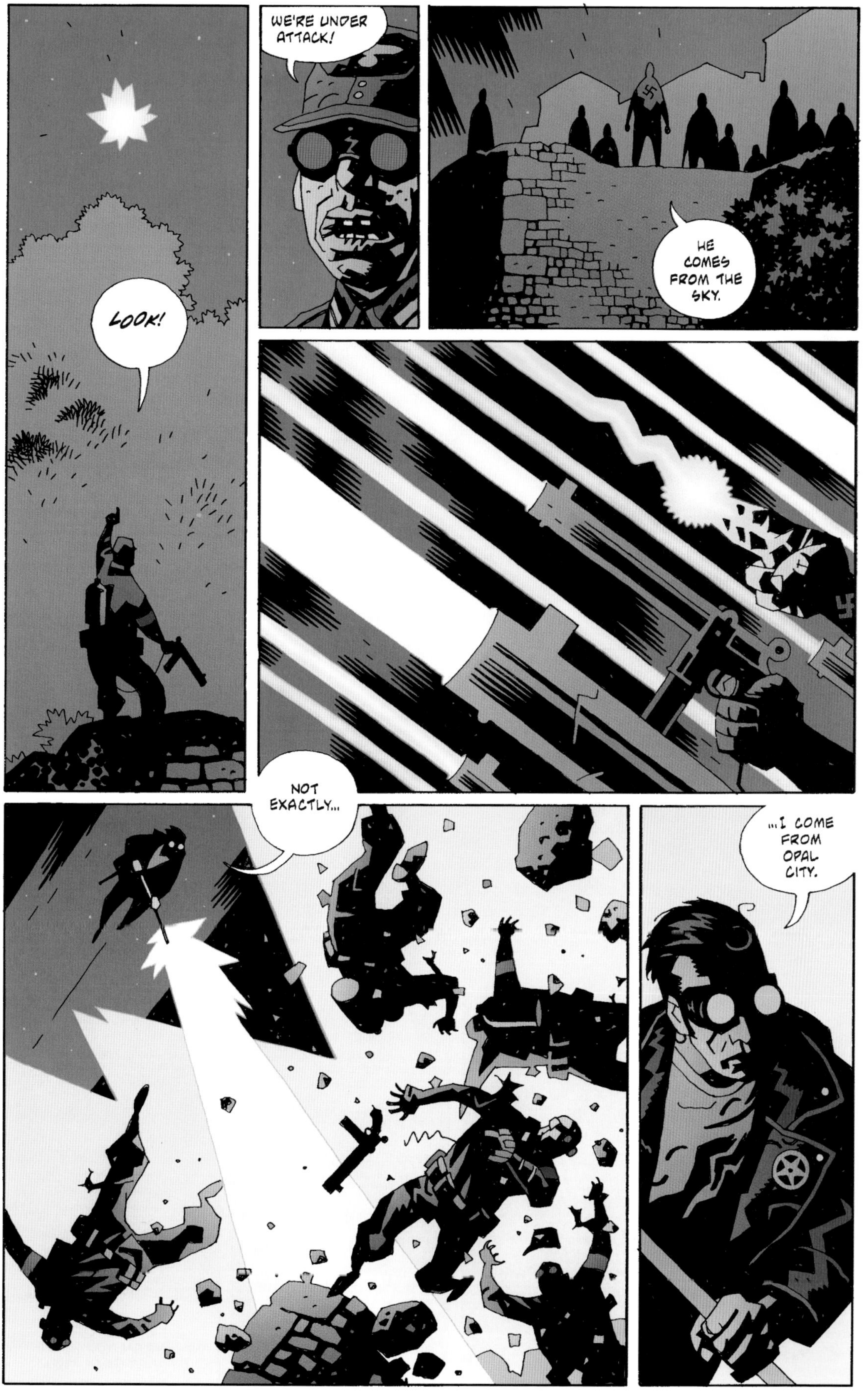
LOOK!
WE'RE UNDER ATTACK!
HE COMES FROM THE SKY.
NOT EXACTLY...
...I COME FROM OPAL CITY.

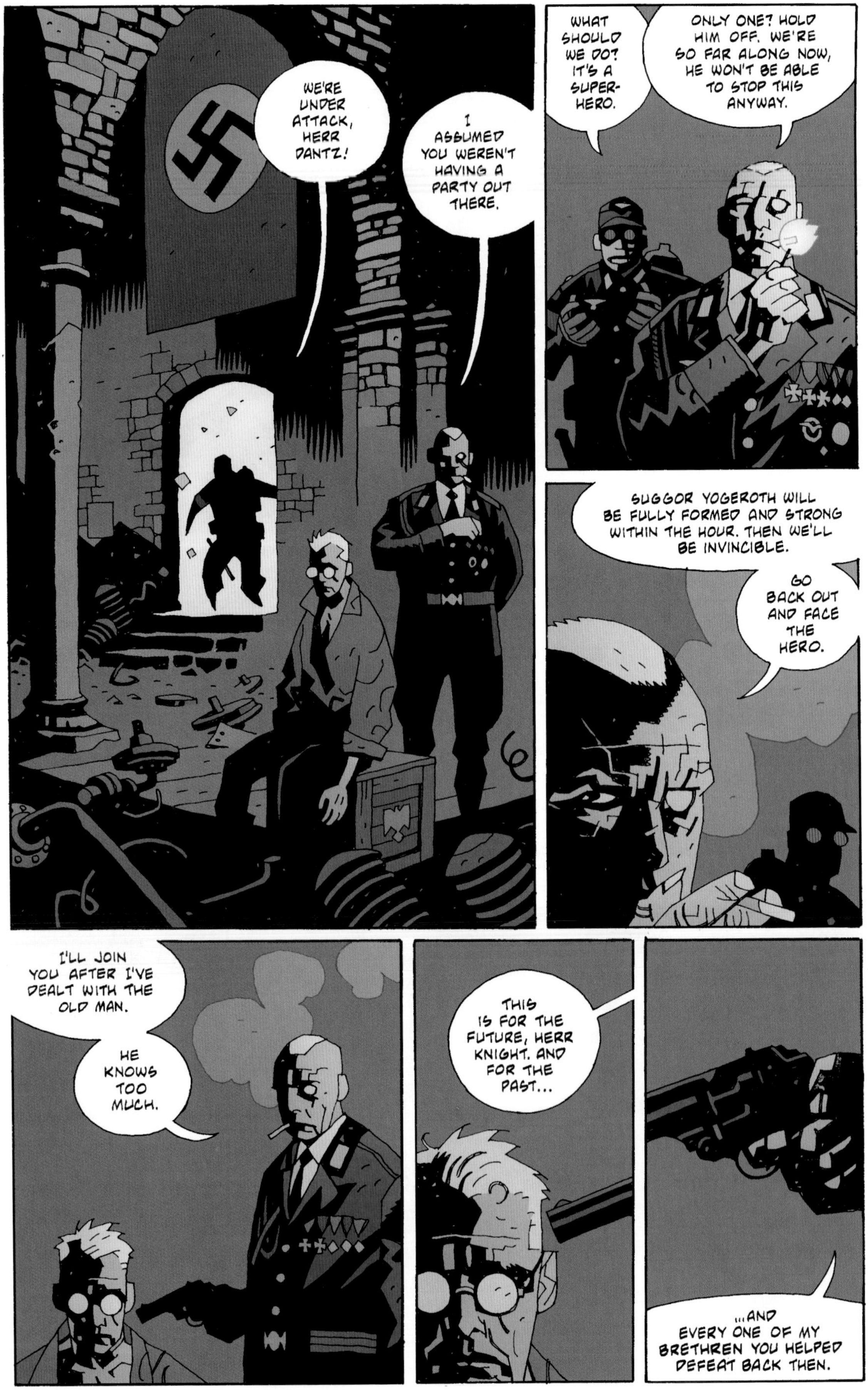
WE'RE UNDER ATTACK, HERR DANTZ!
I ASSUMED YOU WEREN'T HAVING A PARTY OUT THERE.
WHAT SHOULD WE DO? IT'S A SUPER-HERO.
ONLY ONE? HOLD HIM OFF. WE'RE SO FAR ALONG NOW, HE WON'T BE ABLE TO STOP THIS ANYWAY.
SUGGOR YOGEROTH WILL BE FULLY FORMED AND STRONG WITHIN THE HOUR. THEN WE'LL BE INVINCIBLE.
GO BACK OUT AND FACE THE HERO.
I'LL JOIN YOU AFTER I'VE DEALT WITH THE OLD MAN.
HE KNOWS TOO MUCH.
THIS IS FOR THE FUTURE, HERR KNIGHT. AND FOR THE PAST...
...AND EVERY ONE OF MY BRETHREN YOU HELPED DEFEAT BACK THEN.

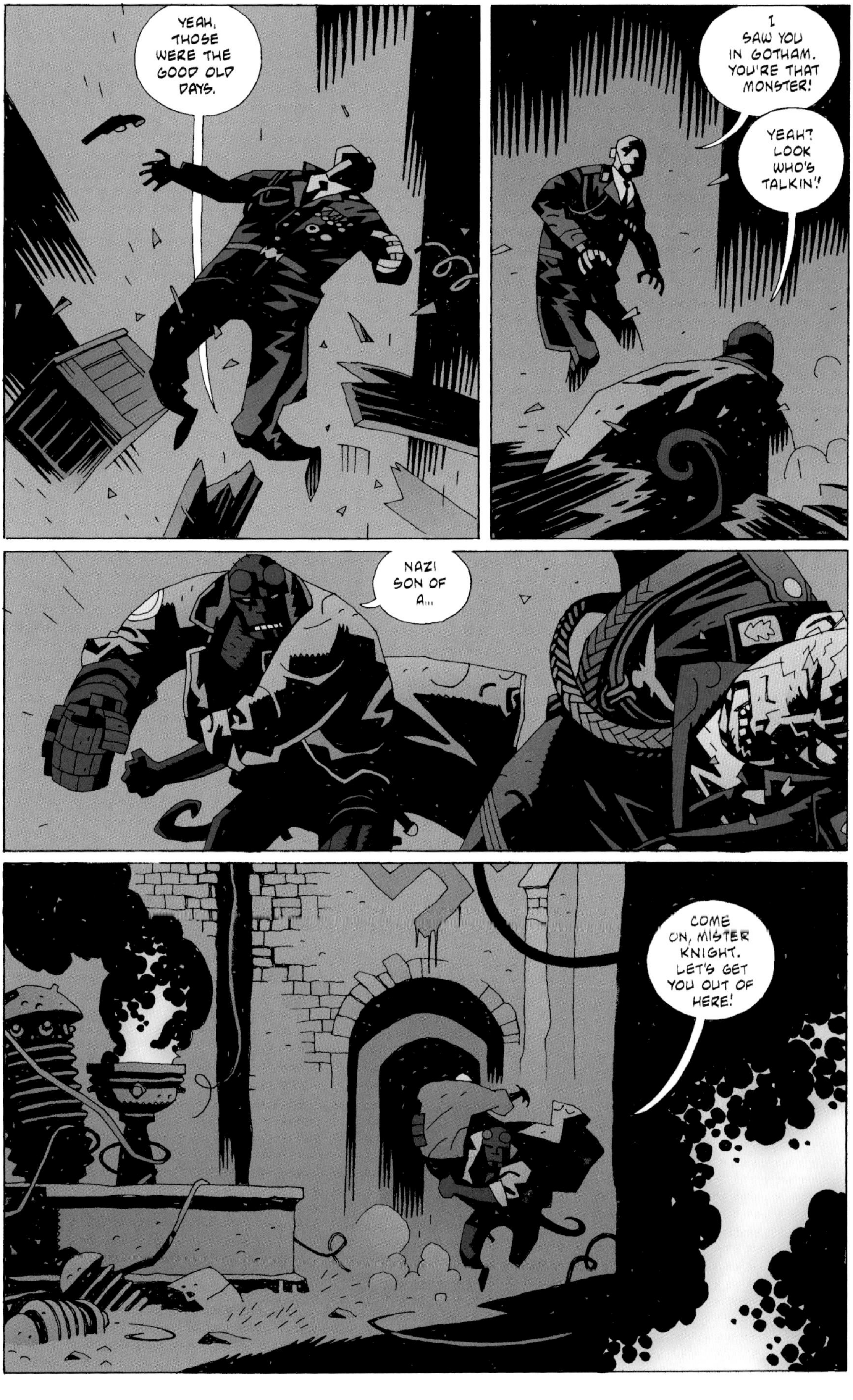
YEAH, THOSE WERE THE GOOD OLD DAYS.
I SAW YOU IN GOTHAM. YOU'RE THAT MONSTER!
YEAH? LOOK WHO'S TALKIN'!
NAZI SON OF A...
COME ON, MISTER KNIGHT. LET'S GET YOU OUT OF HERE!

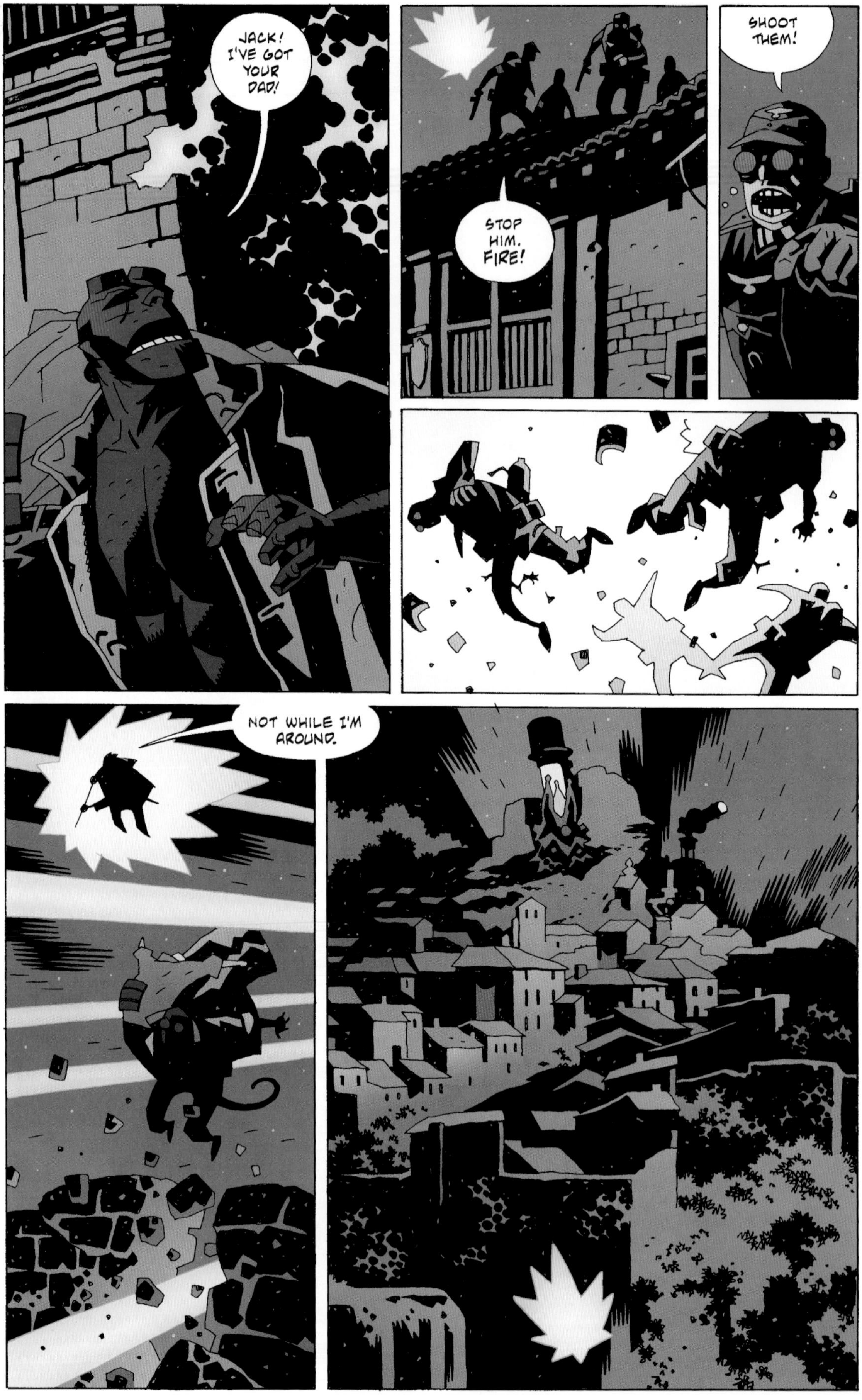
JACK! I'VE GOT YOUR DAD!
STOP HIM. FIRE!
SHOOT THEM!
NOT WHILE I'M AROUND.

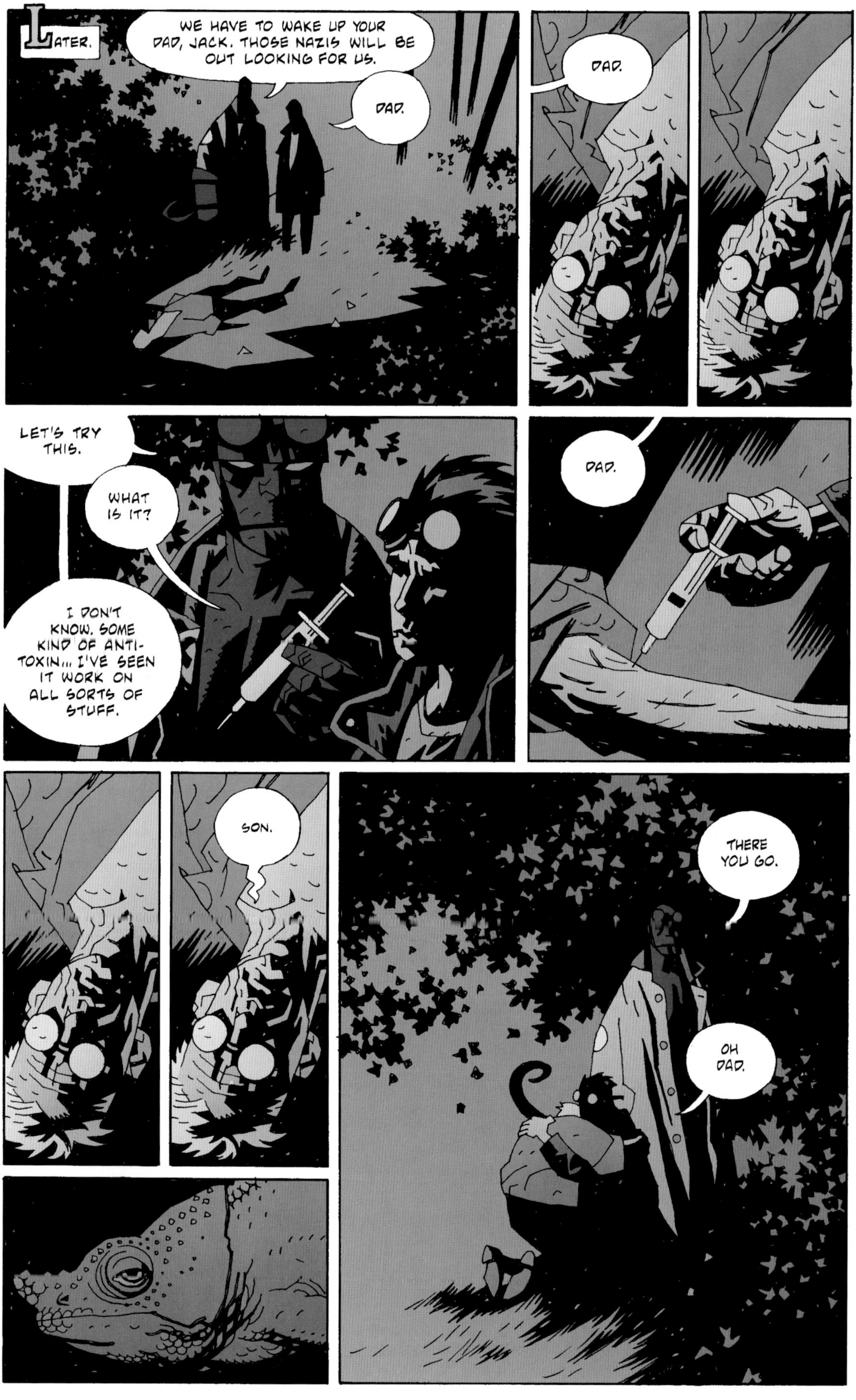
LATER.
WE HAVE TO WAKE UP YOUR DAD, JACK. THOSE NAZIS WILL BE OUT LOOKING FOR US.
DAD.
DAD.
LET'S TRY THIS.
WHAT IS IT?
I DON'T KNOW. SOME KIND OF ANTI-TOXIN... I'VE SEEN IT WORK ON ALL SORTS OF STUFF.
DAD.
SON.
THERE YOU GO.
OH DAD.

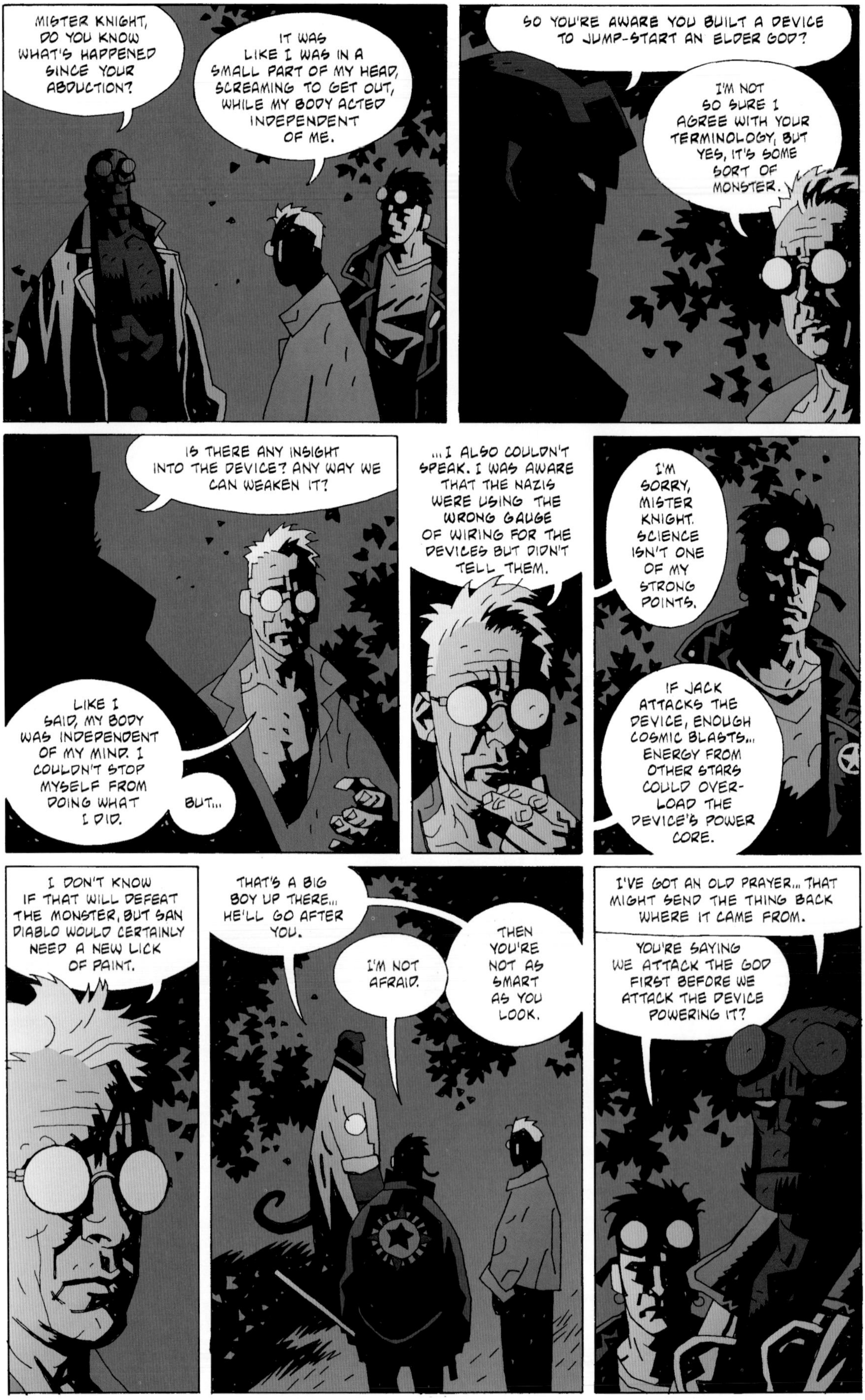
MISTER KNIGHT, DO YOU KNOW WHAT'S HAPPENED SINCE YOUR ABDUCTION?
IT WAS LIKE I WAS IN A SMALL PART OF MY HEAD, SCREAMING TO GET OUT, WHILE MY BODY ACTED INDEPENDENT OF ME.
SO YOU'RE AWARE YOU BUILT A DEVICE TO JUMP-START AN ELDER GOD?
I'M NOT SO SURE I AGREE WITH YOUR TERMINOLOGY, BUT YES, IT'S SOME SORT OF MONSTER.
IS THERE ANY INSIGHT INTO THE DEVICE? ANY WAY WE CAN WEAKEN IT?
LIKE I SAID, MY BODY WAS INDEPENDENT OF MY MIND. I COULDN'T STOP MYSELF FROM DOING WHAT I DID.
BUT...
...I ALSO COULDN'T SPEAK. I WAS AWARE THAT THE NAZIS WERE USING THE WRONG GAUGE OF WIRING FOR THE DEVICES BUT DIDN'T TELL THEM.
I'M SORRY, MISTER KNIGHT. SCIENCE ISN'T ONE OF MY STRONG POINTS.
IF JACK ATTACKS THE DEVICE, ENOUGH COSMIC BLASTS... ENERGY FROM OTHER STARS COULD OVER-LOAD THE DEVICE'S POWER CORE.
I DON'T KNOW IF THAT WILL DEFEAT THE MONSTER, BUT SAN DIABLO WOULD CERTAINLY NEED A NEW LICK OF PAINT.
THAT'S A BIG BOY UP THERE... HE'LL GO AFTER YOU.
I'M NOT AFRAID.
THEN YOU'RE NOT AS SMART AS YOU LOOK.
I'VE GOT AN OLD PRAYER... THAT MIGHT SEND THE THING BACK WHERE IT CAME FROM.
YOU'RE SAYING WE ATTACK THE GOD FIRST BEFORE WE ATTACK THE DEVICE POWERING IT?

"NO..."

HERE HE COMES AGAIN.

THE FLYING MAN.

SHOOT HIM DOWN.

"...I'M SAYING *YOU* ATTACK THE CREATURE. WEAKEN IT..."

ANGLE THE ECTOPLASMIC ROCKET CANNON.

AIM FOR HIM. WIPE HIM FROM THE EARTH.

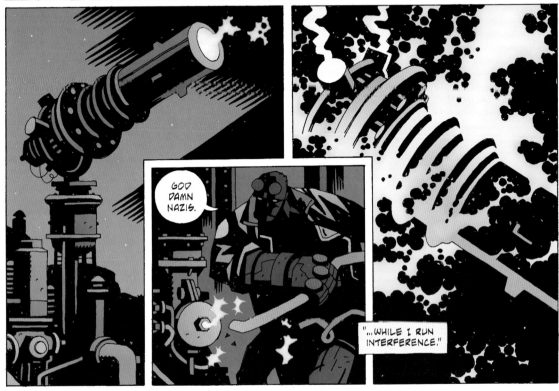

GOD DAMN NAZIS.

"...WHILE I RUN INTERFERENCE."

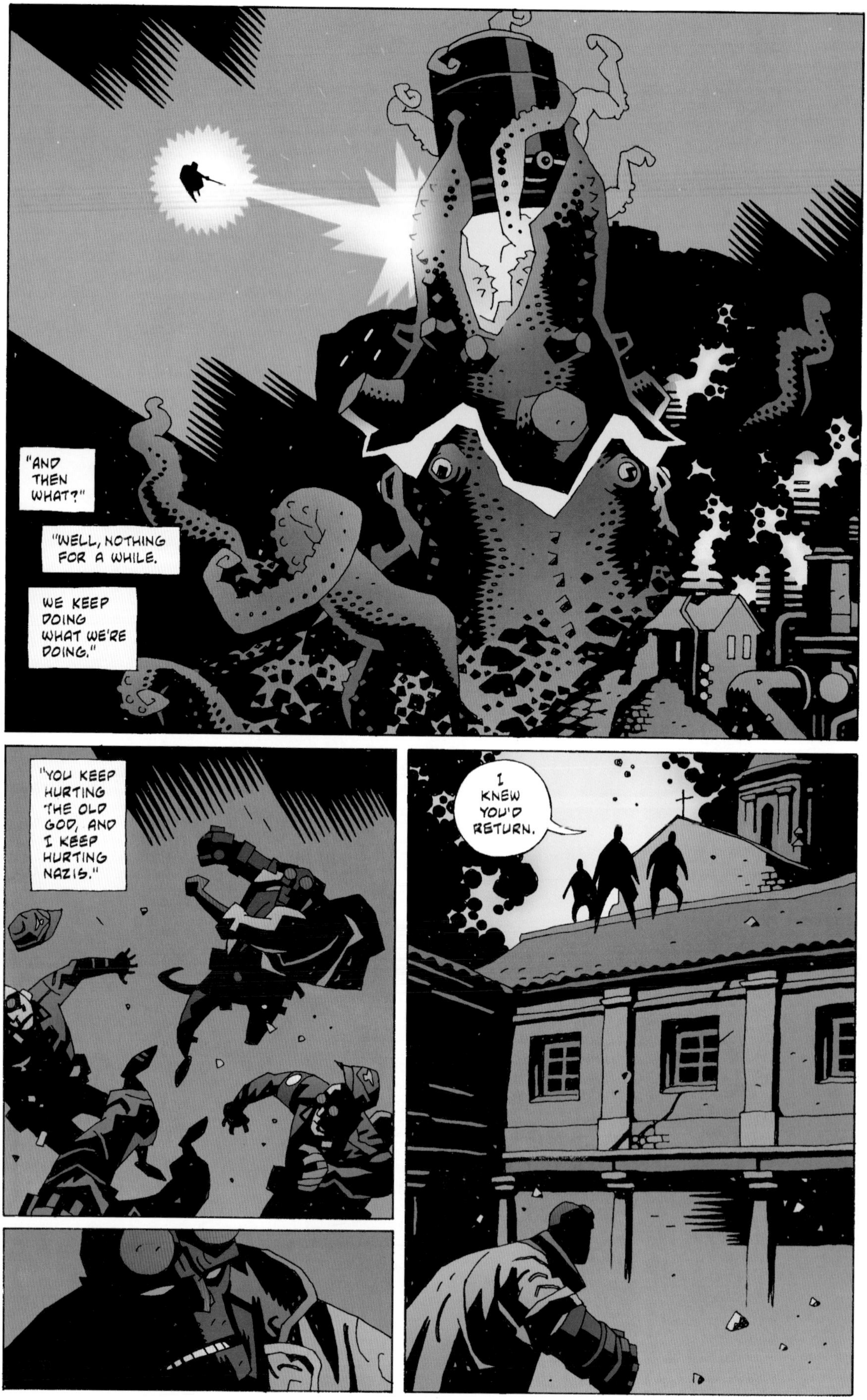
"AND THEN WHAT?"
"WELL, NOTHING FOR A WHILE.
WE KEEP DOING WHAT WE'RE DOING."
"YOU KEEP HURTING THE OLD GOD, AND I KEEP HURTING NAZIS."
I KNEW YOU'D RETURN.

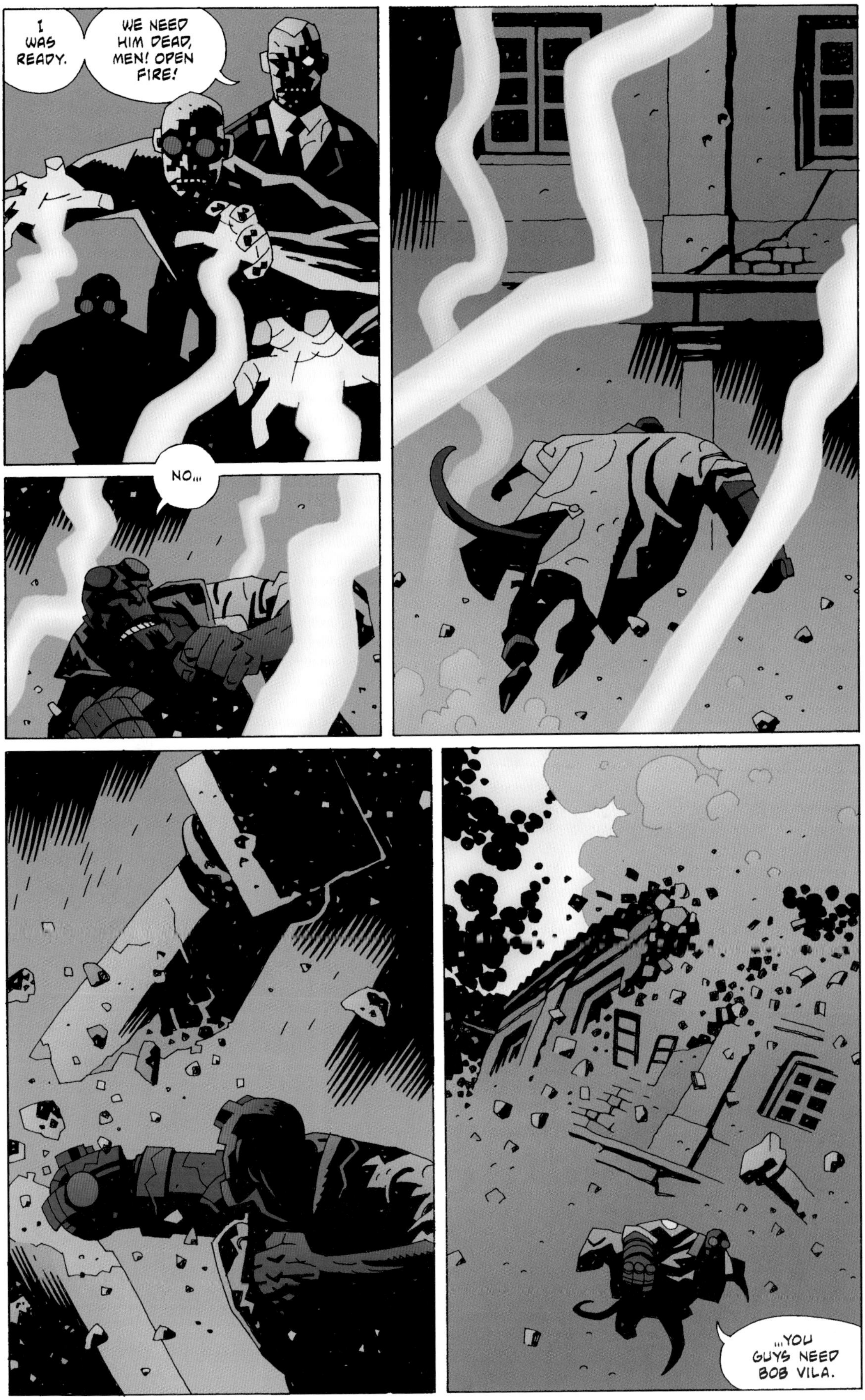
I WAS READY.
WE NEED HIM DEAD, MEN! OPEN FIRE!
NO...
...YOU GUYS NEED BOB VILA.

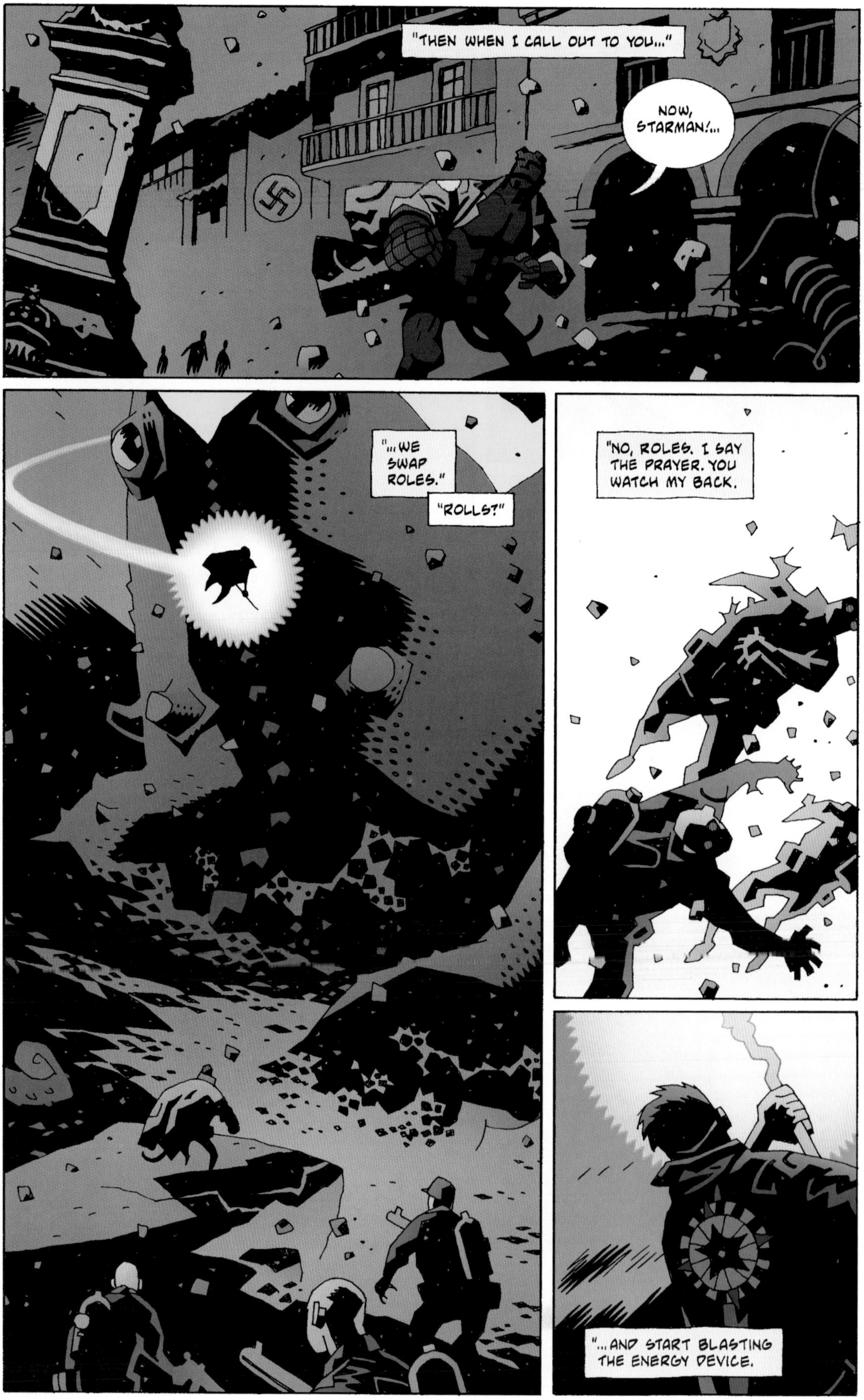
"THEN WHEN I CALL OUT TO YOU..."
NOW, STARMAN!...
"...WE SWAP ROLES."
"ROLLS?"
"NO, ROLES. I SAY THE PRAYER. YOU WATCH MY BACK.
"...AND START BLASTING THE ENERGY DEVICE.

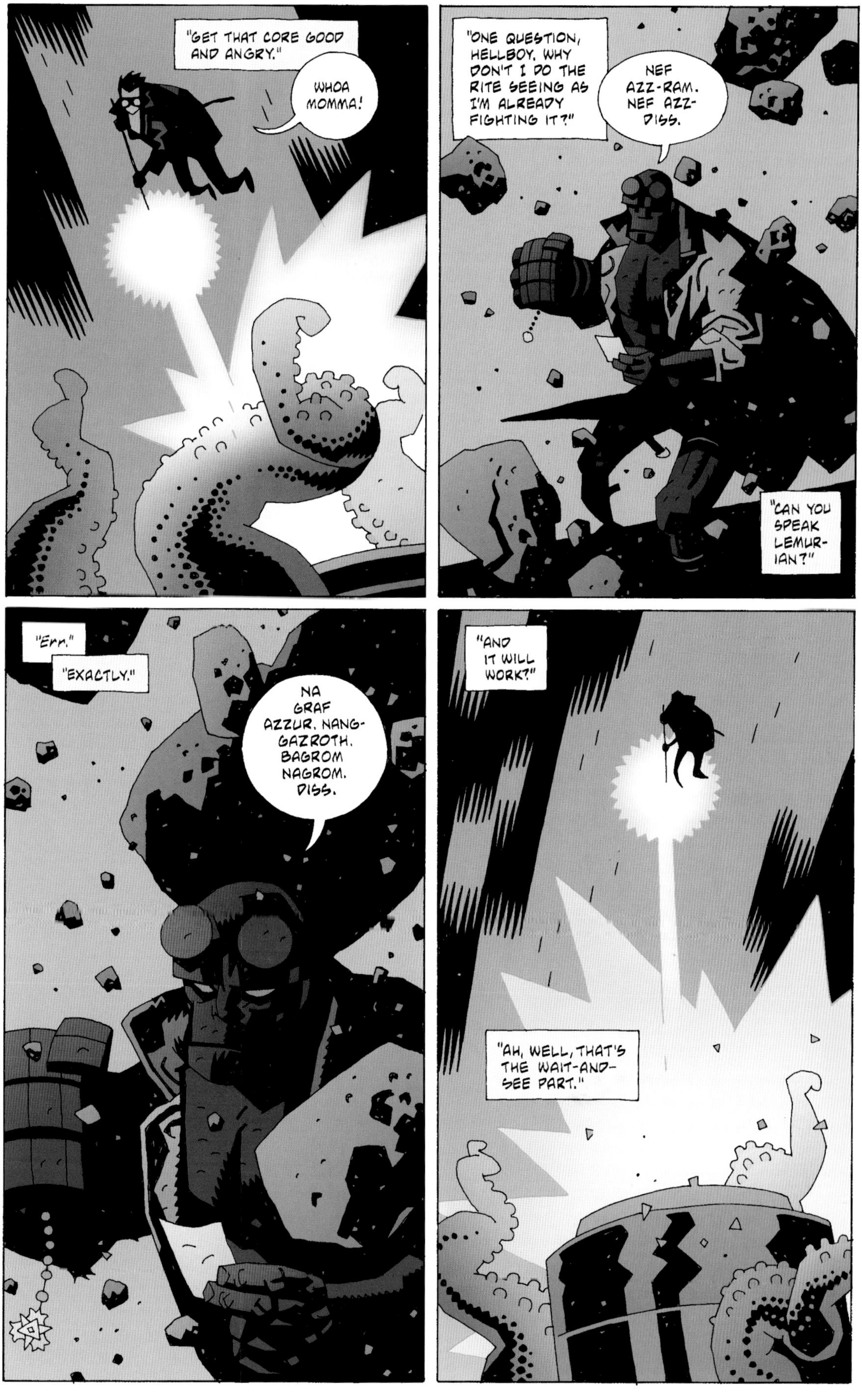
"GET THAT CORE GOOD AND ANGRY."
WHOA MOMMA!
"ONE QUESTION, HELLBOY. WHY DON'T I DO THE RITE SEEING AS I'M ALREADY FIGHTING IT?"
NEF AZZ-RAM. NEF AZZ-DISS.
"CAN YOU SPEAK LEMURIAN?"
"Err."
"EXACTLY."
NA GRAF AZZUR. NANG-GAZROTH. BAGROM NAGROM. DISS.
"AND IT WILL WORK?"
"AH, WELL, THAT'S THE WAIT-AND-SEE PART."

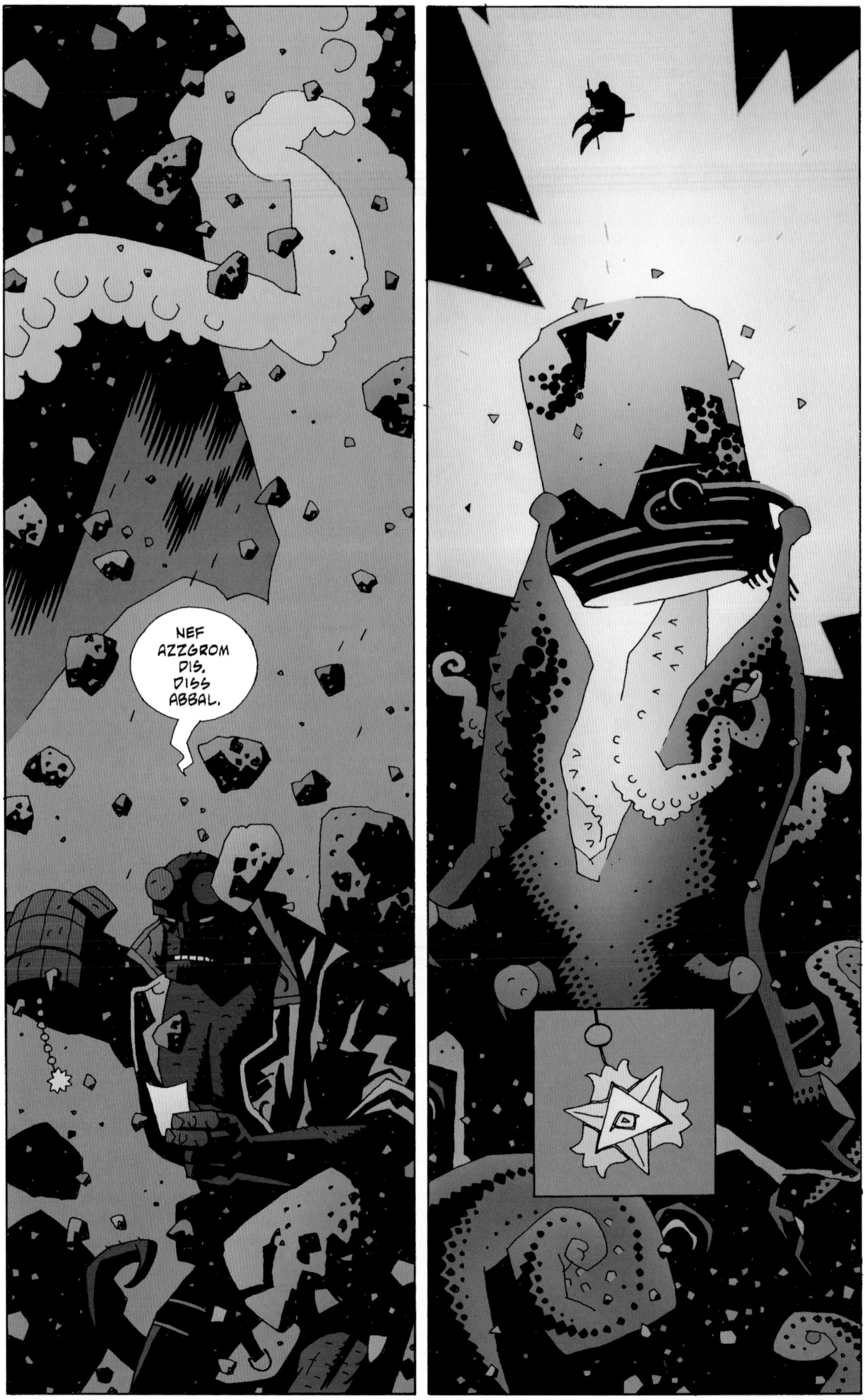
NEF AZZGROM DIS. DISS ABBAL.

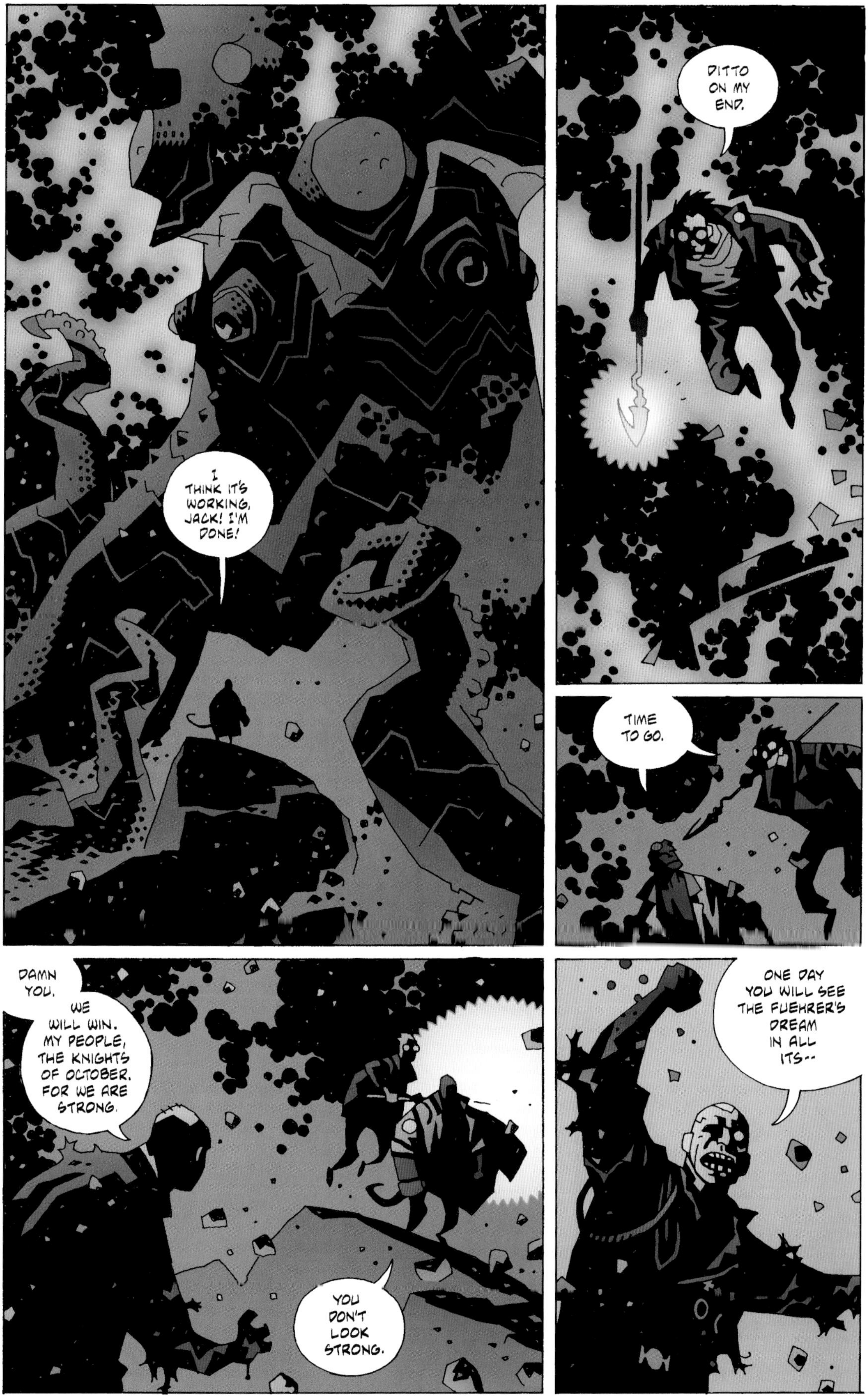
I THINK IT'S WORKING, JACK! I'M DONE!
DITTO ON MY END.
TIME TO GO.
DAMN YOU.
WE WILL WIN. MY PEOPLE, THE KNIGHTS OF OCTOBER. FOR WE ARE STRONG.
YOU DON'T LOOK STRONG.
ONE DAY YOU WILL SEE THE FUEHRER'S DREAM IN ALL ITS--

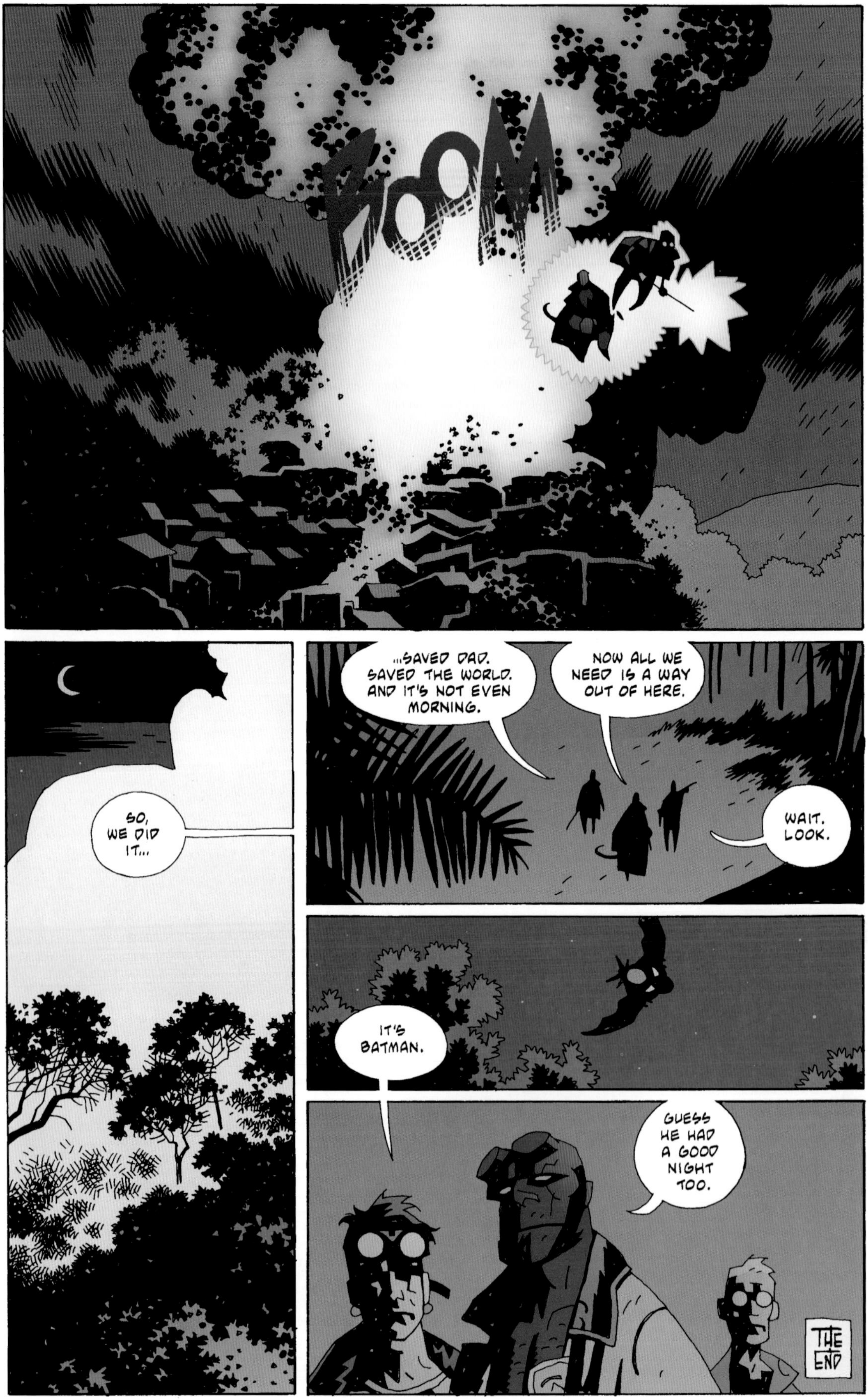
BOOM
SO, WE DID IT...
...SAVED DAD. SAVED THE WORLD. AND IT'S NOT EVEN MORNING.
NOW ALL WE NEED IS A WAY OUT OF HERE.
WAIT. LOOK.
IT'S BATMAN.
GUESS HE HAD A GOOD NIGHT TOO.
THE END

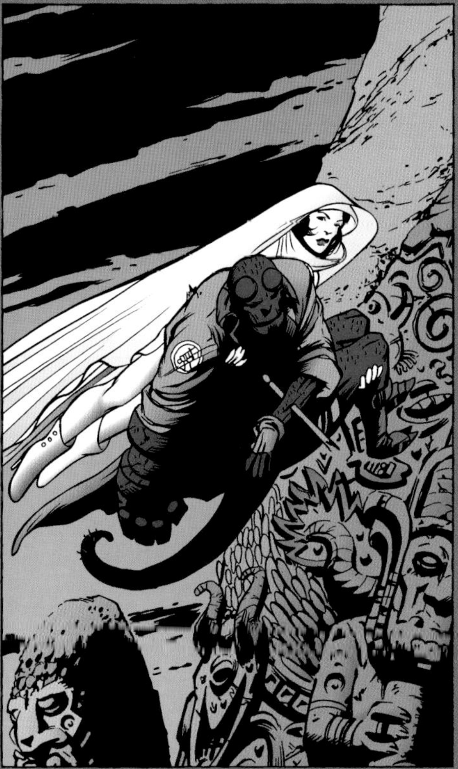

MIGNOLA

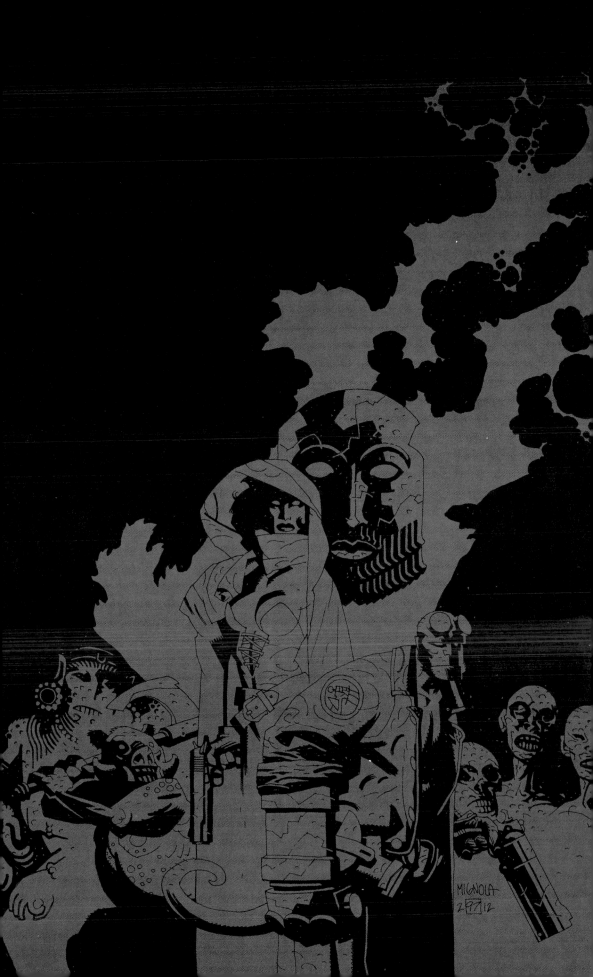

CHAPTER ONE

MIGNOLA
95

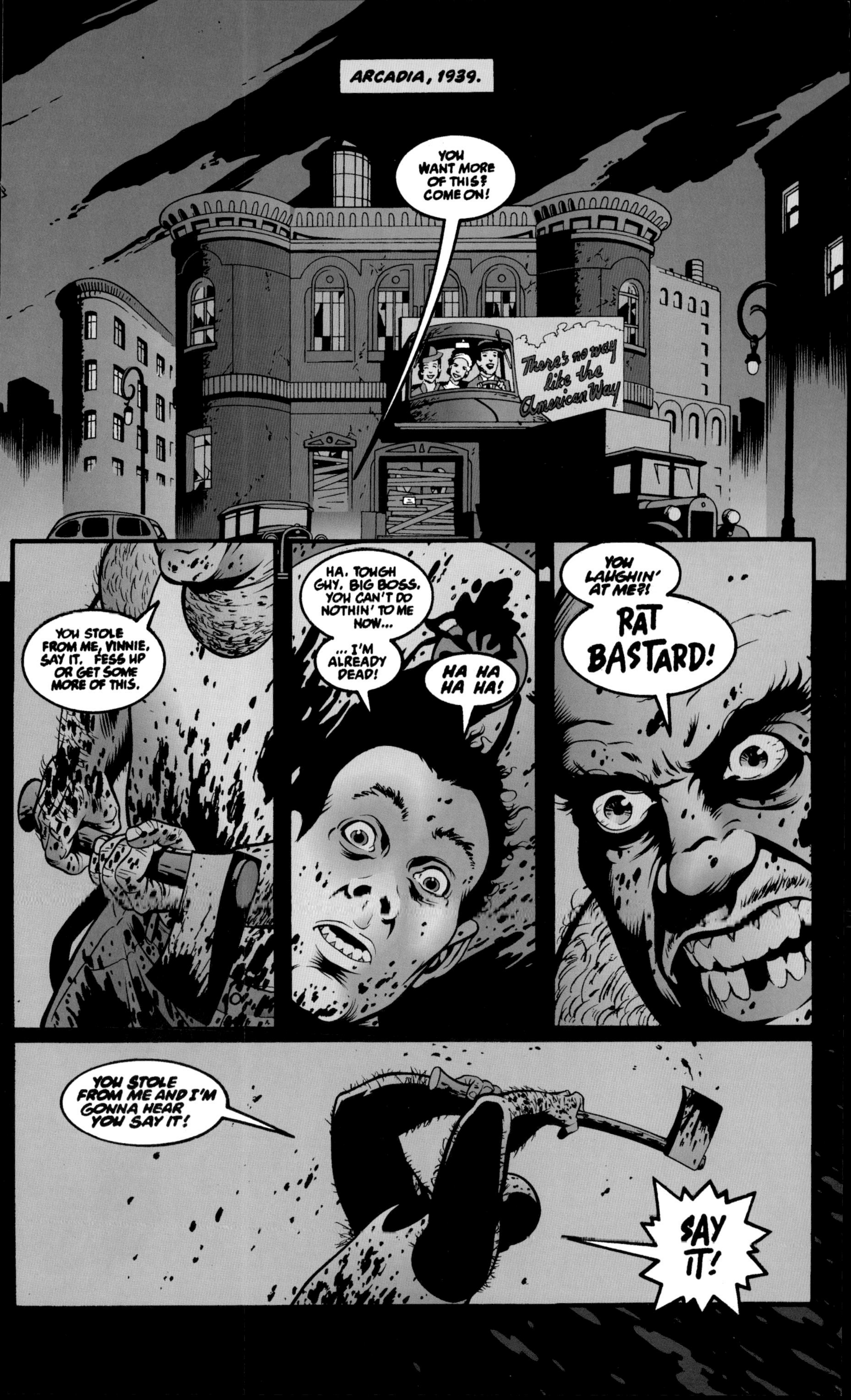
ARCADIA, 1939.
YOU WANT MORE OF THIS? COME ON!
There's no way like the American Way
YOU STOLE FROM ME, VINNIE. SAY IT. FESS UP OR GET SOME MORE OF THIS.
HA. TOUGH GUY. BIG BOSS. YOU CAN'T DO NOTHIN' TO ME NOW...
... I'M ALREADY DEAD!
HA HA HA HA!
YOU LAUGHIN' AT ME?!
RAT BASTARD!
YOU STOLE FROM ME AND I'M GONNA HEAR YOU SAY IT!
SAY IT!

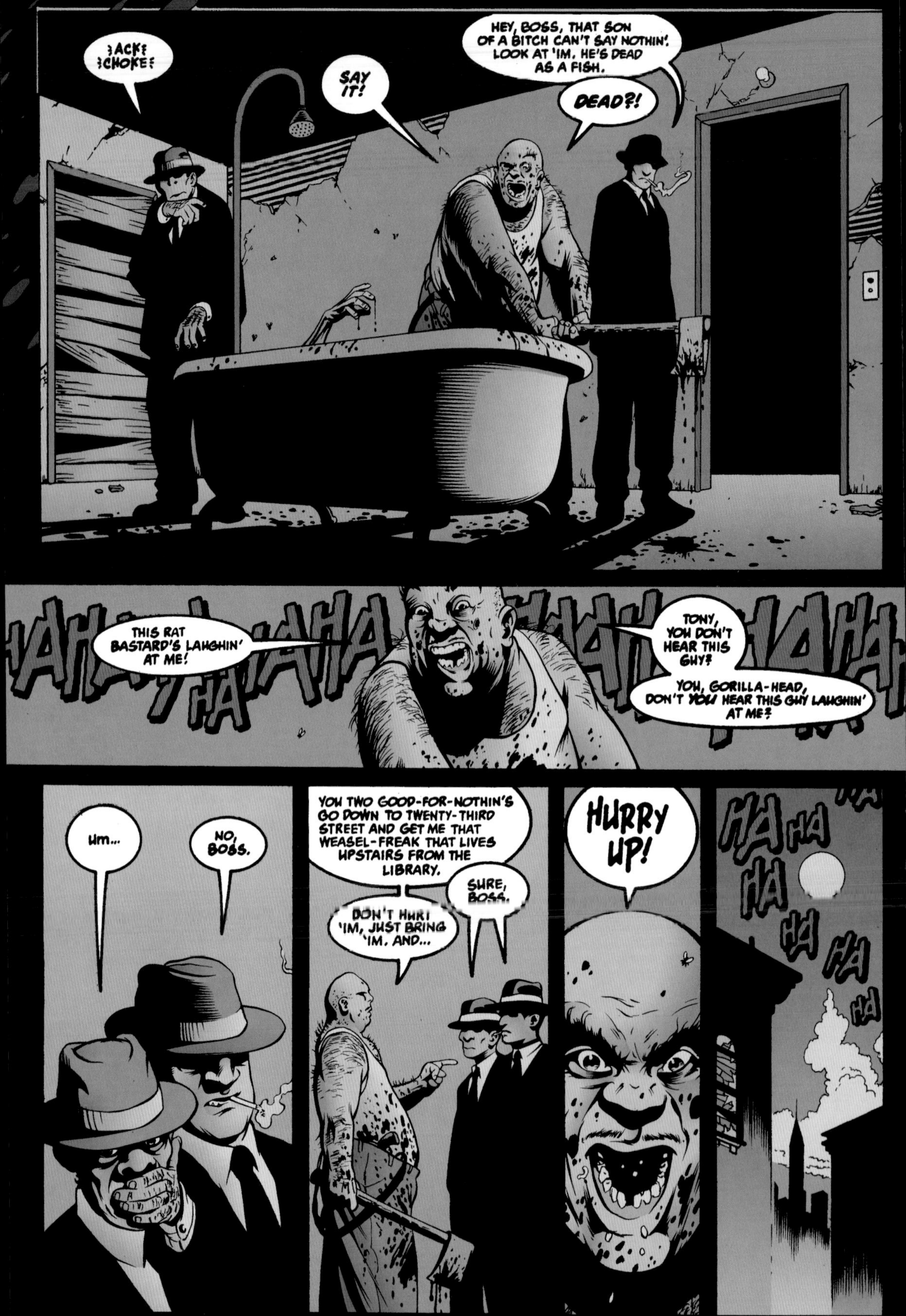
ACK
CHOKE
SAY IT!
HEY, BOSS, THAT SON OF A BITCH CAN'T SAY NOTHIN'. LOOK AT 'IM. HE'S DEAD AS A FISH.
DEAD?!
HAHAHAHA
THIS RAT BASTARD'S LAUGHIN' AT ME!
TONY, YOU DON'T HEAR THIS GUY?
YOU, GORILLA-HEAD, DON'T YOU HEAR THIS GUY LAUGHIN' AT ME?
UM...
NO, BOSS.
YOU TWO GOOD-FOR-NOTHIN'S GO DOWN TO TWENTY-THIRD STREET AND GET ME THAT WEASEL-FREAK THAT LIVES UPSTAIRS FROM THE LIBRARY.
DON'T HURT 'IM, JUST BRING 'IM. AND...
SURE, BOSS.
HURRY UP!
HA HA HA HA HA HA HA HA

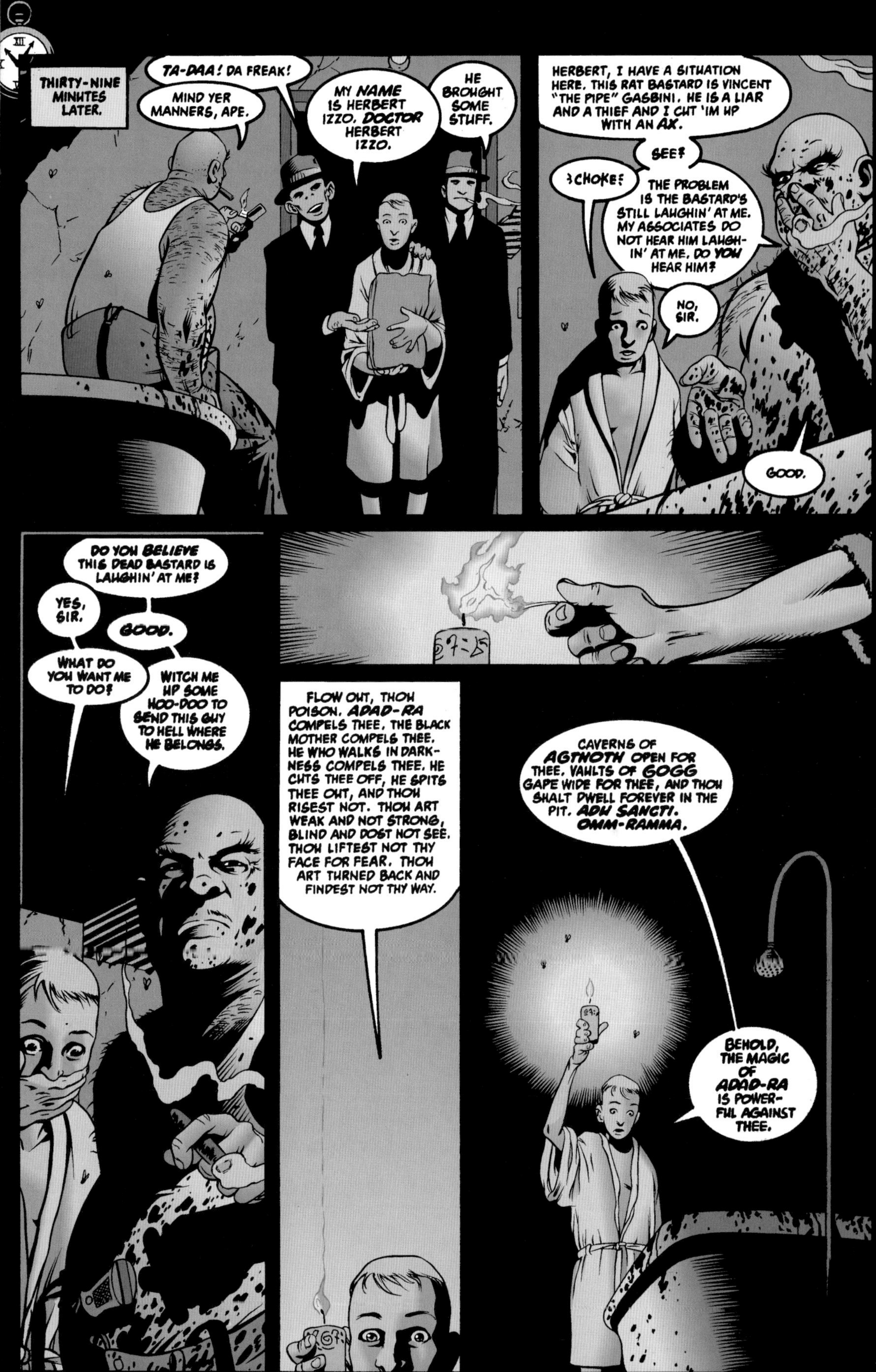
THIRTY-NINE MINUTES LATER.
TA-DAA! DA FREAK!
MIND YER MANNERS, APE.
MY NAME IS HERBERT IZZO. DOCTOR HERBERT IZZO.
HE BROUGHT SOME STUFF.
HERBERT, I HAVE A SITUATION HERE. THIS RAT BASTARD IS VINCENT "THE PIPE" GASBINI. HE IS A LIAR AND A THIEF AND I CUT 'IM UP WITH AN AX.
SEE?
CHOKE
THE PROBLEM IS THE BASTARD'S STILL LAUGHIN' AT ME. MY ASSOCIATES DO NOT HEAR HIM LAUGHIN' AT ME. DO YOU HEAR HIM?
NO, SIR.
GOOD.
DO YOU BELIEVE THIS DEAD BASTARD IS LAUGHIN' AT ME?
YES, SIR.
GOOD.
WHAT DO YOU WANT ME TO DO?
WITCH ME UP SOME HOO-DOO TO SEND THIS GUY TO HELL WHERE HE BELONGS.
FLOW OUT, THOU POISON. ADAD-RA COMPELS THEE. THE BLACK MOTHER COMPELS THEE. HE WHO WALKS IN DARKNESS COMPELS THEE. HE CUTS THEE OFF, HE SPITS THEE OUT, AND THOU RISEST NOT. THOU ART WEAK AND NOT STRONG, BLIND AND DOST NOT SEE. THOU LIFTEST NOT THY FACE FOR FEAR. THOU ART TURNED BACK AND FINDEST NOT THY WAY.
CAVERNS OF AGTNOTH OPEN FOR THEE. VAULTS OF GOGG GAPE WIDE FOR THEE, AND THOU SHALT DWELL FOREVER IN THE PIT. ADU SANCTI. OMM-RAMMA.
BEHOLD, THE MAGIC OF ADAD-RA IS POWERFUL AGAINST THEE.

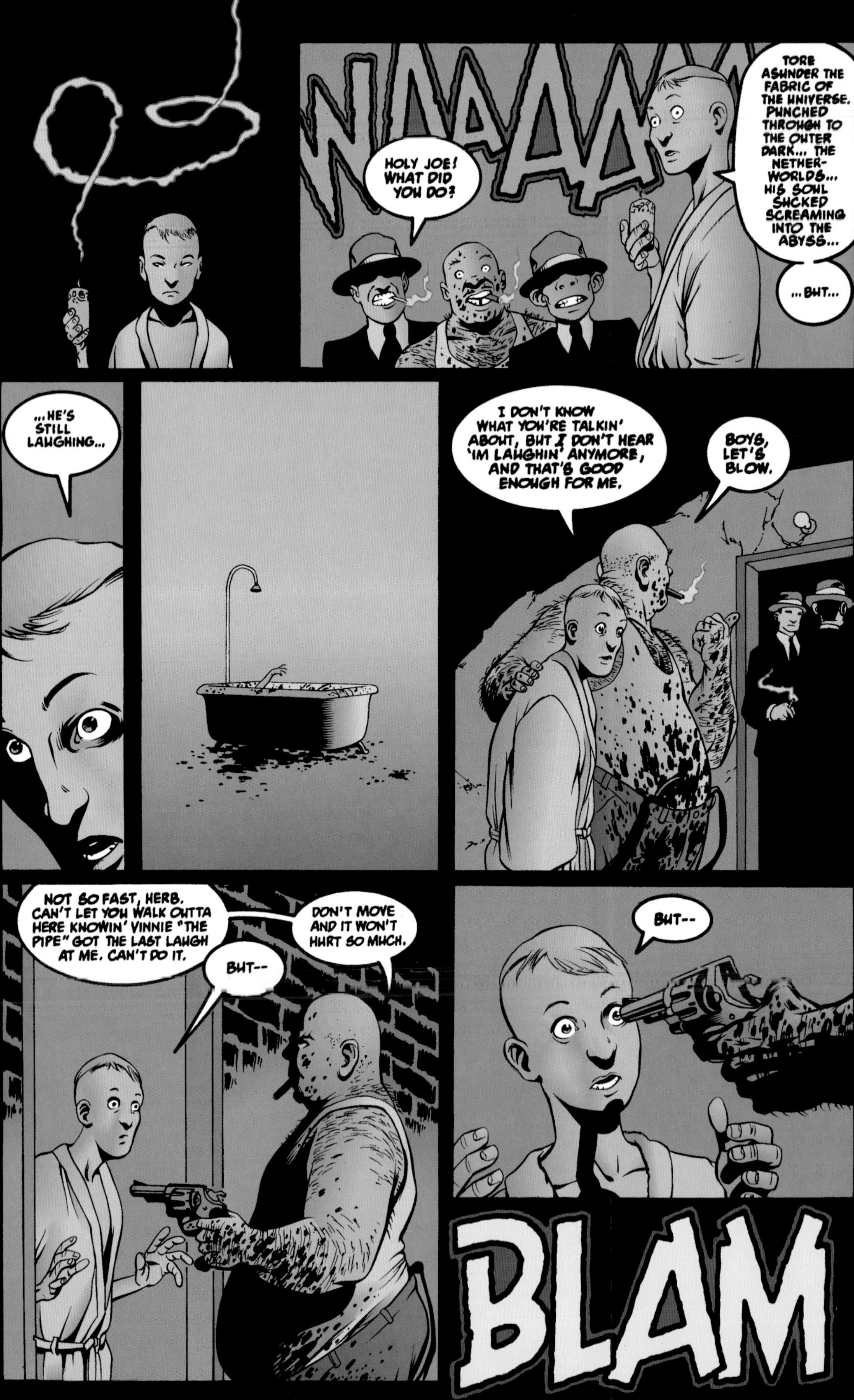
NAAAAA
HOLY JOE! WHAT DID YOU DO?
TORE ASUNDER THE FABRIC OF THE UNIVERSE. PUNCHED THROUGH TO THE OUTER DARK... THE NETHER-WORLDS... HIS SOUL SUCKED SCREAMING INTO THE ABYSS...
...BUT...
...HE'S STILL LAUGHING...
I DON'T KNOW WHAT YOU'RE TALKIN' ABOUT, BUT I DON'T HEAR 'IM LAUGHIN' ANYMORE, AND THAT'S GOOD ENOUGH FOR ME.
BOYS, LET'S BLOW.
NOT SO FAST, HERB. CAN'T LET YOU WALK OUTTA HERE KNOWIN' VINNIE "THE PIPE" GOT THE LAST LAUGH AT ME. CAN'T DO IT.
BUT--
DON'T MOVE AND IT WON'T HURT SO MUCH.
BUT--
BLAM

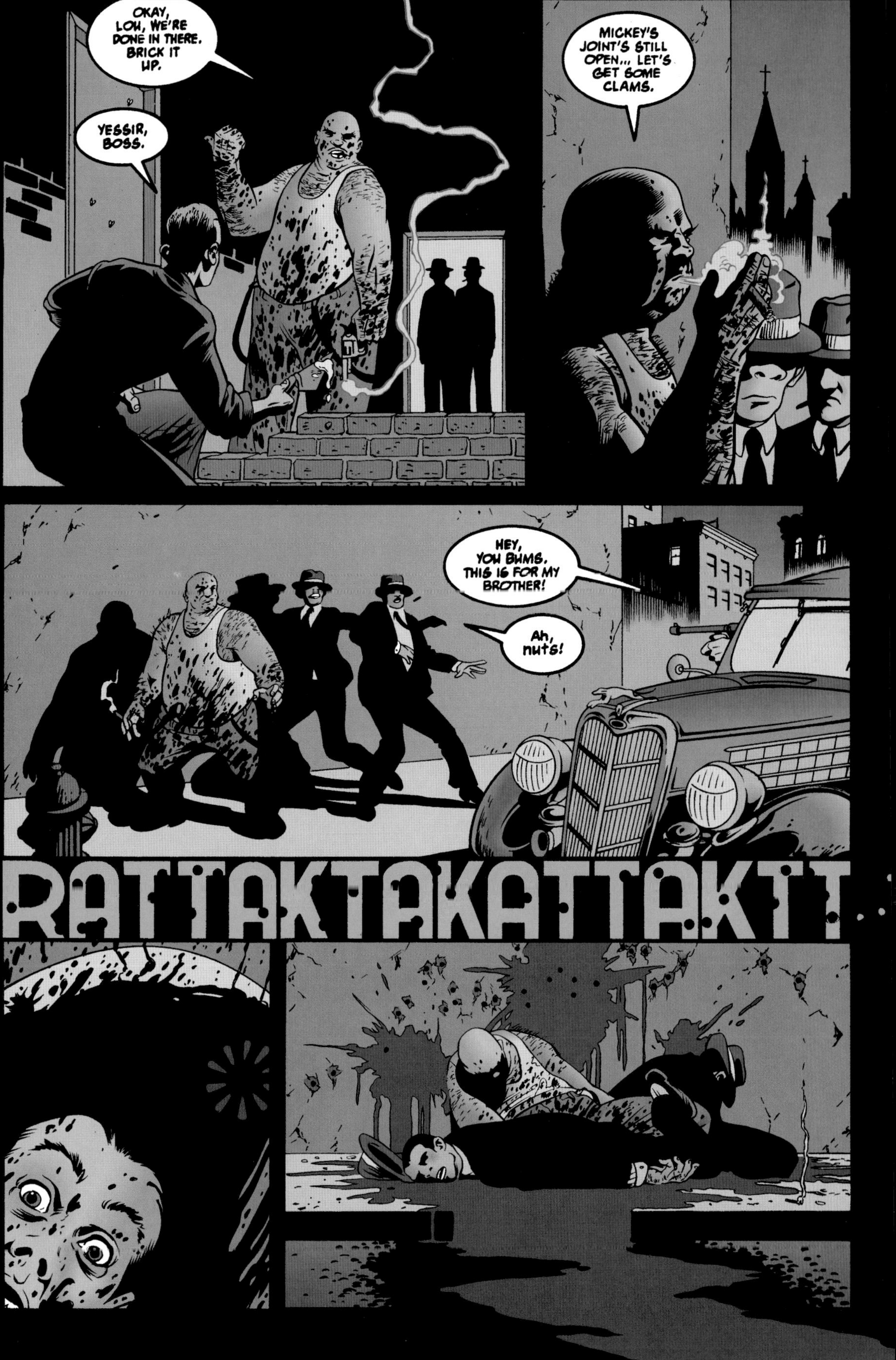
OKAY, LOU, WE'RE DONE IN THERE. BRICK IT UP.
YESSIR, BOSS.
MICKEY'S JOINT'S STILL OPEN... LET'S GET SOME CLAMS.
HEY, YOU BUMS. THIS IS FOR MY BROTHER!
Ah, nuts!
RATTAKTAKATTAKTT

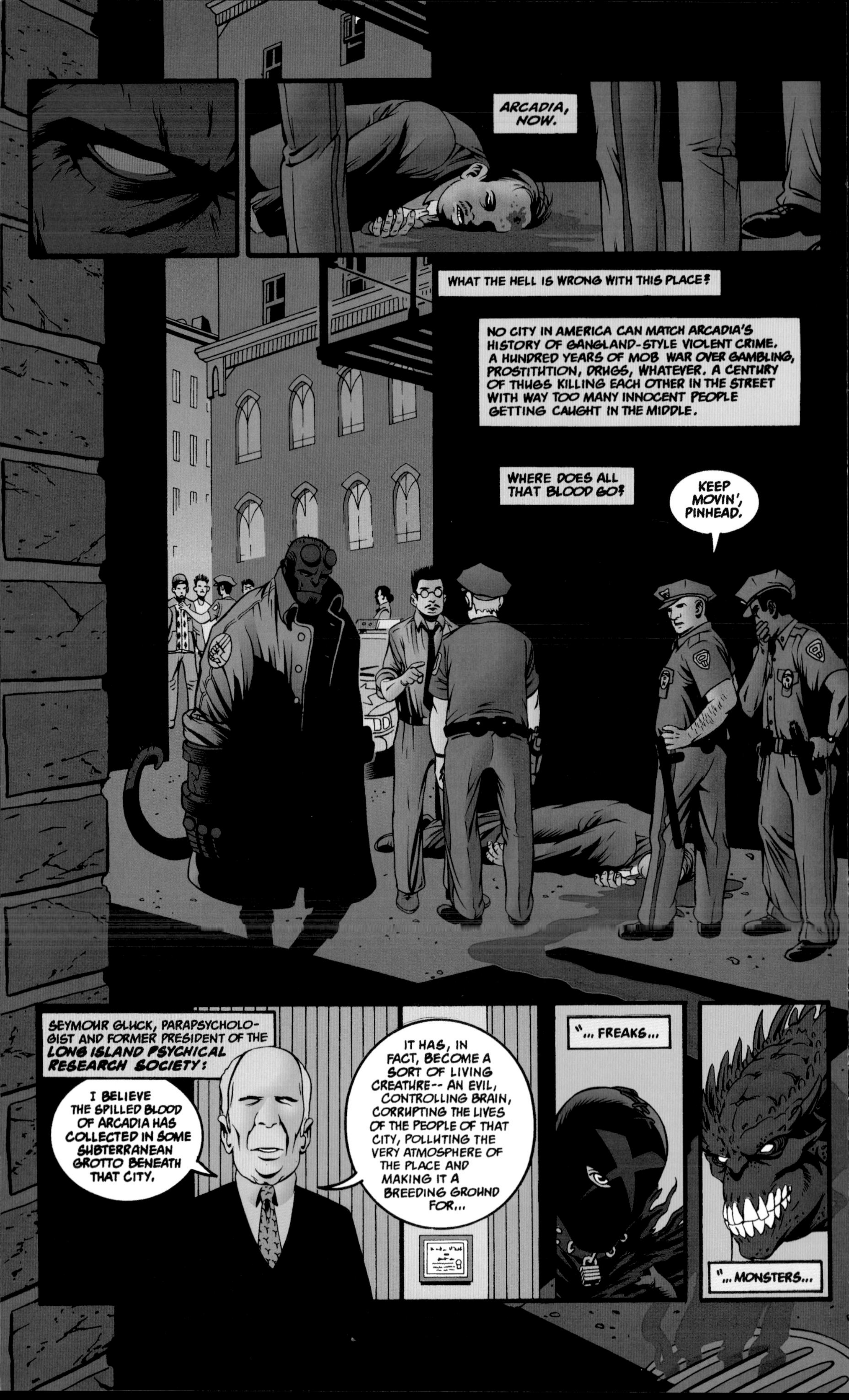
ARCADIA, NOW.
WHAT THE HELL IS WRONG WITH THIS PLACE?
NO CITY IN AMERICA CAN MATCH ARCADIA'S HISTORY OF GANGLAND-STYLE VIOLENT CRIME. A HUNDRED YEARS OF MOB WAR OVER GAMBLING, PROSTITUTION, DRUGS, WHATEVER. A CENTURY OF THUGS KILLING EACH OTHER IN THE STREET WITH WAY TOO MANY INNOCENT PEOPLE GETTING CAUGHT IN THE MIDDLE.
WHERE DOES ALL THAT BLOOD GO?
KEEP MOVIN', PINHEAD.
SEYMOUR GLUCK, PARAPSYCHOLOGIST AND FORMER PRESIDENT OF THE LONG ISLAND PSYCHICAL RESEARCH SOCIETY:
I BELIEVE THE SPILLED BLOOD OF ARCADIA HAS COLLECTED IN SOME SUBTERRANEAN GROTTO BENEATH THAT CITY.
IT HAS, IN FACT, BECOME A SORT OF LIVING CREATURE-- AN EVIL, CONTROLLING BRAIN, CORRUPTING THE LIVES OF THE PEOPLE OF THAT CITY, POLLUTING THE VERY ATMOSPHERE OF THE PLACE AND MAKING IT A BREEDING GROUND FOR...
"... FREAKS...
"... MONSTERS...

"... AND GHOSTS."

SHE'S HERE, HELLBOY. CLOSE.

REAL CLOSE.

YOU SURE IT'S HER, JO? THERE'S A DEAD GUY AROUND THE CORNER.

IT'S HER.

P.R.D.

HOT GIRLS! Call 1•9

JOSEPHINE T. GANT. PSYCHIC. FIELD AGENT FOR THE BUREAU FOR PARANORMAL RESEARCH AND DEFENSE SINCE 1989.

I'VE NEVER FELT ANYTHING LIKE HER. THERE'S ANGER COMING OFF HER LIKE HEAT...

...SHE'S HUNTING...

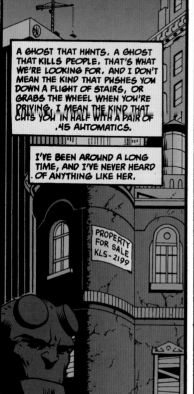

A GHOST THAT HUNTS, A GHOST THAT KILLS PEOPLE. THAT'S WHAT WE'RE LOOKING FOR. AND I DON'T MEAN THE KIND THAT PUSHES YOU DOWN A FLIGHT OF STAIRS, OR GRABS THE WHEEL WHEN YOU'RE DRIVING. I MEAN THE KIND THAT CUTS YOU IN HALF WITH A PAIR OF .45 AUTOMATICS.

I'VE BEEN AROUND A LONG TIME, AND I'VE NEVER HEARD OF ANYTHING LIKE HER.

PROPERTY FOR SALE KL5-2199

IF SHE'S A GHOST-- A REAL GHOST-- THEN SHE'S ONE OF A KIND, AND THE BUREAU WANTS HER. WHATEVER SHE IS, SHE HAS TO STOP SHOOTING PEOPLE...

... EVEN IF SHE IS ONLY SHOOTING THE BAD GUYS.

HEY, MR. MANNETTI, WHERE ARE YA? I DID IT...

YOU GOT MY MONEY?

13

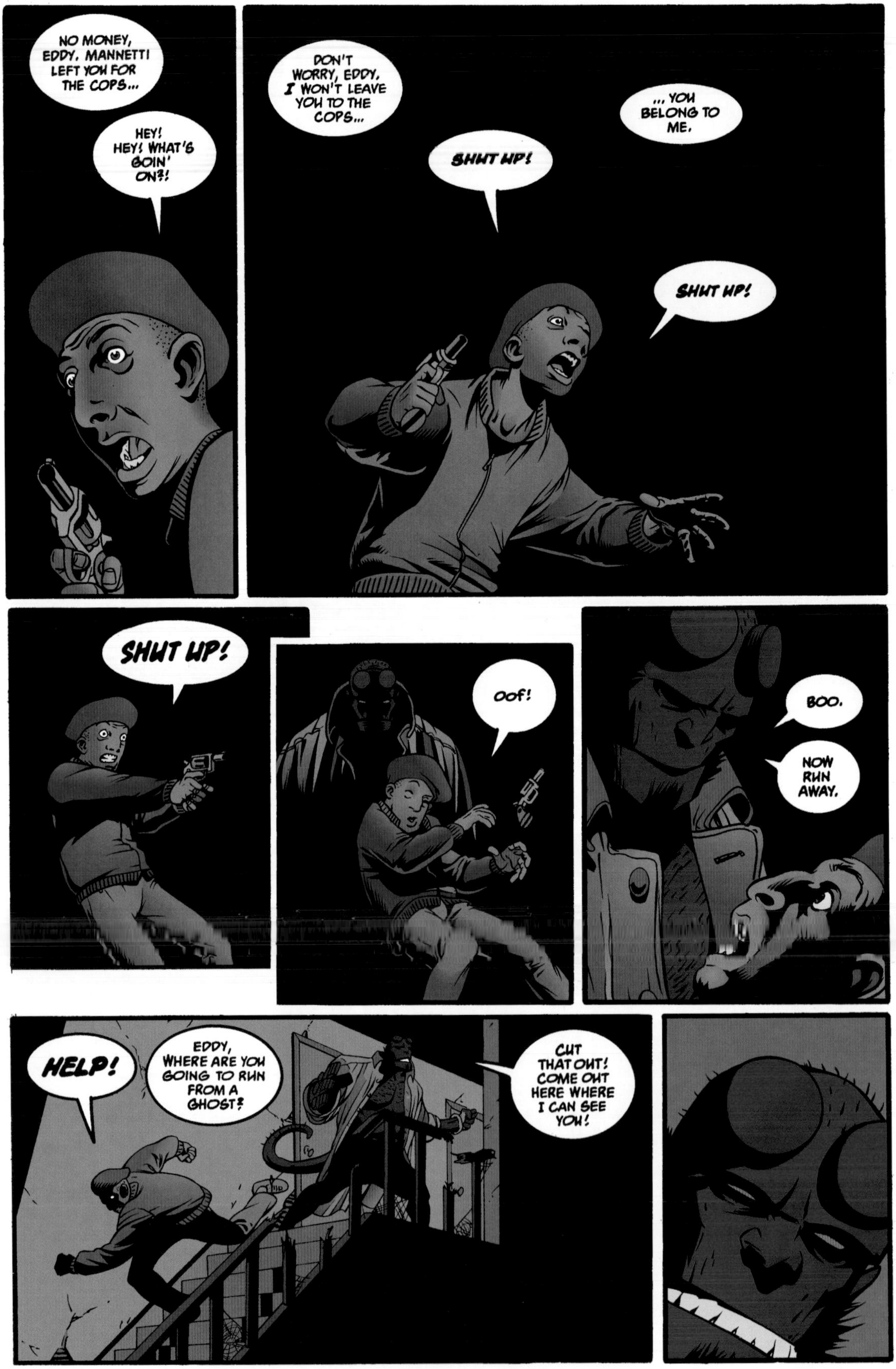

NO MONEY, EDDY. MANNETTI LEFT YOU FOR THE COPS...
HEY! HEY! WHAT'S GOIN' ON?!
DON'T WORRY, EDDY. I WON'T LEAVE YOU TO THE COPS...
SHUT UP!
...YOU BELONG TO ME.
SHUT UP!
SHUT UP!
Oof!
BOO.
NOW RUN AWAY.
HELP!
EDDY, WHERE ARE YOU GOING TO RUN FROM A GHOST?
CUT THAT OUT! COME OUT HERE WHERE I CAN SEE YOU!

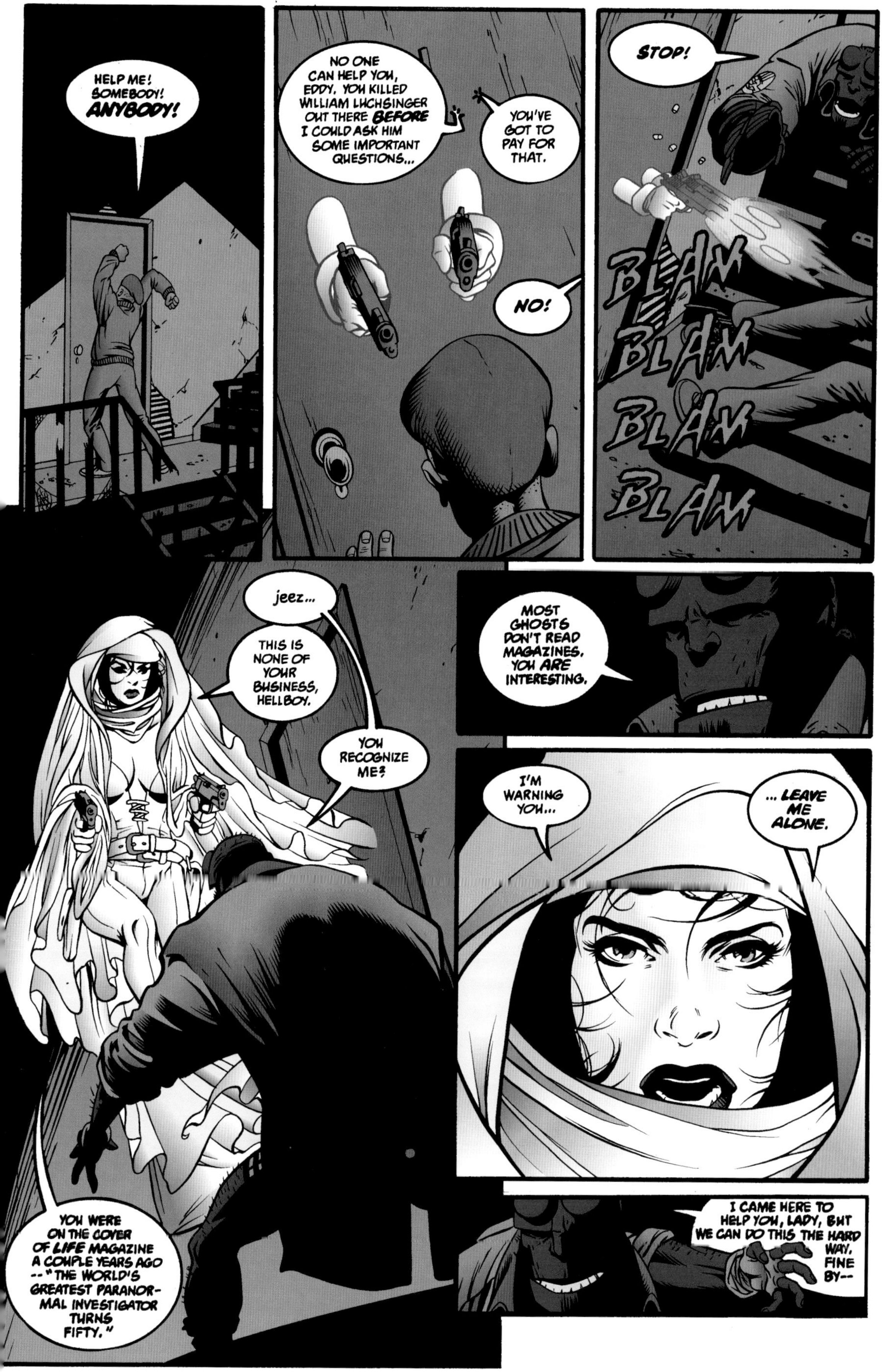
HELP ME! SOMEBODY! ANYBODY!
NO ONE CAN HELP YOU, EDDY. YOU KILLED WILLIAM LUCHSINGER OUT THERE BEFORE I COULD ASK HIM SOME IMPORTANT QUESTIONS...
YOU'VE GOT TO PAY FOR THAT.
NO!
STOP!
BLAM BLAM BLAM BLAM
jeez...
THIS IS NONE OF YOUR BUSINESS, HELLBOY.
YOU RECOGNIZE ME?
YOU WERE ON THE COVER OF LIFE MAGAZINE A COUPLE YEARS AGO -- "THE WORLD'S GREATEST PARANORMAL INVESTIGATOR TURNS FIFTY."
MOST GHOSTS DON'T READ MAGAZINES. YOU ARE INTERESTING.
I'M WARNING YOU...
... LEAVE ME ALONE.
I CAME HERE TO HELP YOU, LADY, BUT WE CAN DO THIS THE HARD WAY. FINE BY--

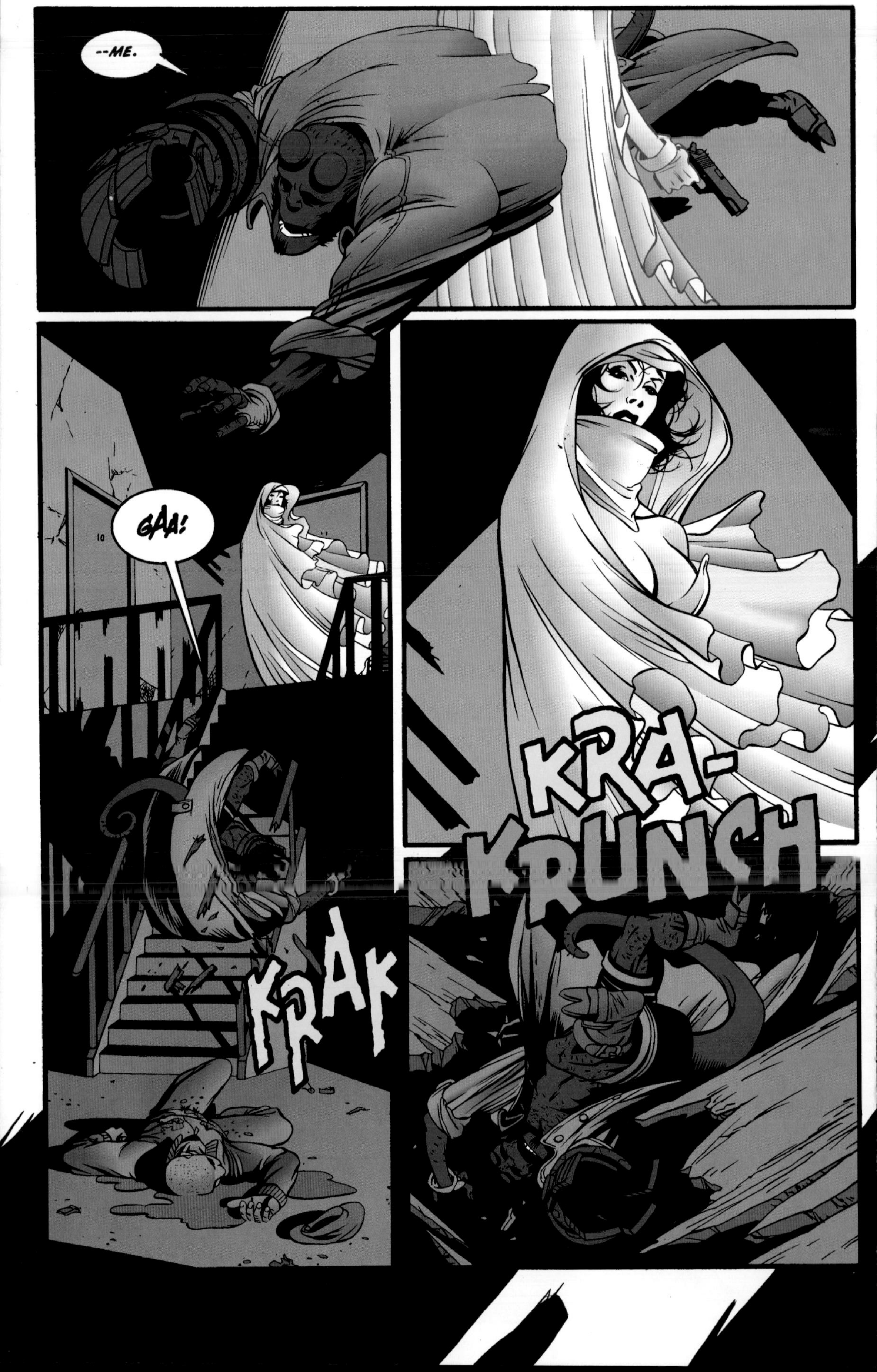
--ME.
GAA!
KRA-
KRUNCH
KRAK

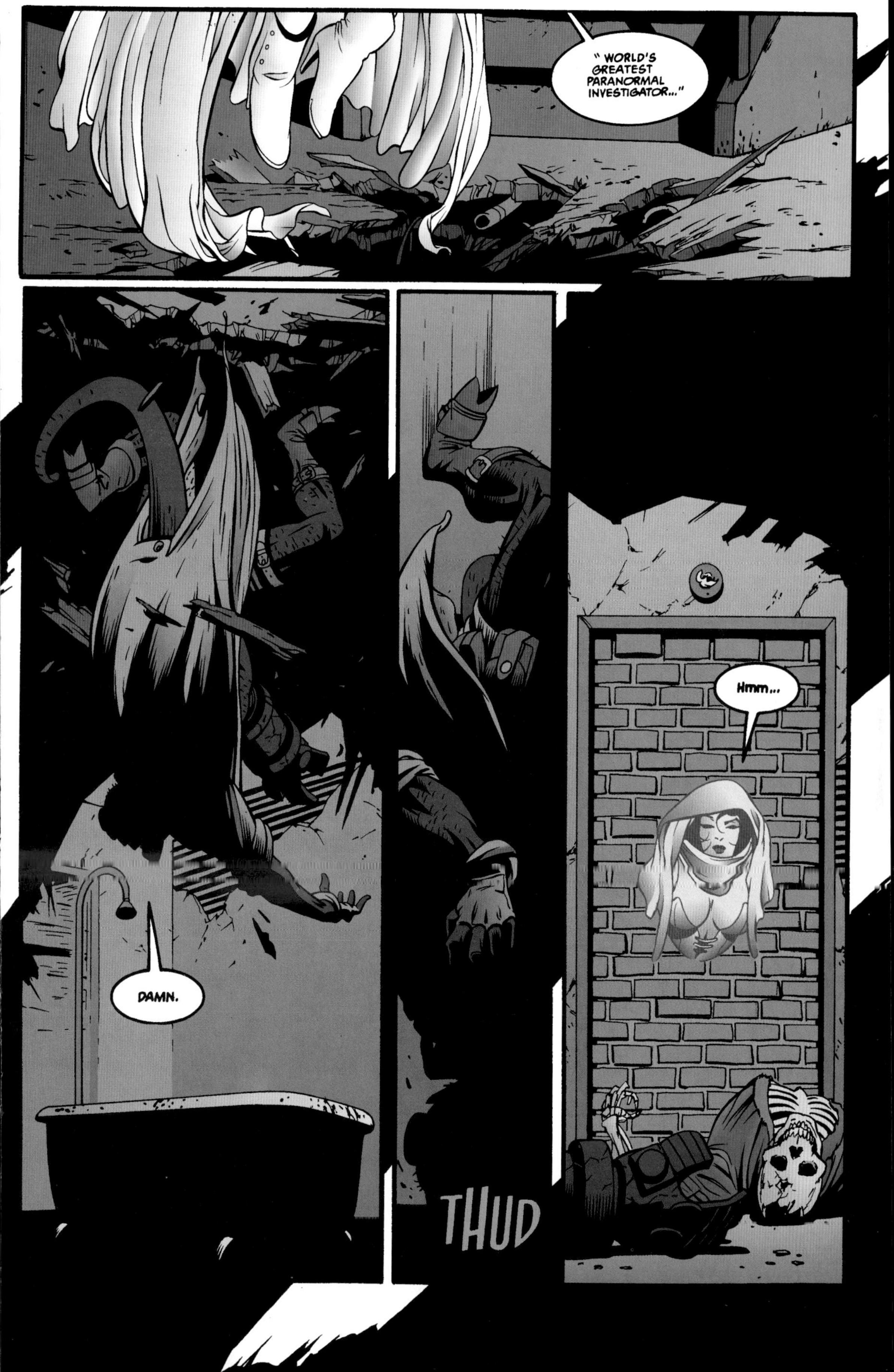
" WORLD'S GREATEST PARANORMAL INVESTIGATOR..."
DAMN.
Hmm...
THUD

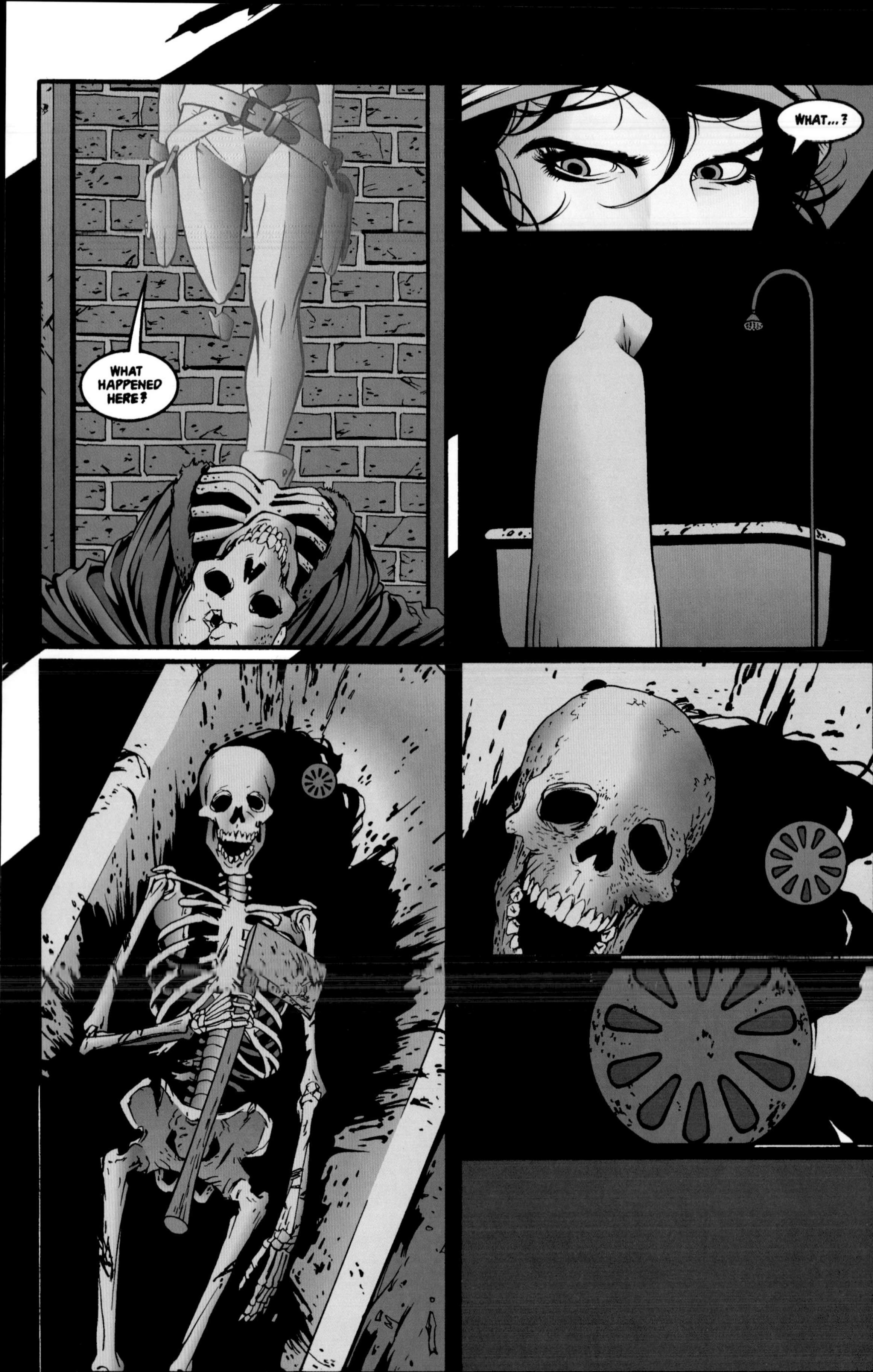
WHAT HAPPENED HERE?
WHAT...?

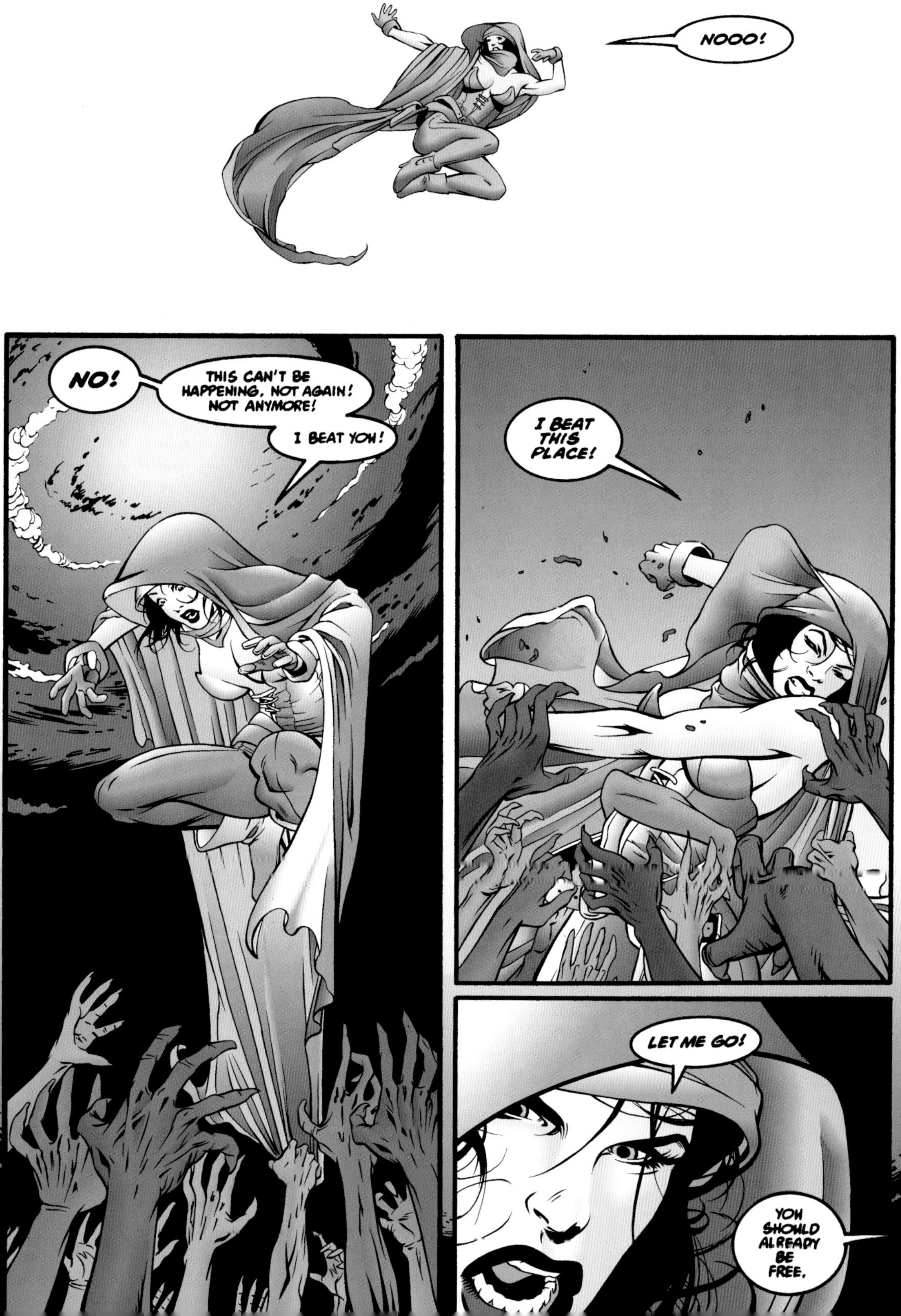
NOOO!
NO!
THIS CAN'T BE HAPPENING, NOT AGAIN! NOT ANYMORE!
I BEAT YOU!
I BEAT THIS PLACE!
LET ME GO!
YOU SHOULD ALREADY BE FREE.

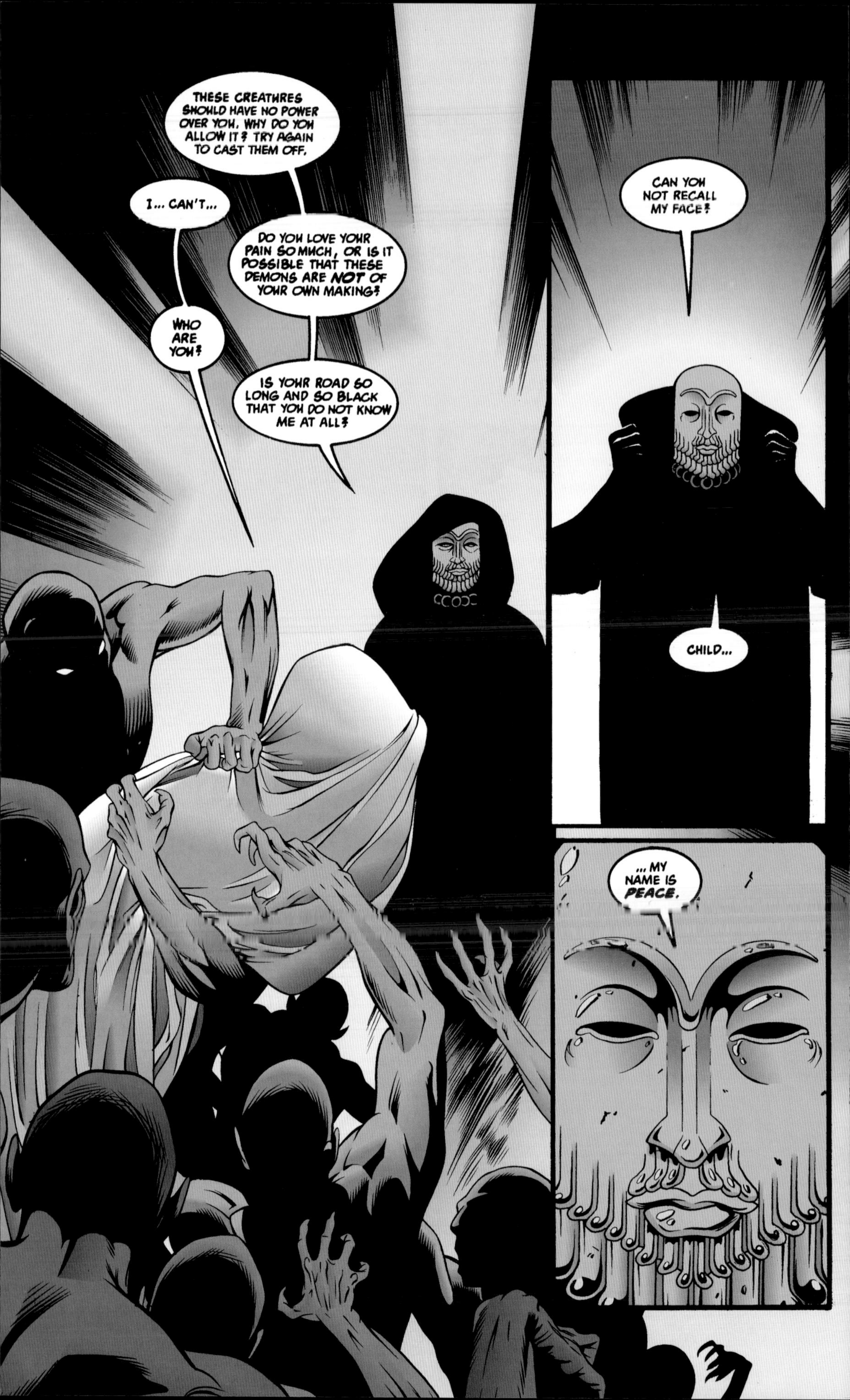
THESE CREATURES SHOULD HAVE NO POWER OVER YOU. WHY DO YOU ALLOW IT? TRY AGAIN TO CAST THEM OFF.
I... CAN'T...
DO YOU LOVE YOUR PAIN SO MUCH, OR IS IT POSSIBLE THAT THESE DEMONS ARE NOT OF YOUR OWN MAKING?
WHO ARE YOU?
IS YOUR ROAD SO LONG AND SO BLACK THAT YOU DO NOT KNOW ME AT ALL?
CAN YOU NOT RECALL MY FACE?
CHILD...
... MY NAME IS PEACE.

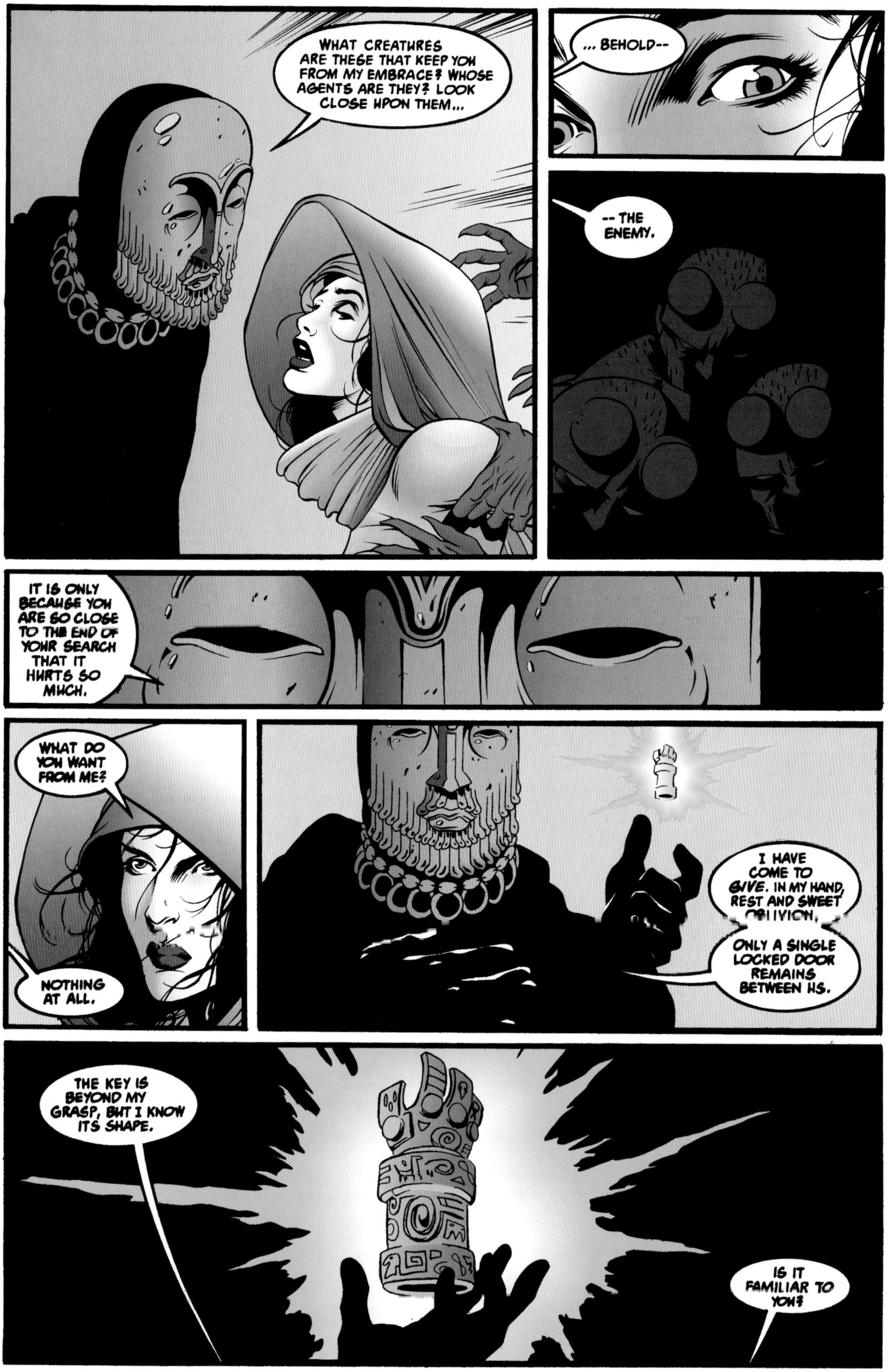
WHAT CREATURES ARE THESE THAT KEEP YOU FROM MY EMBRACE? WHOSE AGENTS ARE THEY? LOOK CLOSE UPON THEM...
...BEHOLD--
--THE ENEMY.
IT IS ONLY BECAUSE YOU ARE SO CLOSE TO THE END OF YOUR SEARCH THAT IT HURTS SO MUCH.
WHAT DO YOU WANT FROM ME?
NOTHING AT ALL.
I HAVE COME TO GIVE. IN MY HAND, REST AND SWEET
ONLY A SINGLE LOCKED DOOR REMAINS BETWEEN US.
THE KEY IS BEYOND MY GRASP, BUT I KNOW ITS SHAPE.
IS IT FAMILIAR TO YOU?

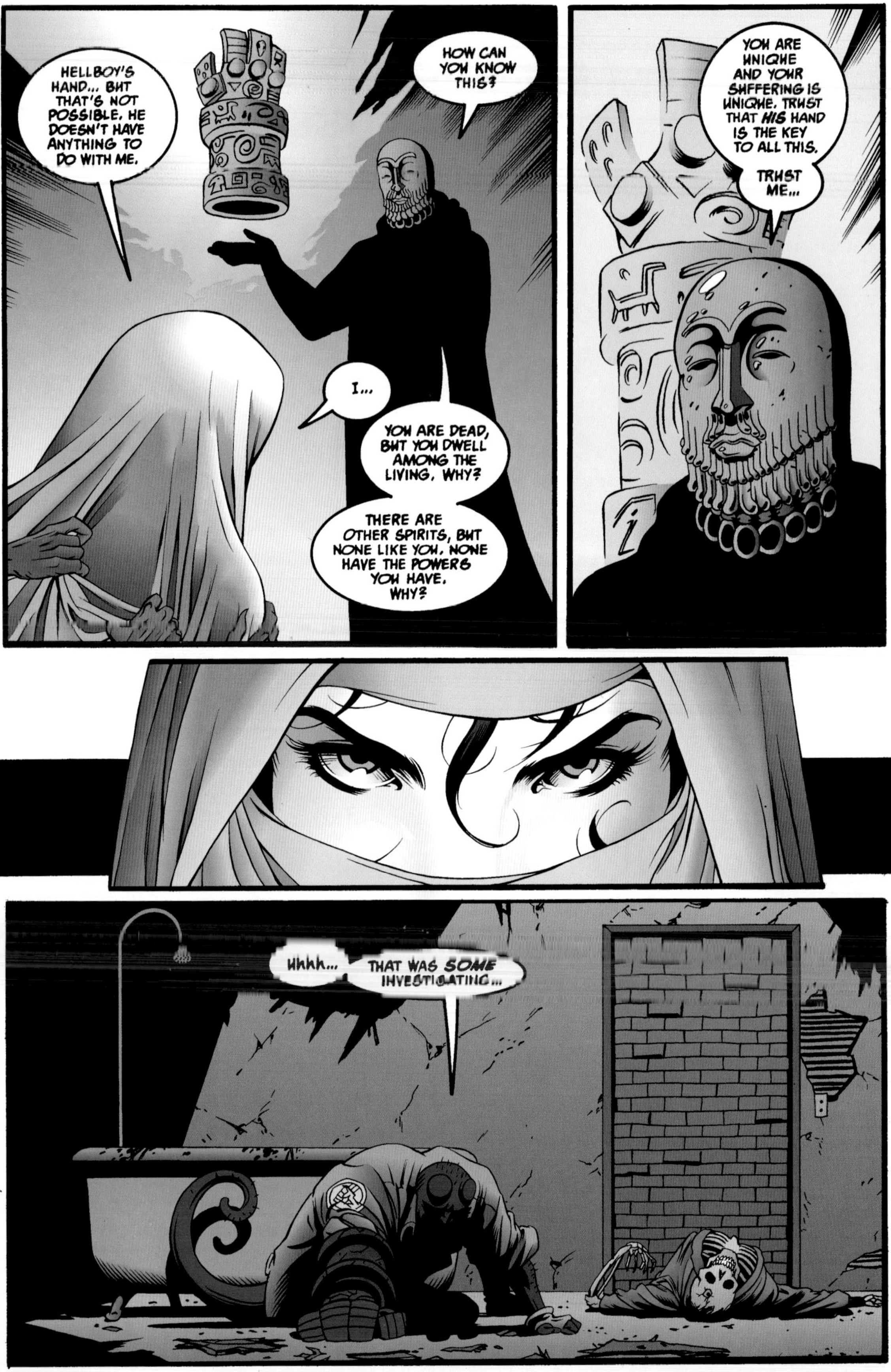
HELLBOY'S HAND... BUT THAT'S NOT POSSIBLE. HE DOESN'T HAVE ANYTHING TO DO WITH ME.
HOW CAN YOU KNOW THIS?
I...
YOU ARE DEAD, BUT YOU DWELL AMONG THE LIVING. WHY?
THERE ARE OTHER SPIRITS, BUT NONE LIKE YOU. NONE HAVE THE POWERS YOU HAVE. WHY?
YOU ARE UNIQUE AND YOUR SUFFERING IS UNIQUE. TRUST THAT HIS HAND IS THE KEY TO ALL THIS.
TRUST ME...
UHHH...
THAT WAS SOME INVESTIGATING...

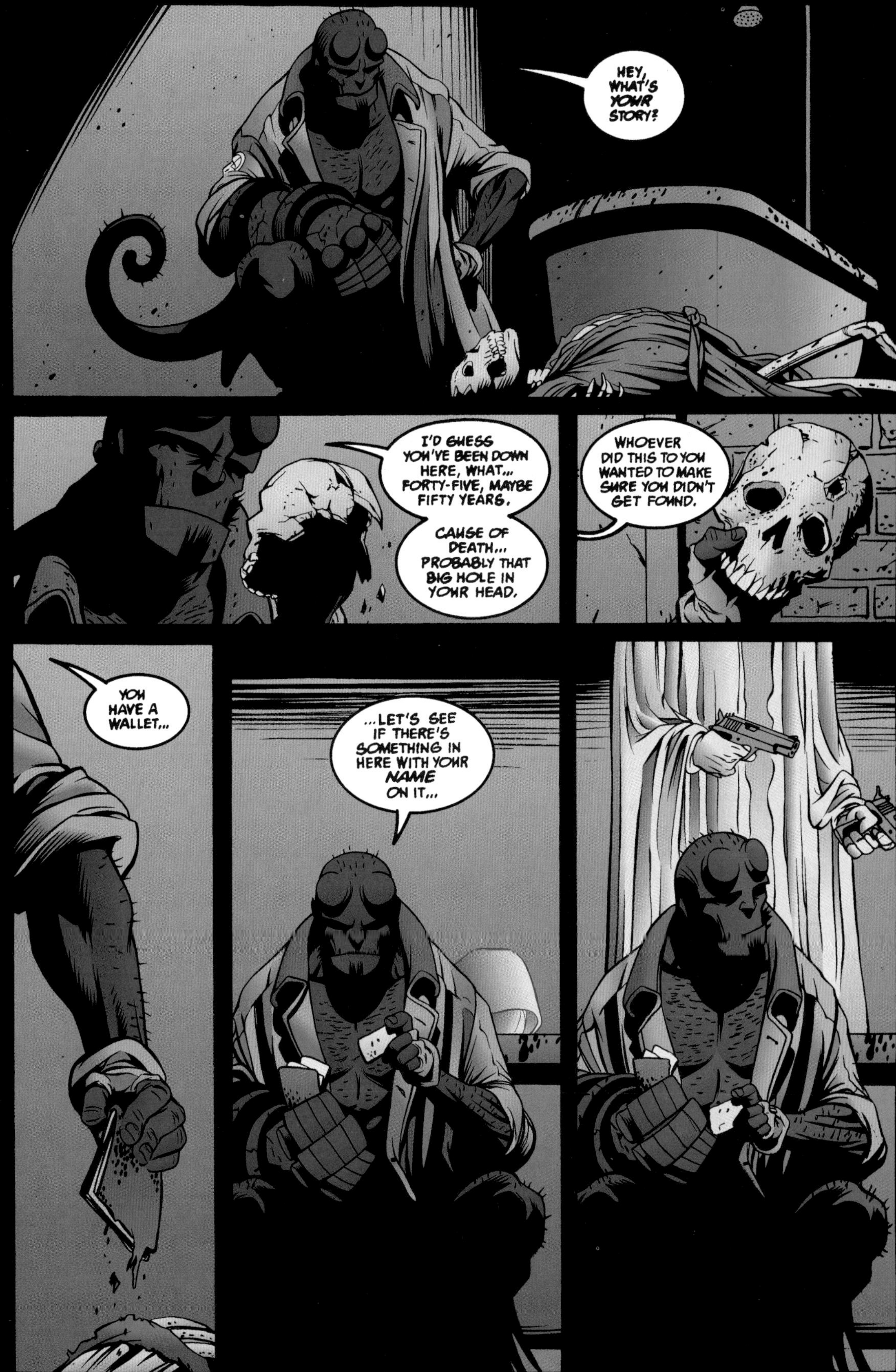
HEY, WHAT'S YOUR STORY?
I'D GUESS YOU'VE BEEN DOWN HERE, WHAT... FORTY-FIVE, MAYBE FIFTY YEARS.
CAUSE OF DEATH... PROBABLY THAT BIG HOLE IN YOUR HEAD.
WHOEVER DID THIS TO YOU WANTED TO MAKE SURE YOU DIDN'T GET FOUND.
YOU HAVE A WALLET...
...LET'S SEE IF THERE'S SOMETHING IN HERE WITH YOUR NAME ON IT...

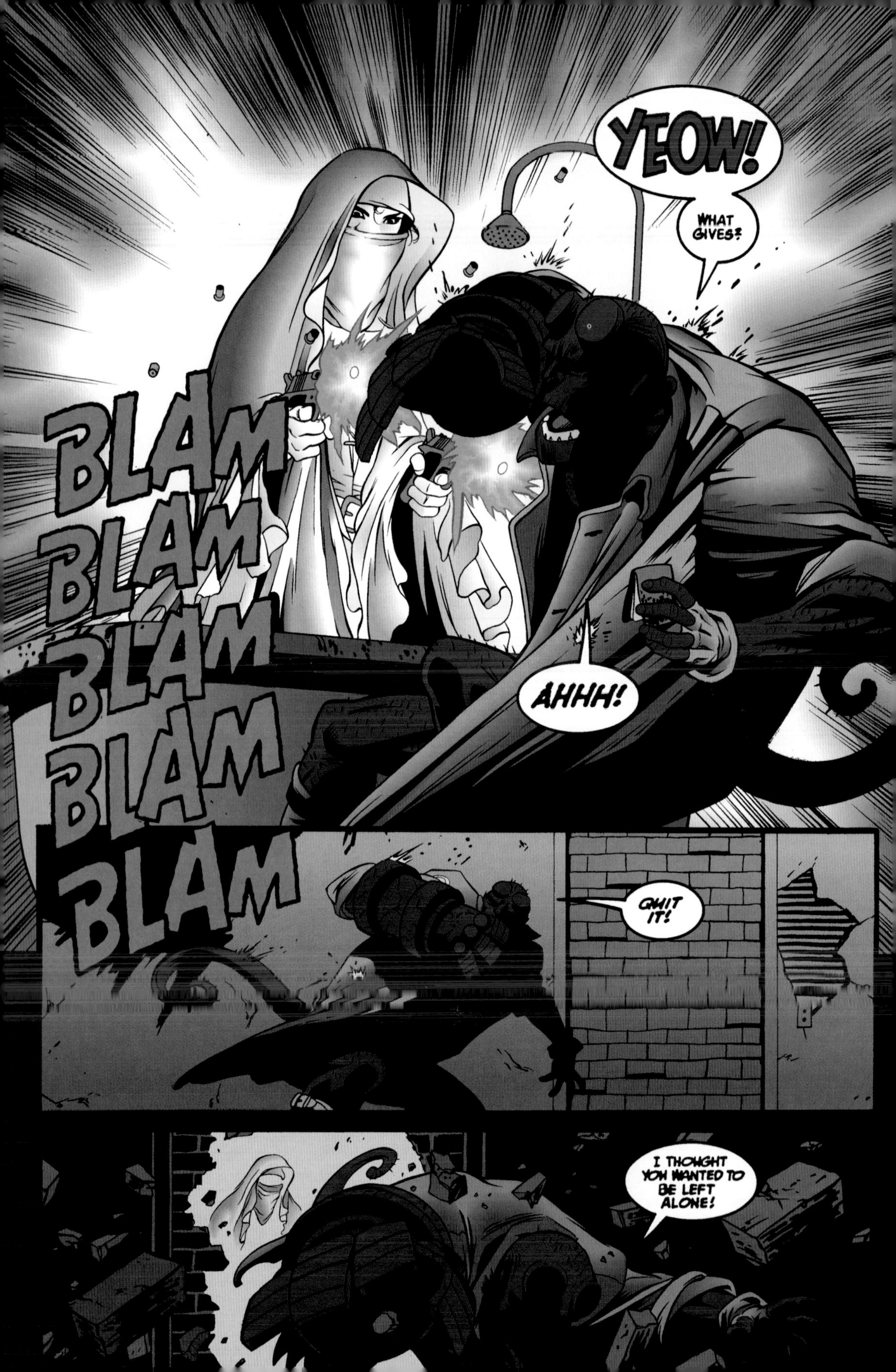
YEOW!
WHAT GIVES?
BLAM BLAM BLAM BLAM BLAM BLAM
AHHH!
QUIT IT!
I THOUGHT YOU WANTED TO BE LEFT ALONE!

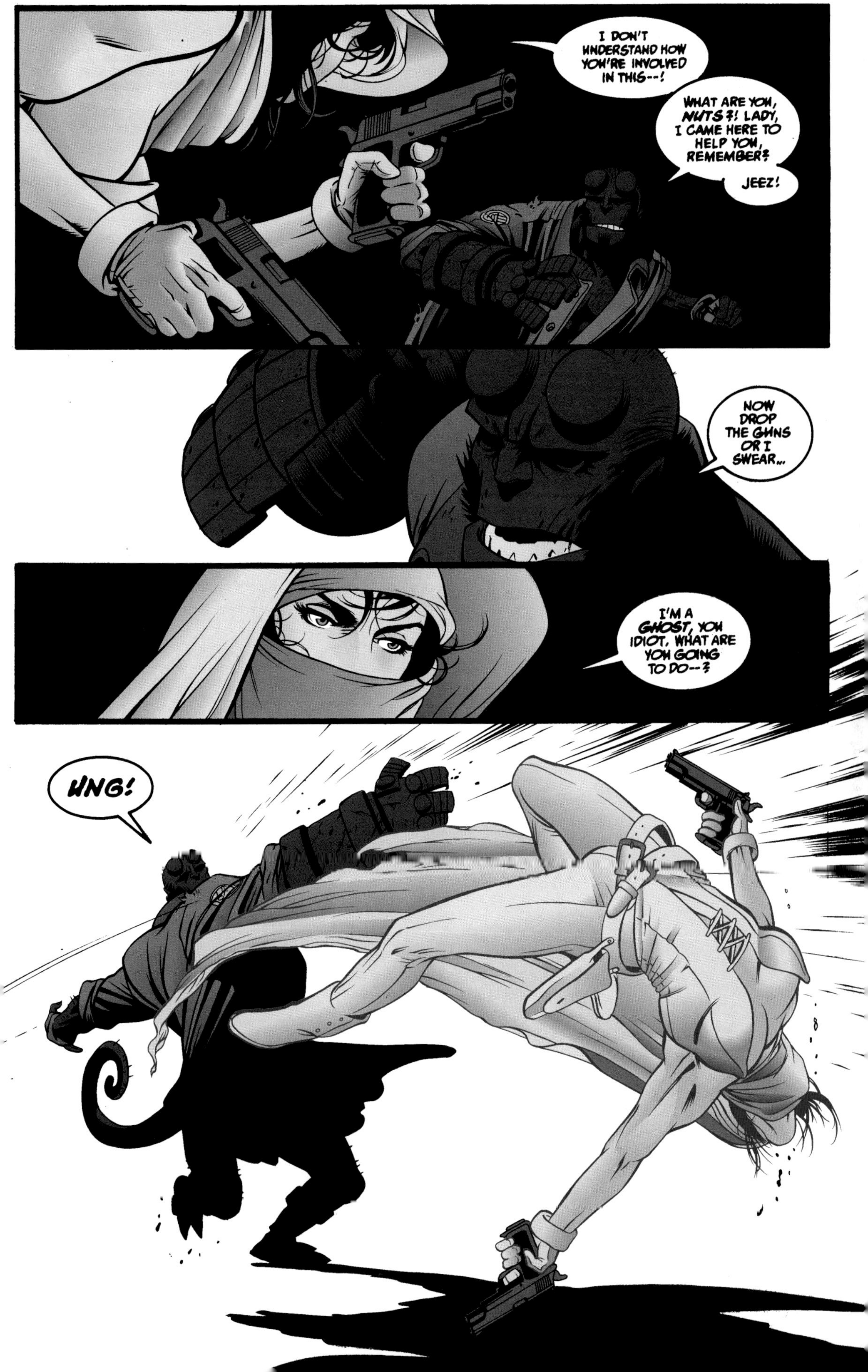

I DON'T UNDERSTAND HOW YOU'RE INVOLVED IN THIS--!
WHAT ARE YOU, NUTS?! LADY, I CAME HERE TO HELP YOU, REMEMBER?
JEEZ!
NOW DROP THE GUNS OR I SWEAR...
I'M A GHOST, YOU IDIOT, WHAT ARE YOU GOING TO DO--?
UNG!

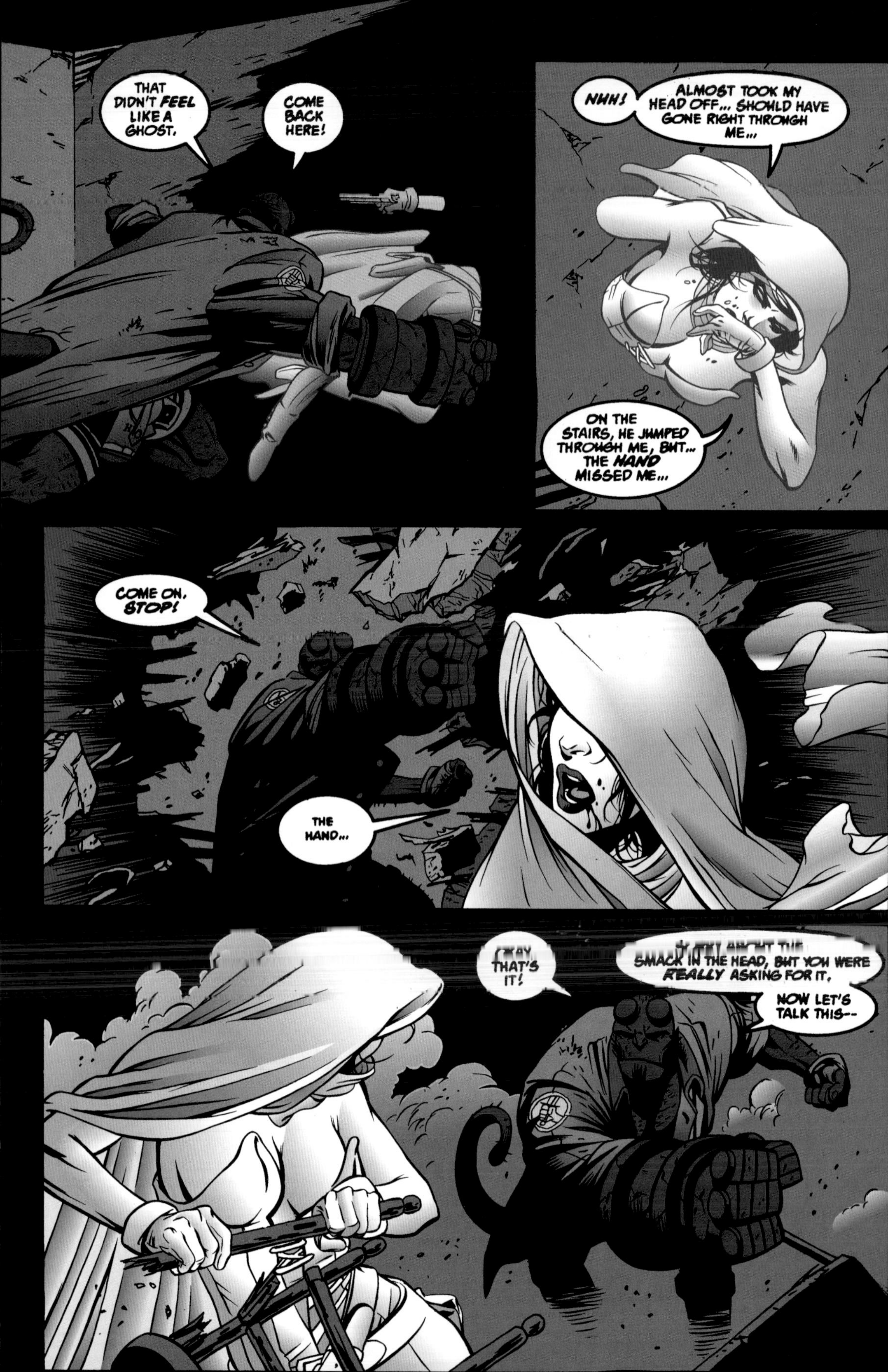
THAT DIDN'T FEEL LIKE A GHOST.
COME BACK HERE!
NUH!
ALMOST TOOK MY HEAD OFF... SHOULD HAVE GONE RIGHT THROUGH ME...
ON THE STAIRS, HE JUMPED THROUGH ME, BUT... THE HAND MISSED ME...
COME ON. STOP!
THE HAND...
THAT'S IT!
SMACK IN THE HEAD, BUT YOU WERE REALLY ASKING FOR IT.
NOW LET'S TALK THIS--

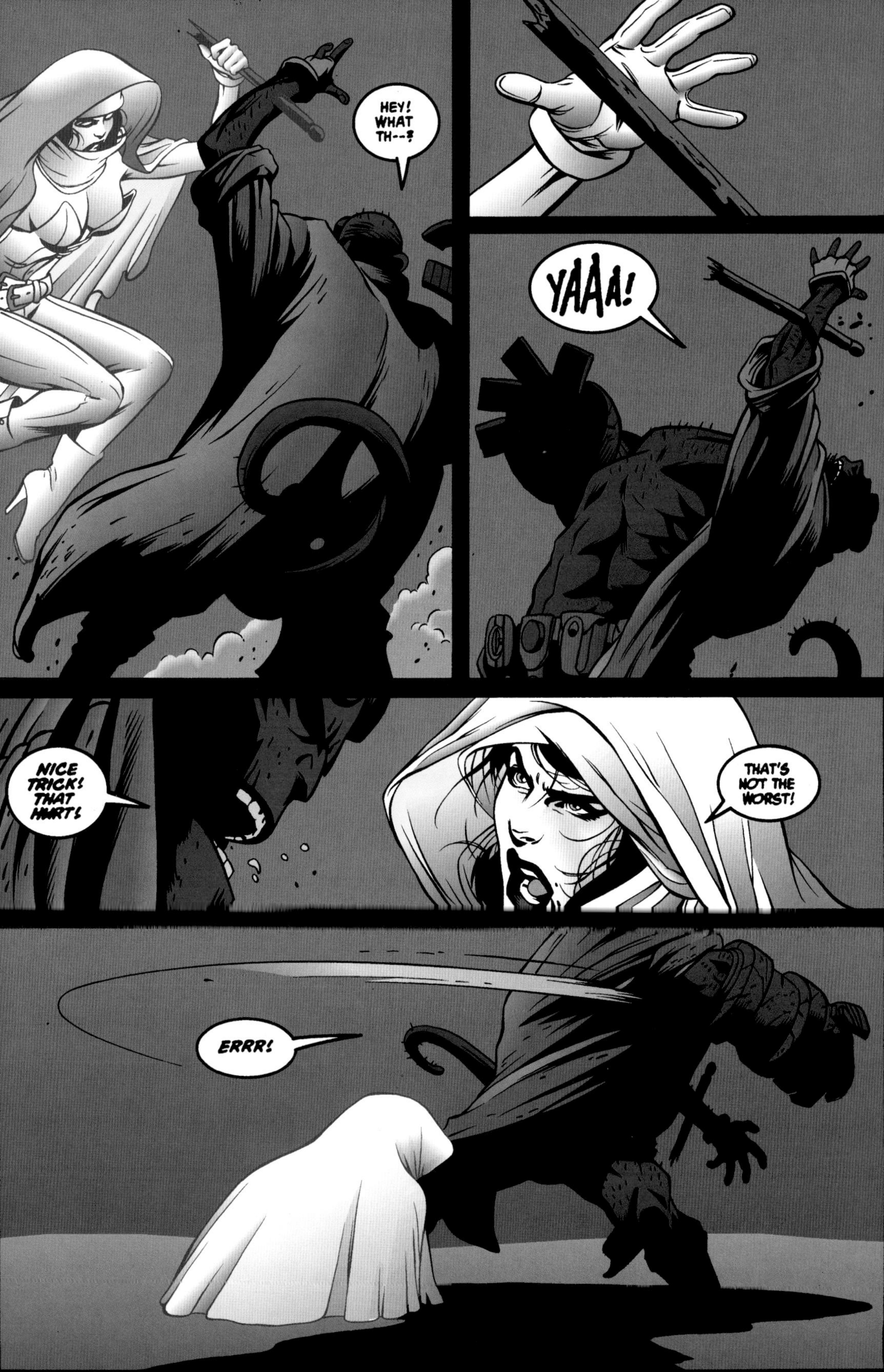
HEY! WHAT TH--?
YAAA!
NICE TRICK! THAT HURT!
THAT'S NOT THE WORST!
ERRR!

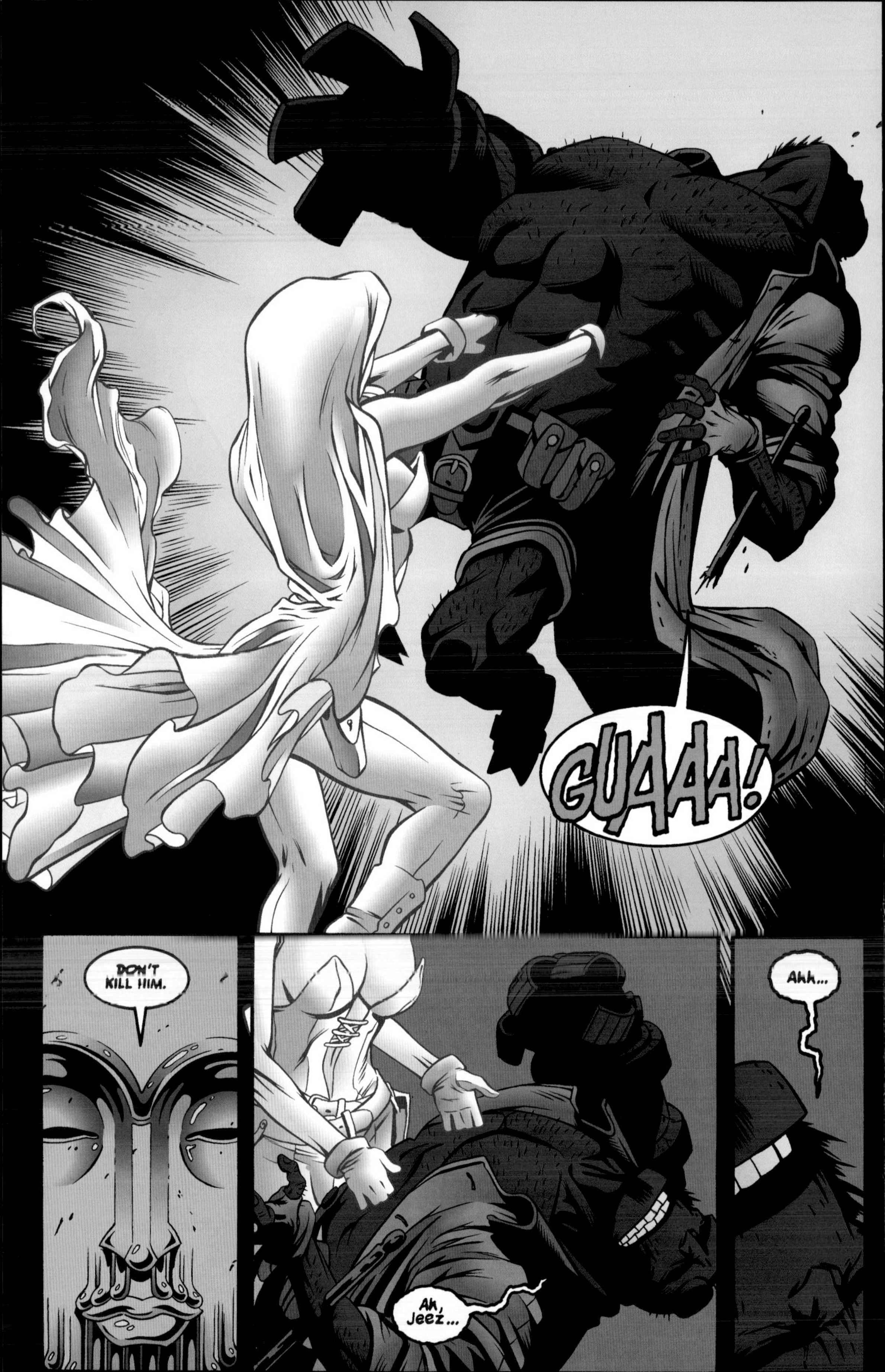
GUAAA!
DON'T KILL HIM.
Ah, Jeez...
Ahh...

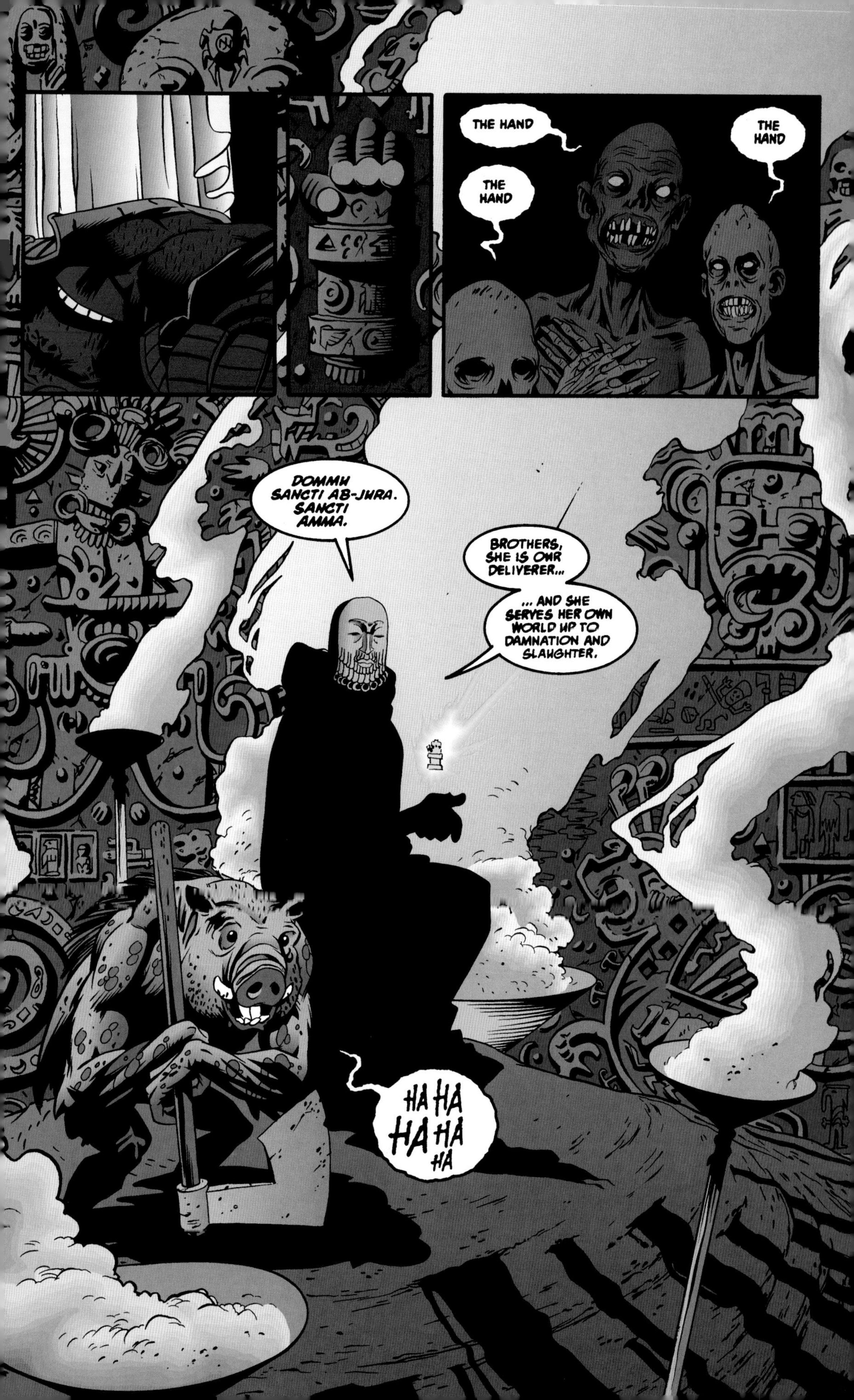
THE HAND
THE HAND
THE HAND
DOMMH SANCTI AB-JURA. SANCTI AMMA.
BROTHERS, SHE IS OMR DELIVERER...
... AND SHE SERVES HER OWN WORLD UP TO DAMNATION AND SLAUGHTER.
HA HA HA HA HA HA

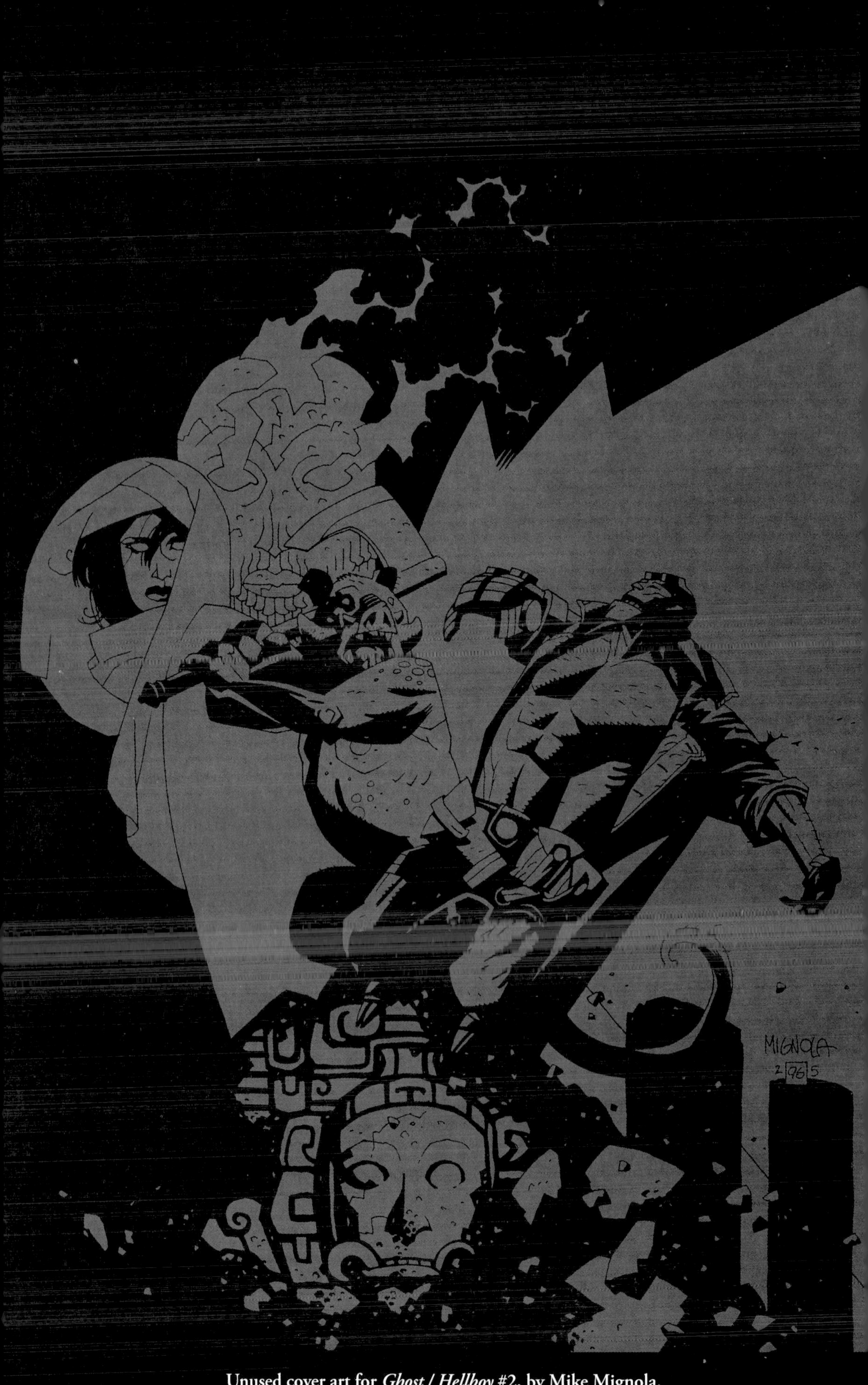
MIGNOLA
2 96 5

Unused cover art for *Ghost / Hellboy* #2, by Mike Mignola.

CHAPTER TWO

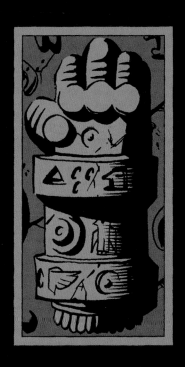

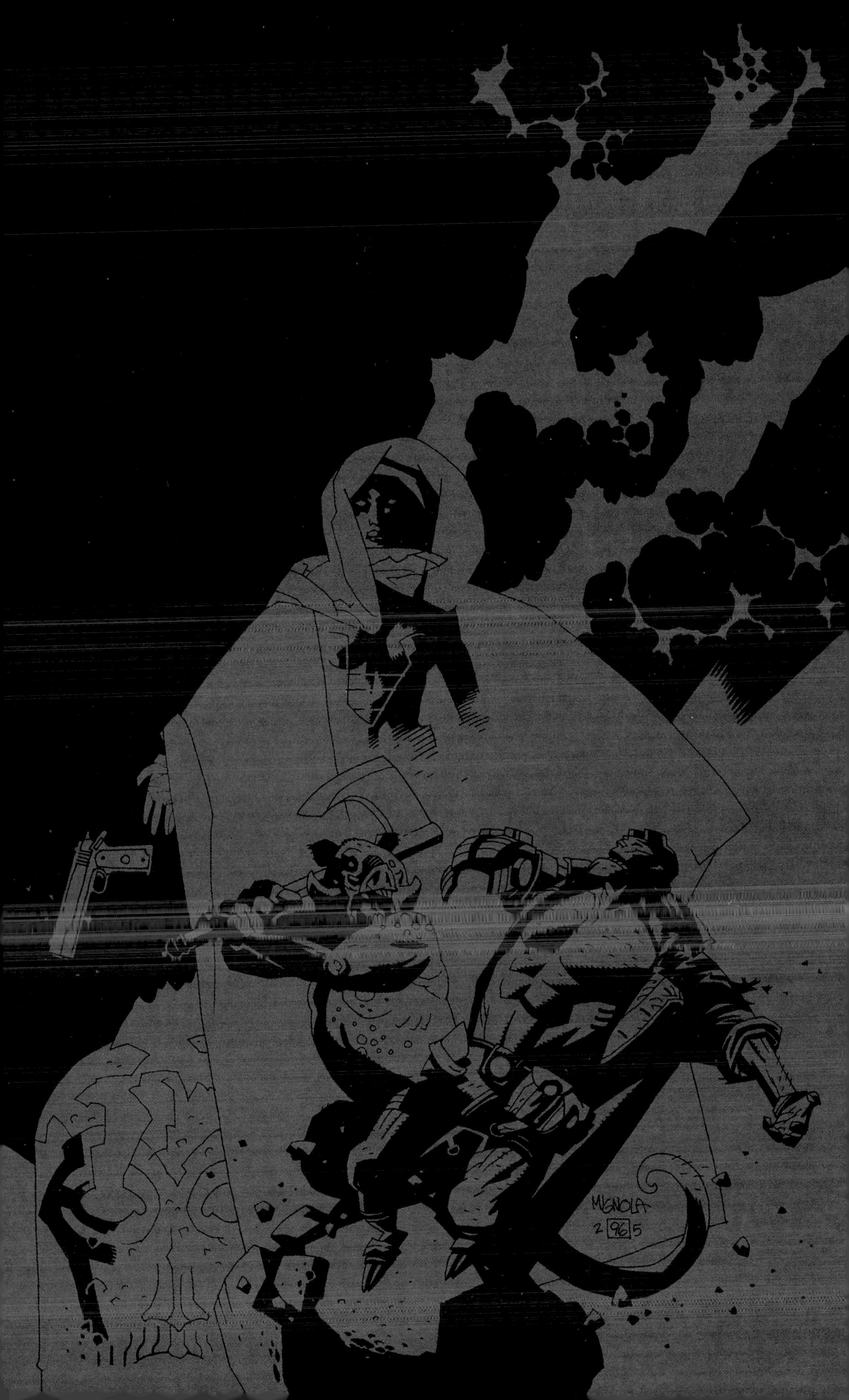
MIGNOLA
2 96 5

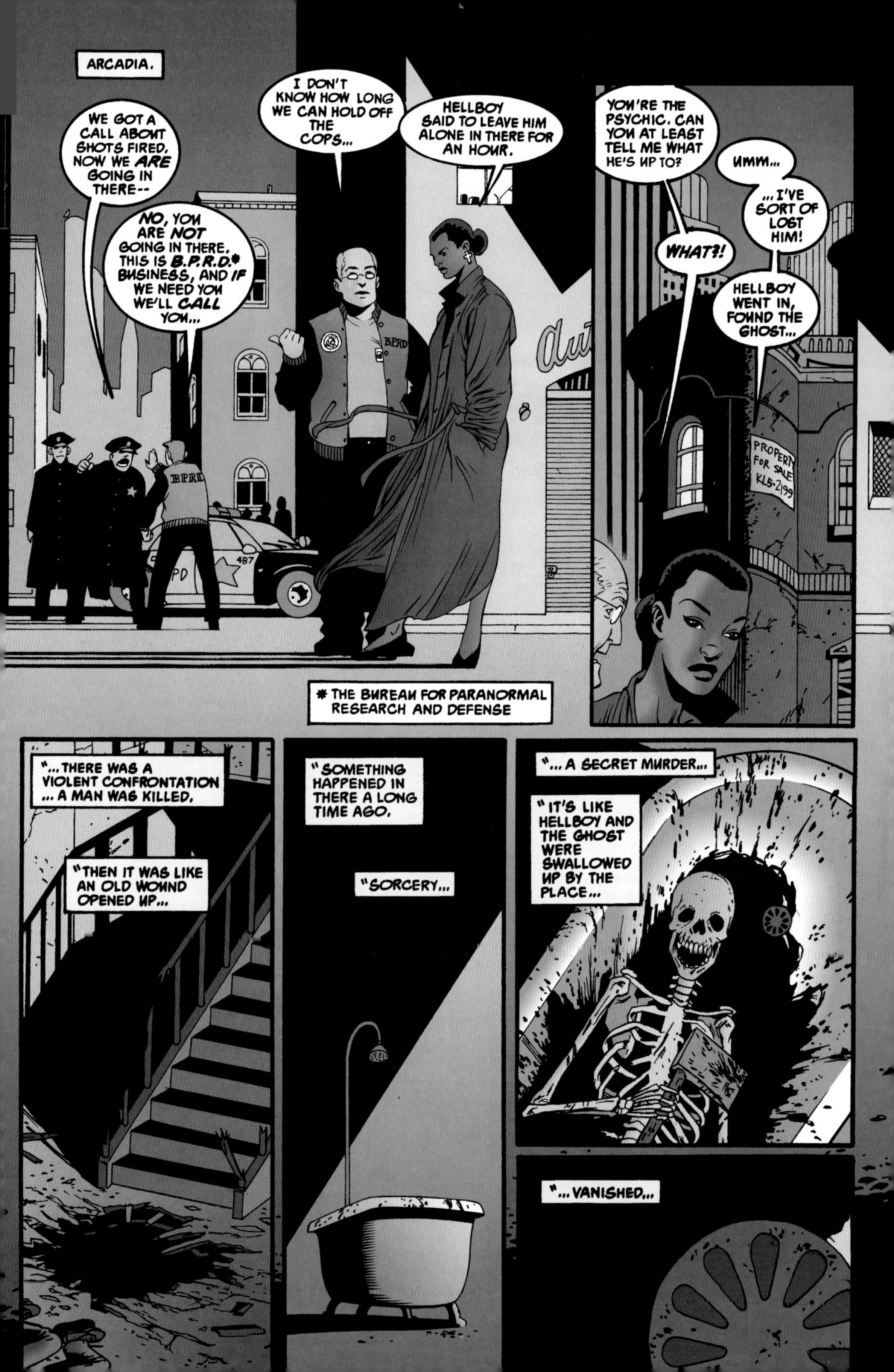
ARCADIA.
WE GOT A CALL ABOUT SHOTS FIRED. NOW WE ARE GOING IN THERE--
NO, YOU ARE NOT GOING IN THERE. THIS IS B.P.R.D.* BUSINESS, AND IF WE NEED YOU WE'LL CALL YOU...
I DON'T KNOW HOW LONG WE CAN HOLD OFF THE COPS...
HELLBOY SAID TO LEAVE HIM ALONE IN THERE FOR AN HOUR.
YOU'RE THE PSYCHIC. CAN YOU AT LEAST TELL ME WHAT HE'S UP TO?
UMM...
...I'VE SORT OF LOST HIM!
WHAT?!
HELLBOY WENT IN, FOUND THE GHOST...
PROPERTY FOR SALE KL5-2199
* THE BUREAU FOR PARANORMAL RESEARCH AND DEFENSE
"...THERE WAS A VIOLENT CONFRONTATION ... A MAN WAS KILLED.
"THEN IT WAS LIKE AN OLD WOUND OPENED UP...
"SOMETHING HAPPENED IN THERE A LONG TIME AGO.
"SORCERY...
"...A SECRET MURDER...
"IT'S LIKE HELLBOY AND THE GHOST WERE SWALLOWED UP BY THE PLACE...
"...VANISHED...

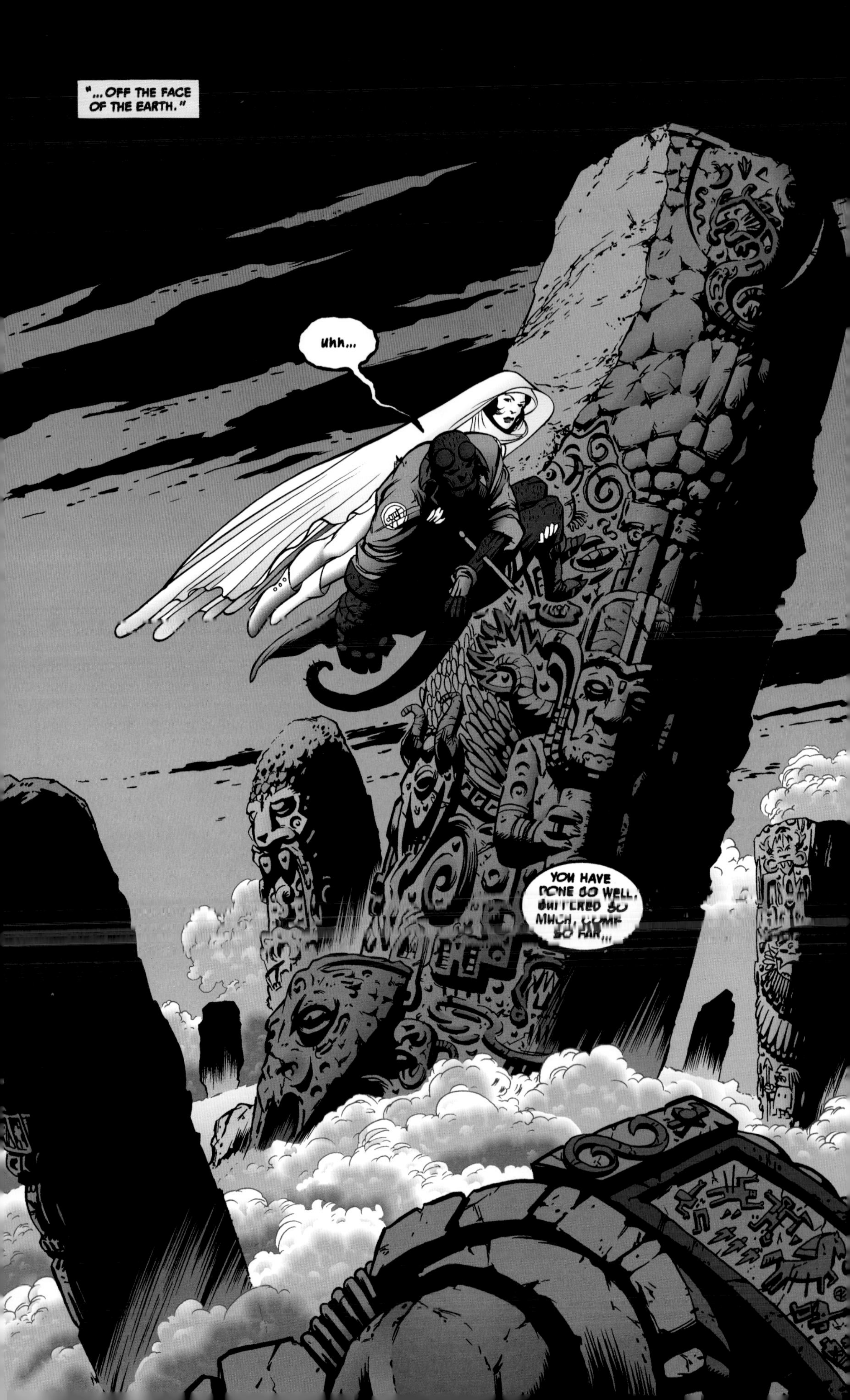
"...OFF THE FACE OF THE EARTH."
Uhh...
YOU HAVE DONE SO WELL, SUFFERED SO MUCH, COME SO FAR...

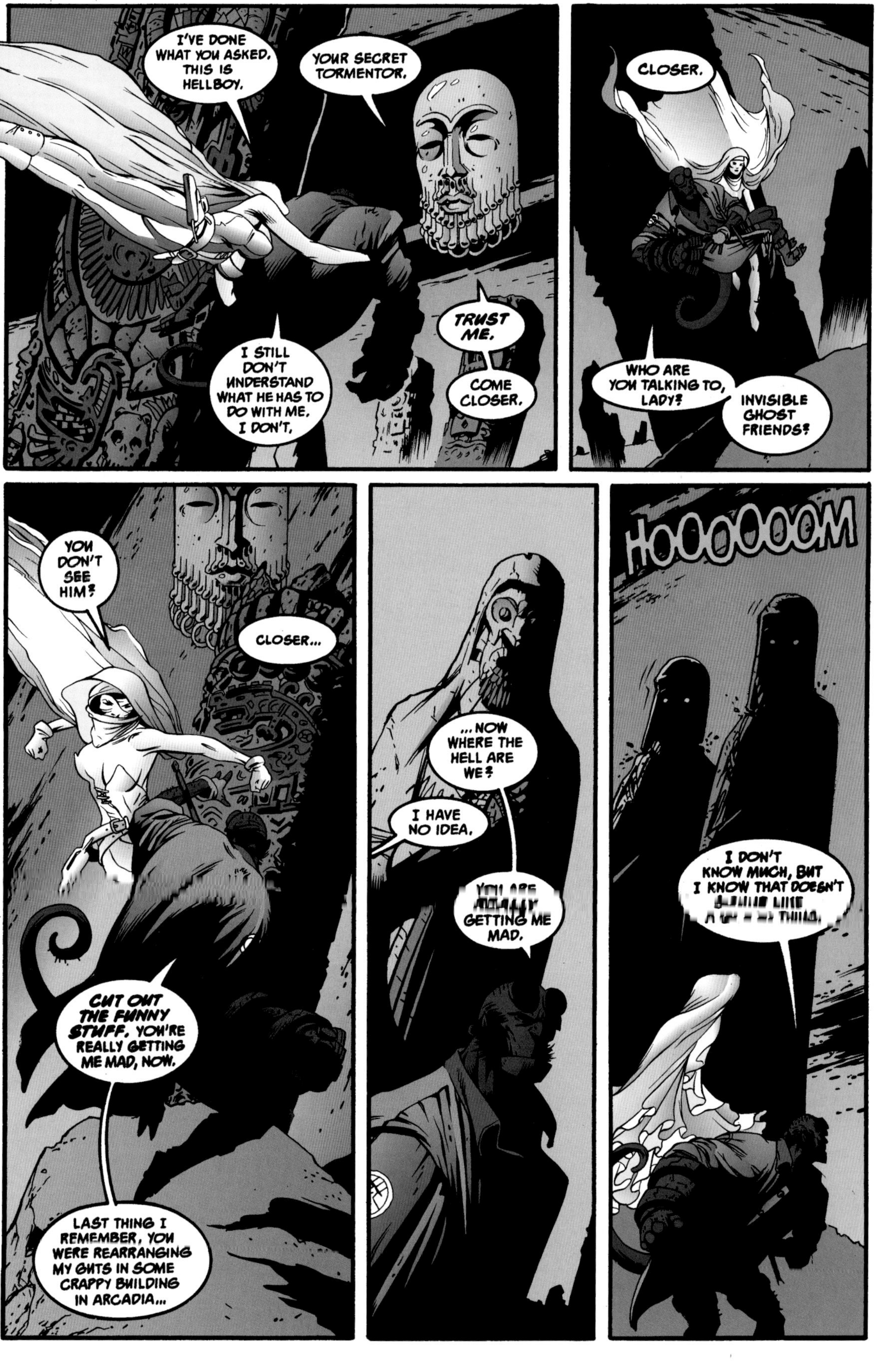
I'VE DONE WHAT YOU ASKED. THIS IS HELLBOY.
YOUR SECRET TORMENTOR.
I STILL DON'T UNDERSTAND WHAT HE HAS TO DO WITH ME. I DON'T.
TRUST ME.
COME CLOSER.
CLOSER.
WHO ARE YOU TALKING TO, LADY?
INVISIBLE GHOST FRIENDS?
YOU DON'T SEE HIM?
CLOSER...
CUT OUT THE FUNNY STUFF. YOU'RE REALLY GETTING ME MAD, NOW.
LAST THING I REMEMBER, YOU WERE REARRANGING MY GUTS IN SOME CRAPPY BUILDING IN ARCADIA...
...NOW WHERE THE HELL ARE WE?
I HAVE NO IDEA.
GETTING ME MAD.
HOOOOOOM
I DON'T KNOW MUCH, BUT I KNOW THAT DOESN'T

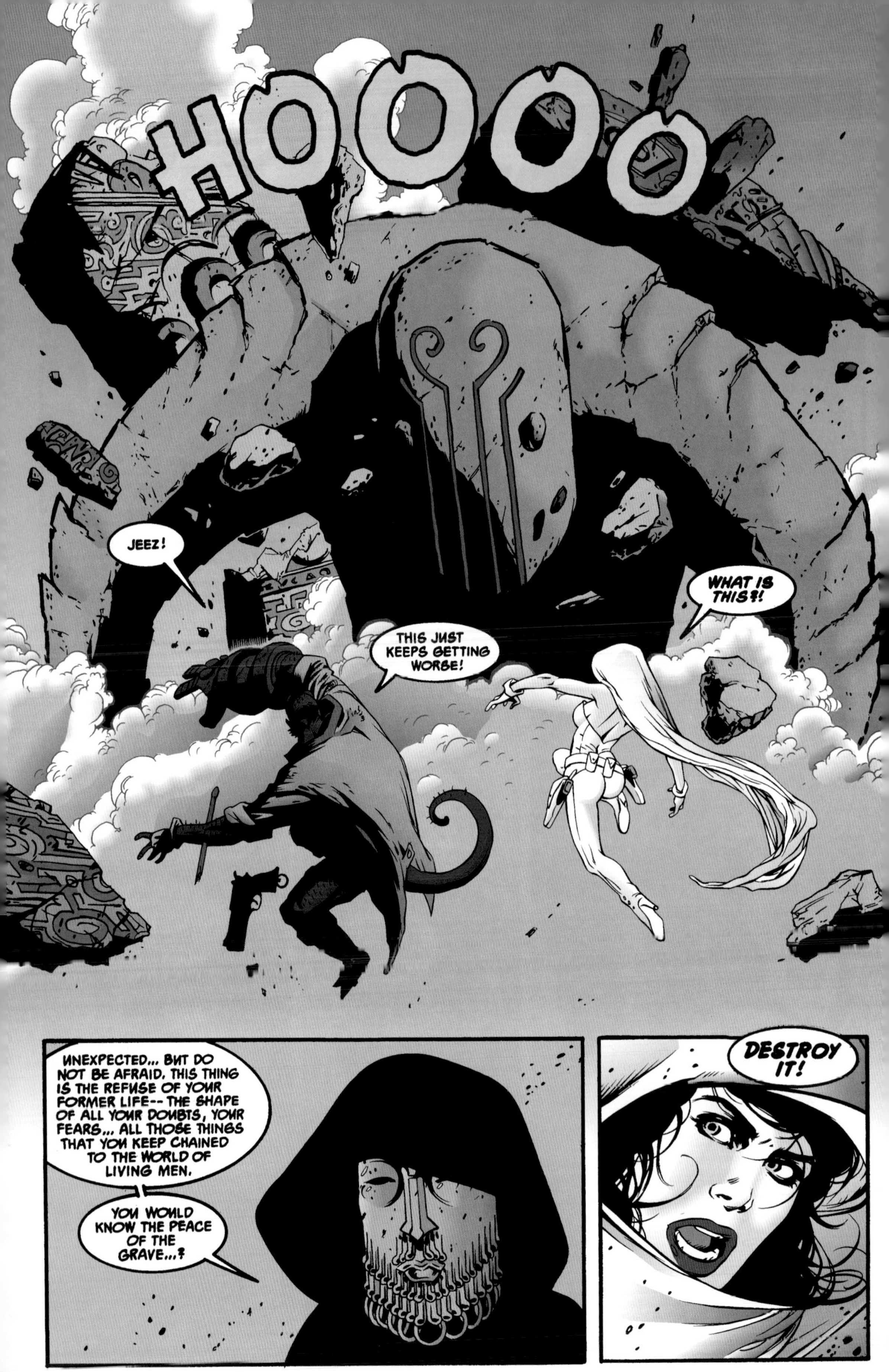
HOOOO
JEEZ!
THIS JUST KEEPS GETTING WORSE!
WHAT IS THIS?!
UNEXPECTED... BUT DO NOT BE AFRAID. THIS THING IS THE REFUSE OF YOUR FORMER LIFE-- THE SHAPE OF ALL YOUR DOUBTS, YOUR FEARS... ALL THOSE THINGS THAT YOU KEEP CHAINED TO THE WORLD OF LIVING MEN.
YOU WOULD KNOW THE PEACE OF THE GRAVE...?
DESTROY IT!

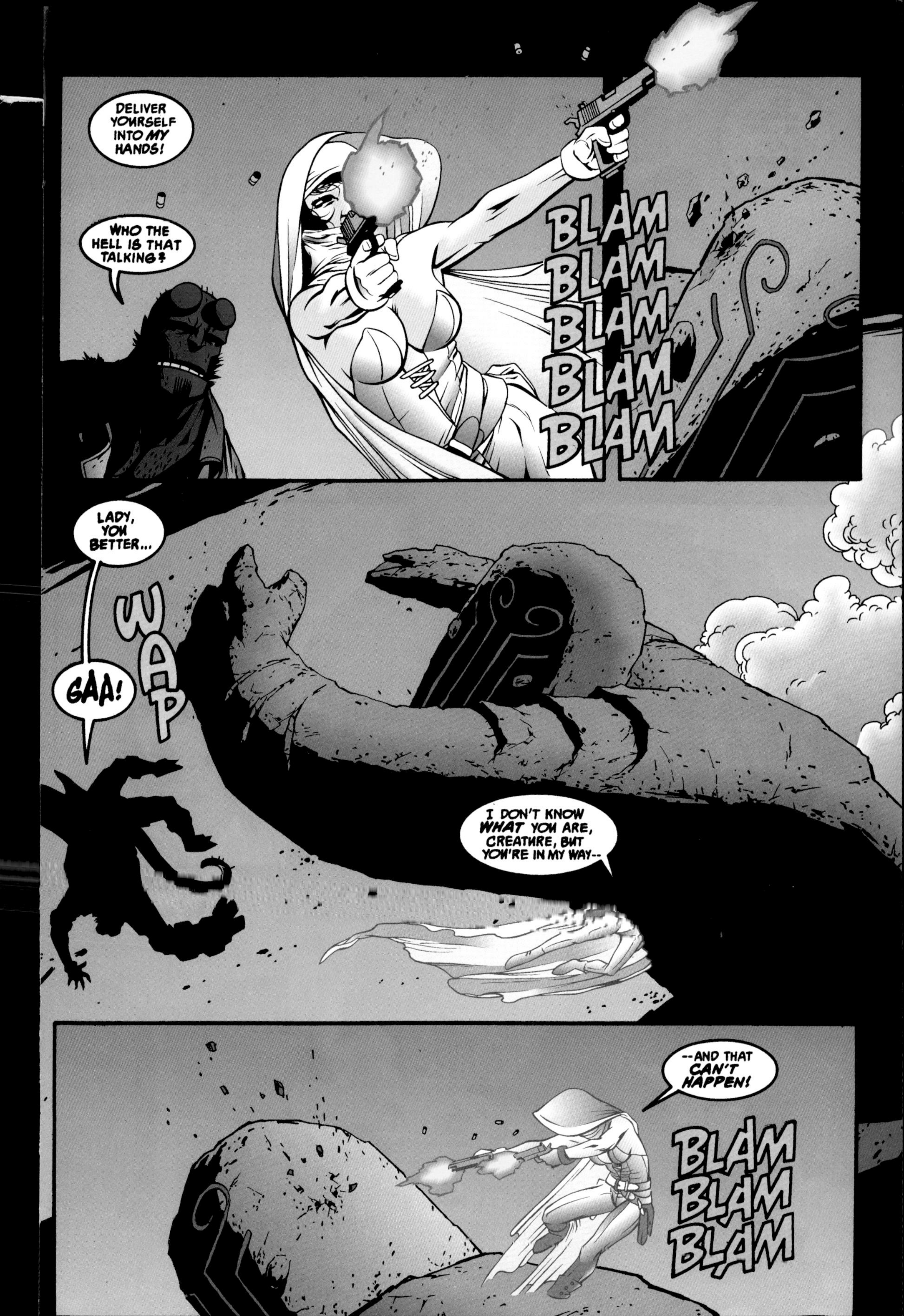
DELIVER YOURSELF INTO MY HANDS!
WHO THE HELL IS THAT TALKING?
BLAM BLAM BLAM BLAM BLAM
LADY, YOU BETTER...
WAP
GAA!
I DON'T KNOW WHAT YOU ARE, CREATURE, BUT YOU'RE IN MY WAY--
--AND THAT CAN'T HAPPEN!
BLAM BLAM BLAM

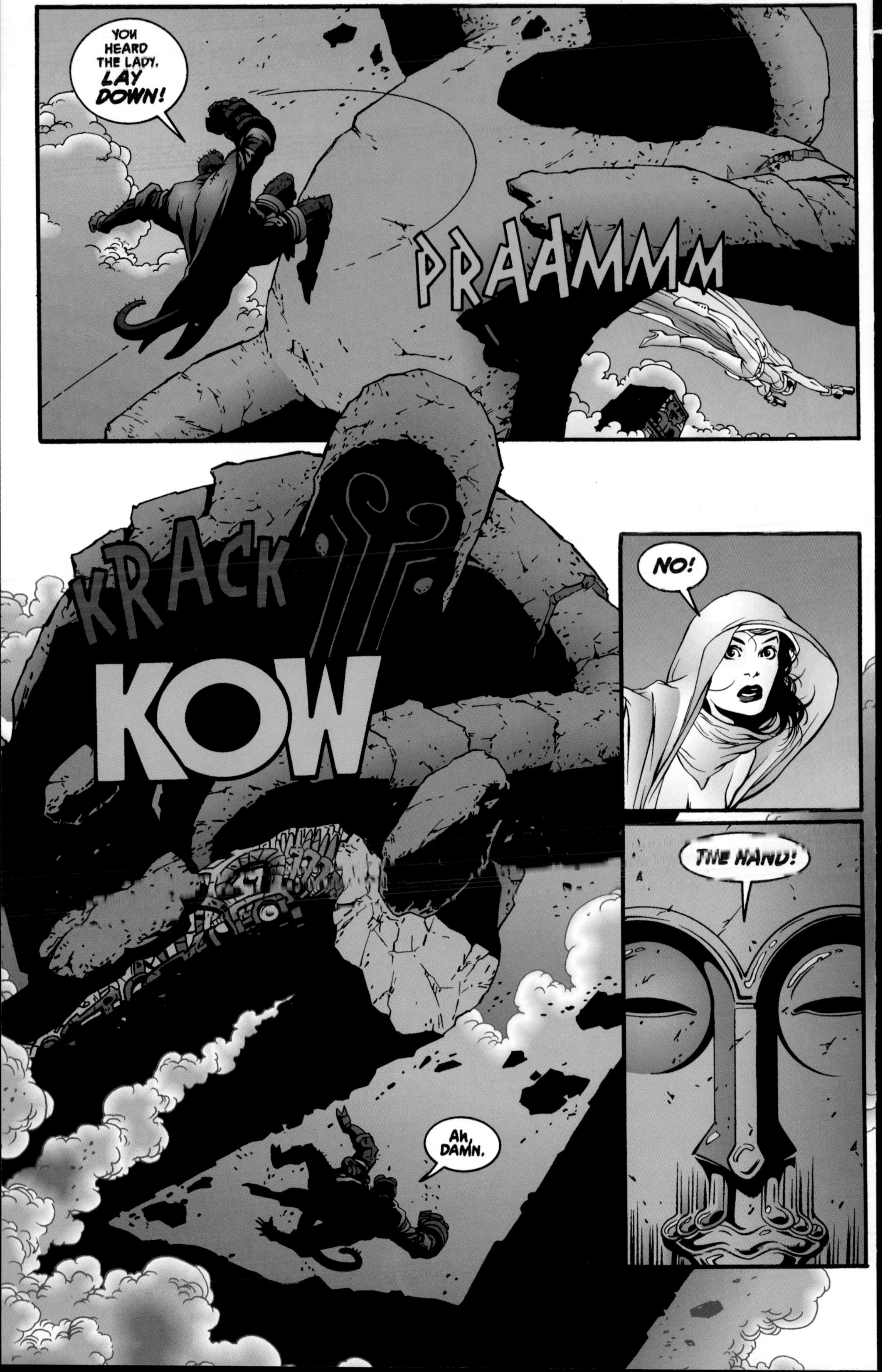
YOU HEARD THE LADY. LAY DOWN!
PRAAMMM
KRACK
KOW
NO!
THE HAND!
AH, DAMN.

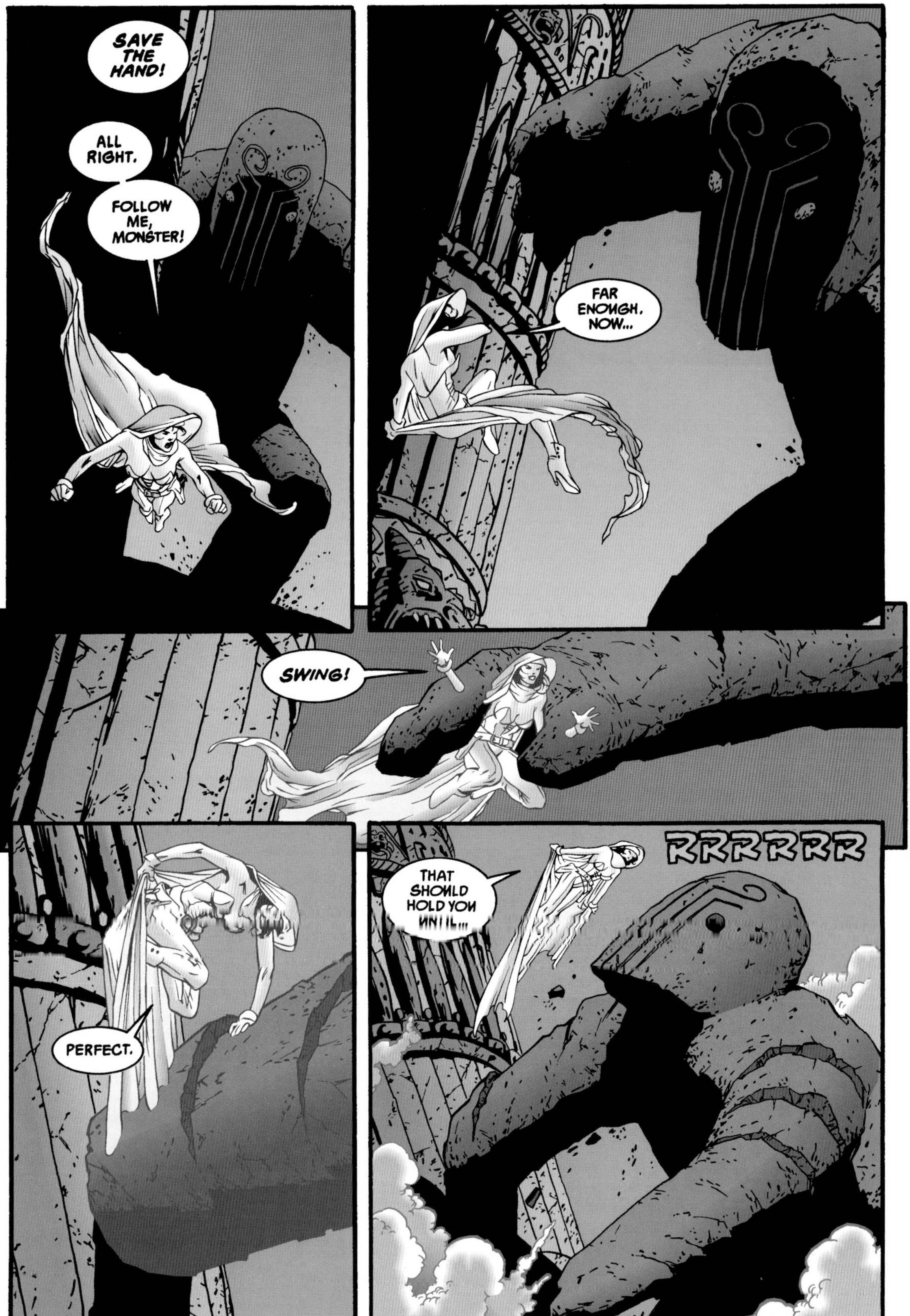
SAVE THE HAND!
ALL RIGHT.
FOLLOW ME, MONSTER!
FAR ENOUGH. NOW...
SWING!
PERFECT.
RRRRRR
THAT SHOULD HOLD YOU UNTIL...

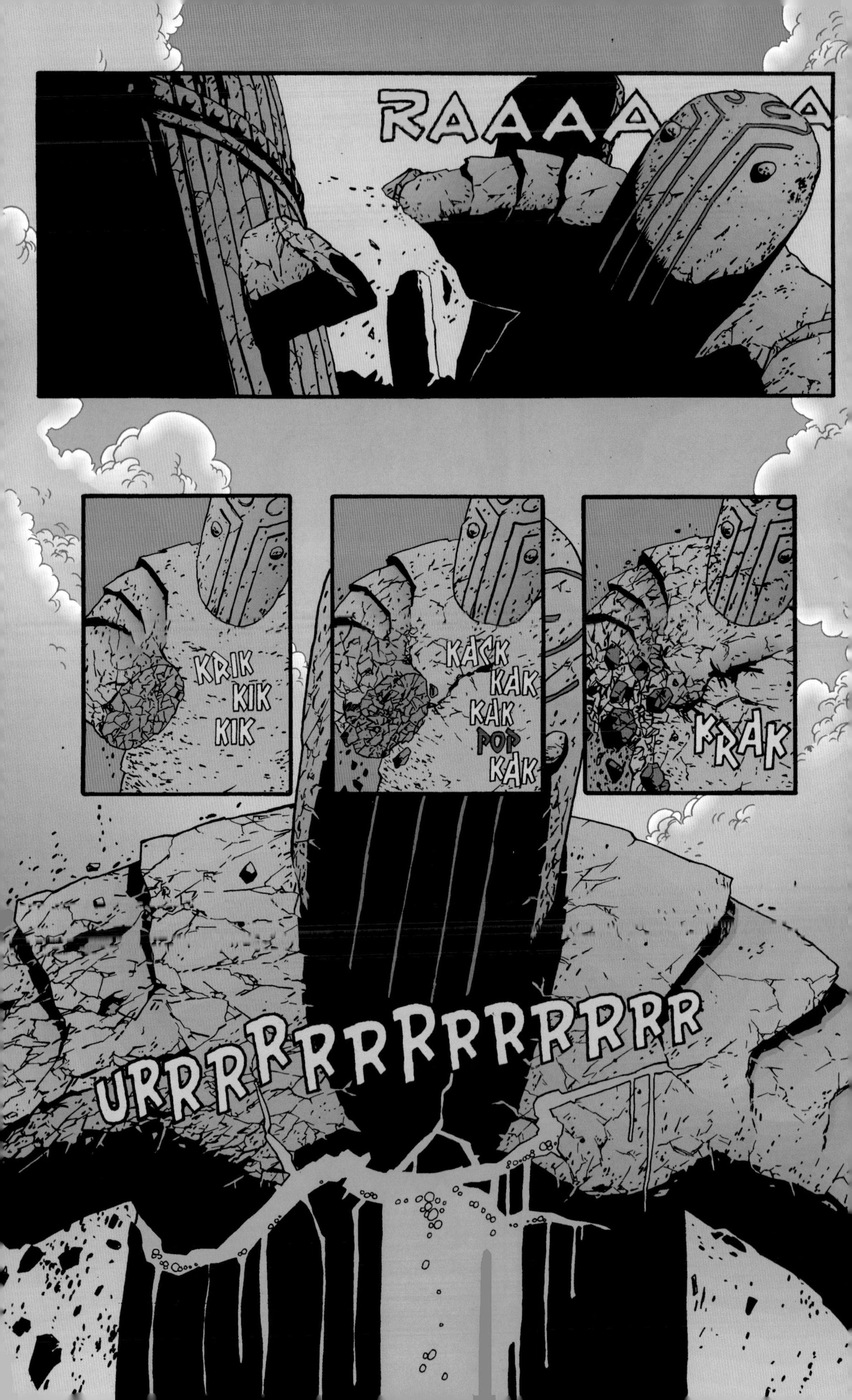
RAAAA
KRIK
KIK
KIK
KACK
KAK
KAK
POP
KAK
KRAK
URRRRRRRRRRRR

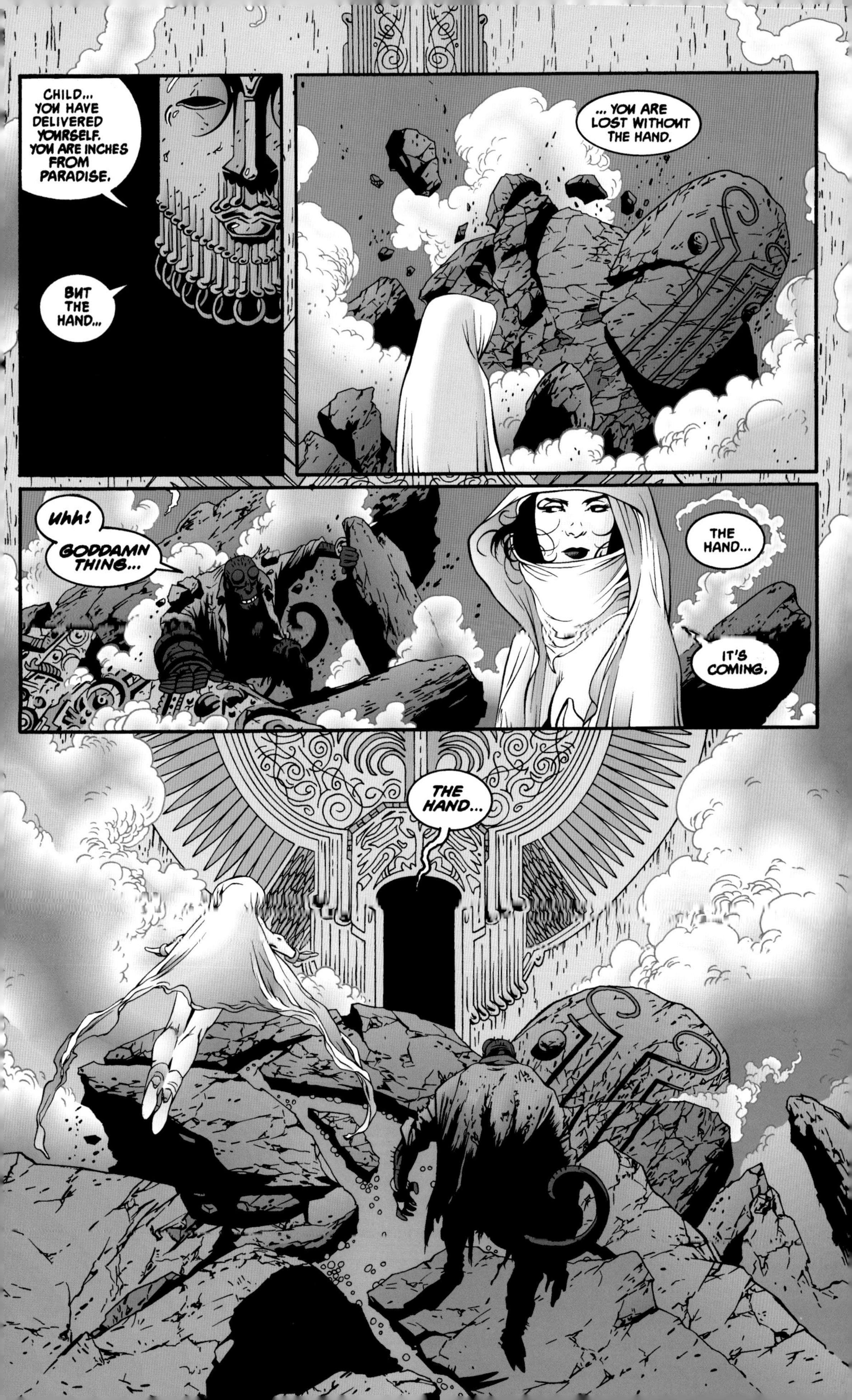

CHILD... YOU HAVE DELIVERED YOURSELF. YOU ARE INCHES FROM PARADISE.
BUT THE HAND...
... YOU ARE LOST WITHOUT THE HAND.
UHH! GODDAMN THING...
THE HAND...
IT'S COMING.
THE HAND...

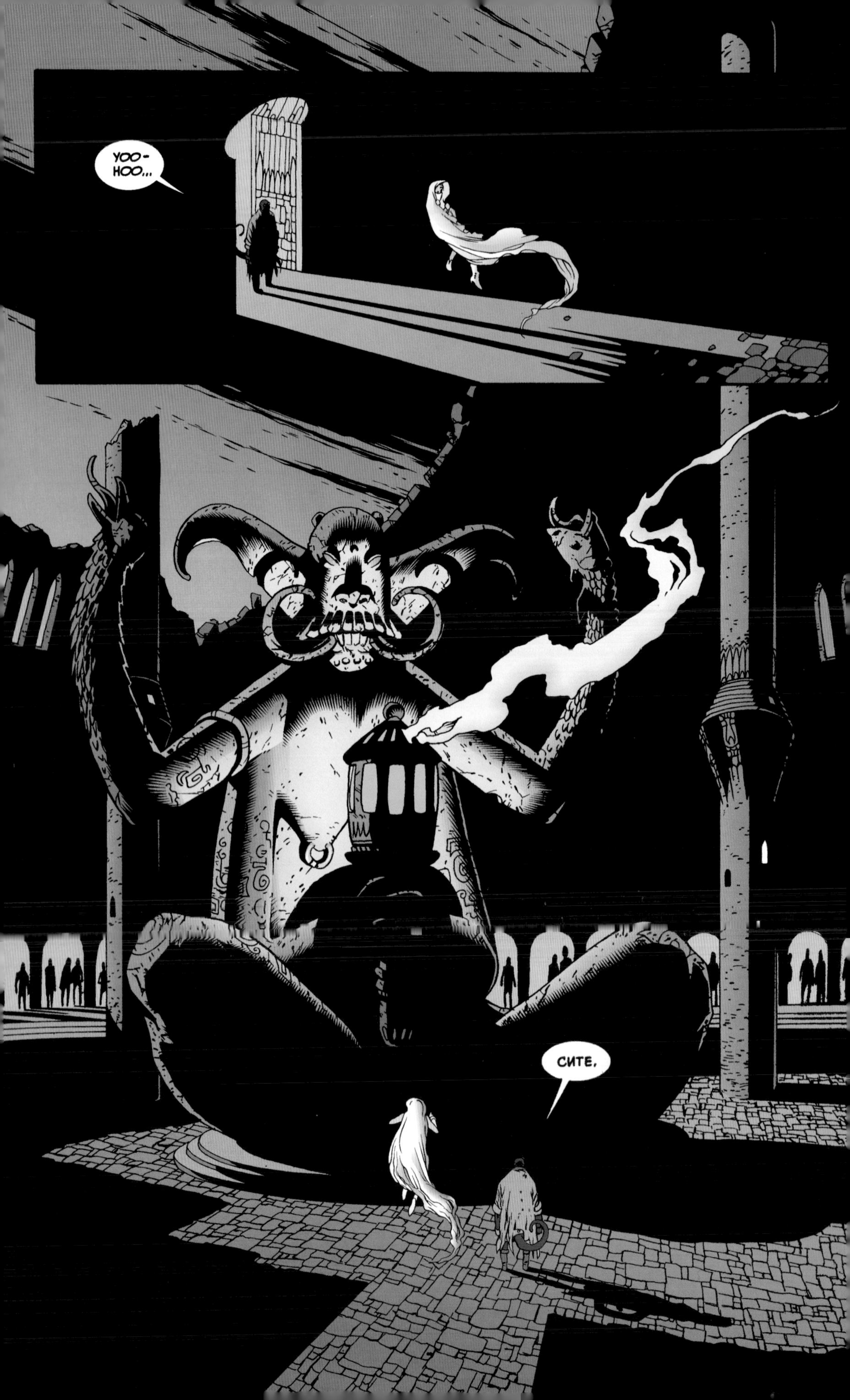
YOO-
HOO...
CUTE,

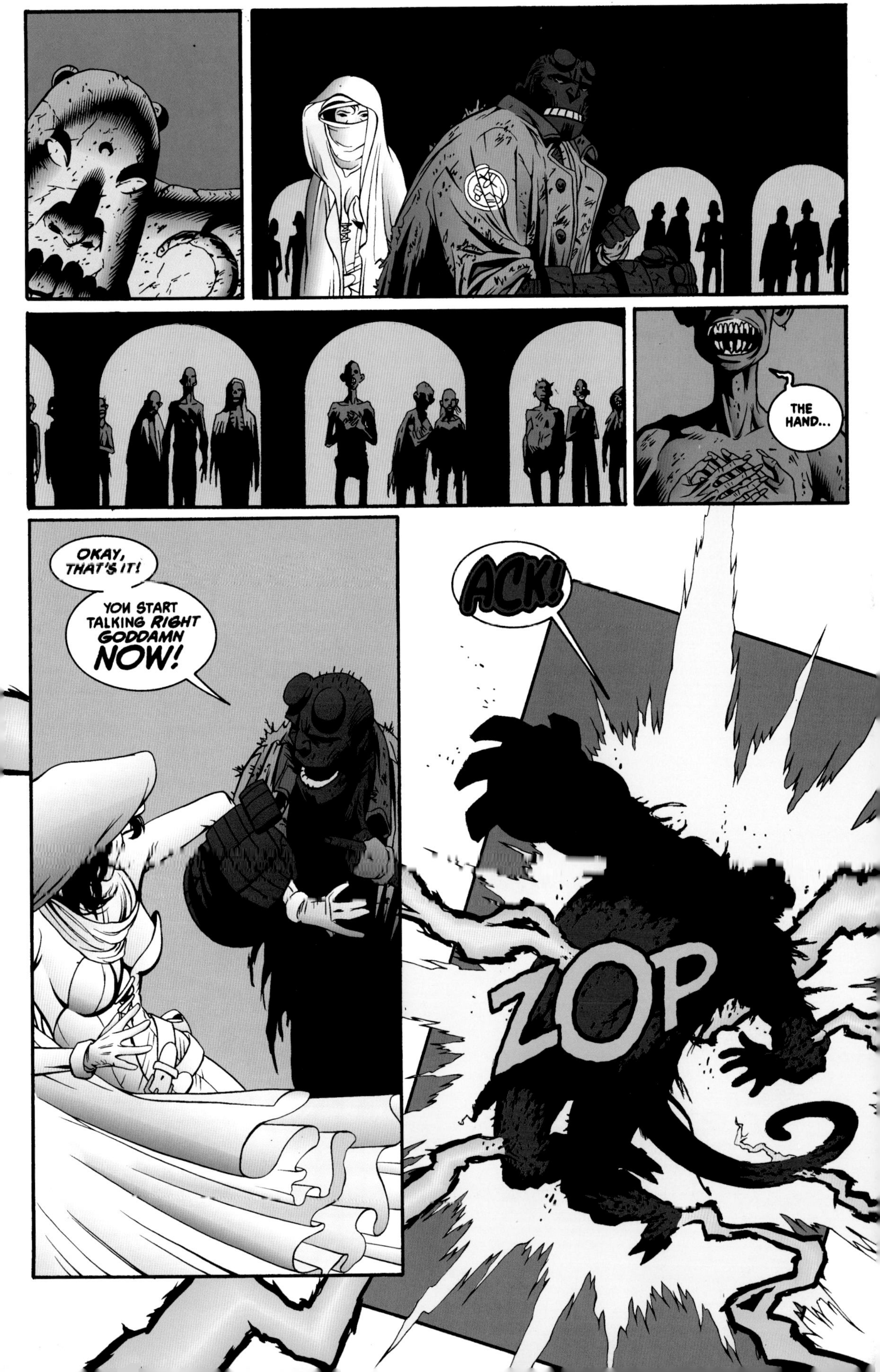
THE HAND...
OKAY, THAT'S IT!
YOU START TALKING RIGHT GODDAMN NOW!
ACK!
ZOP

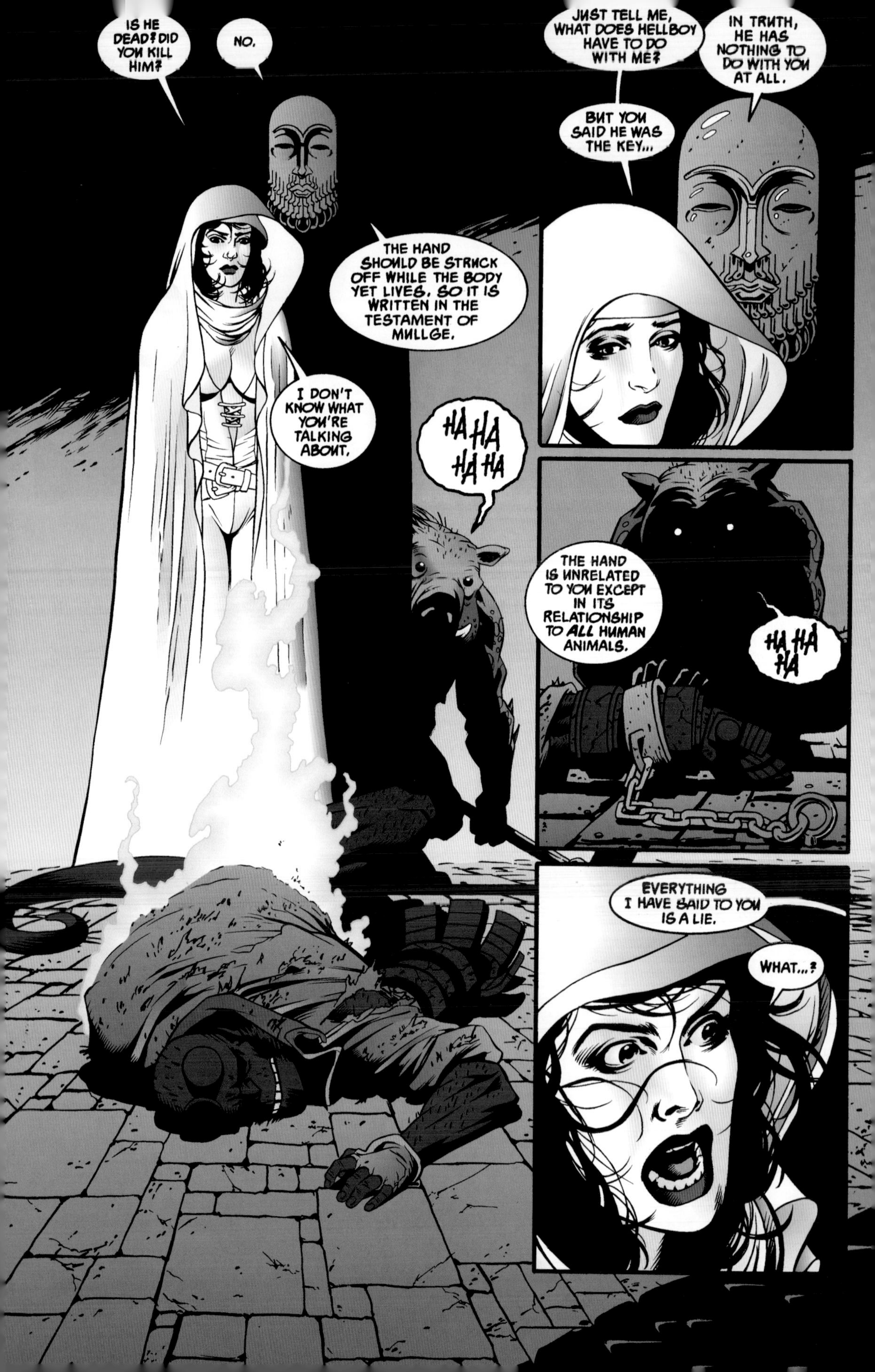
IS HE DEAD? DID YOU KILL HIM?
NO.
THE HAND SHOULD BE STRUCK OFF WHILE THE BODY YET LIVES. SO IT IS WRITTEN IN THE TESTAMENT OF MULLGE.
I DON'T KNOW WHAT YOU'RE TALKING ABOUT.
HA HA HA HA
JUST TELL ME, WHAT DOES HELLBOY HAVE TO DO WITH ME?
BUT YOU SAID HE WAS THE KEY...
IN TRUTH, HE HAS NOTHING TO DO WITH YOU AT ALL.
THE HAND IS UNRELATED TO YOU EXCEPT IN ITS RELATIONSHIP TO ALL HUMAN ANIMALS.
HA HA HA
EVERYTHING I HAVE SAID TO YOU IS A LIE.
WHAT...?

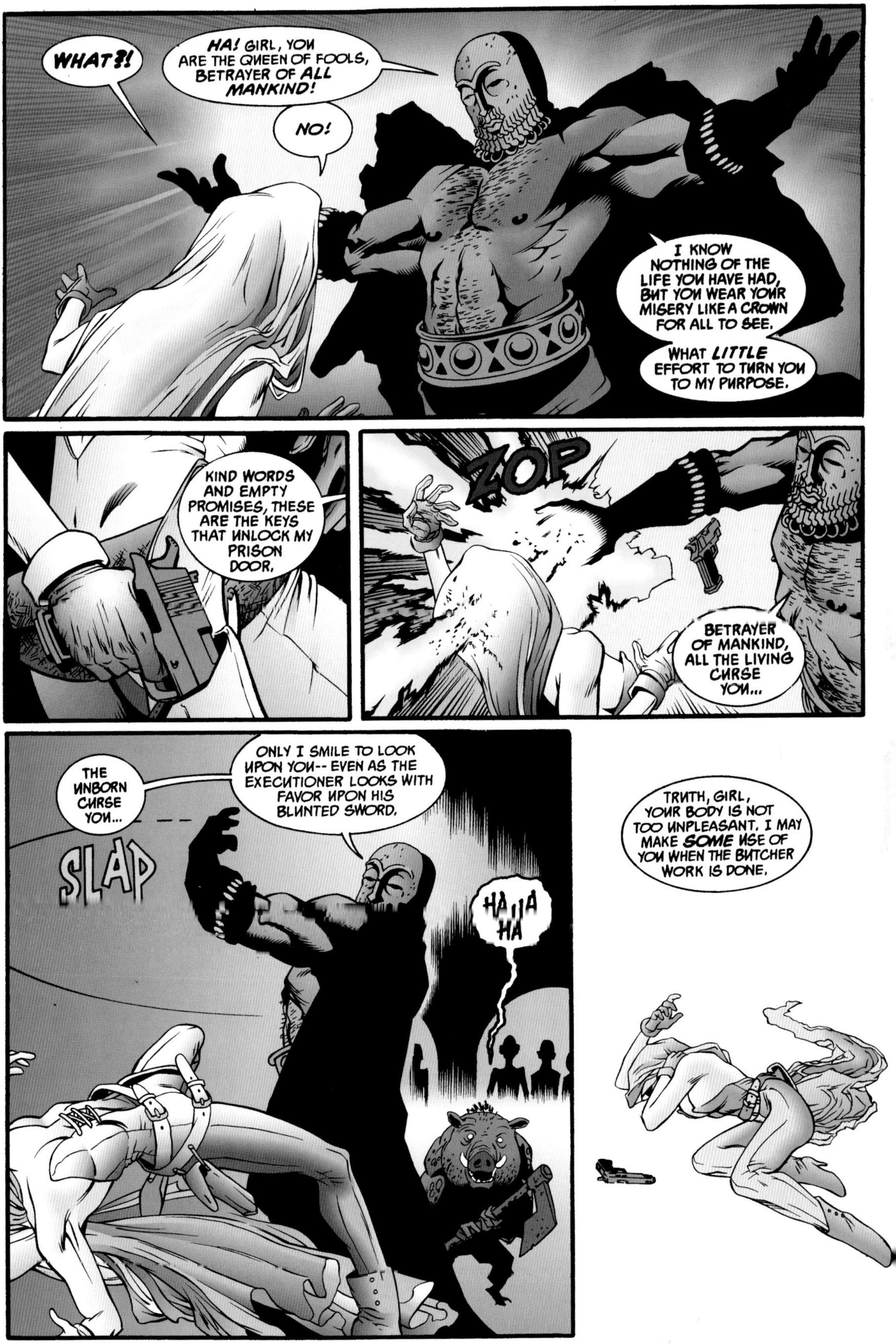
WHAT?!
HA! GIRL, YOU ARE THE QUEEN OF FOOLS, BETRAYER OF ALL MANKIND!
NO!
I KNOW NOTHING OF THE LIFE YOU HAVE HAD, BUT YOU WEAR YOUR MISERY LIKE A CROWN FOR ALL TO SEE.
WHAT LITTLE EFFORT TO TURN YOU TO MY PURPOSE.
KIND WORDS AND EMPTY PROMISES, THESE ARE THE KEYS THAT UNLOCK MY PRISON DOOR.
ZOP
BETRAYER OF MANKIND, ALL THE LIVING CURSE YOU...
THE UNBORN CURSE YOU...
SLAP
ONLY I SMILE TO LOOK UPON YOU-- EVEN AS THE EXECUTIONER LOOKS WITH FAVOR UPON HIS BLUNTED SWORD.
HA HA HA
TRUTH, GIRL, YOUR BODY IS NOT TOO UNPLEASANT. I MAY MAKE SOME USE OF YOU WHEN THE BUTCHER WORK IS DONE.

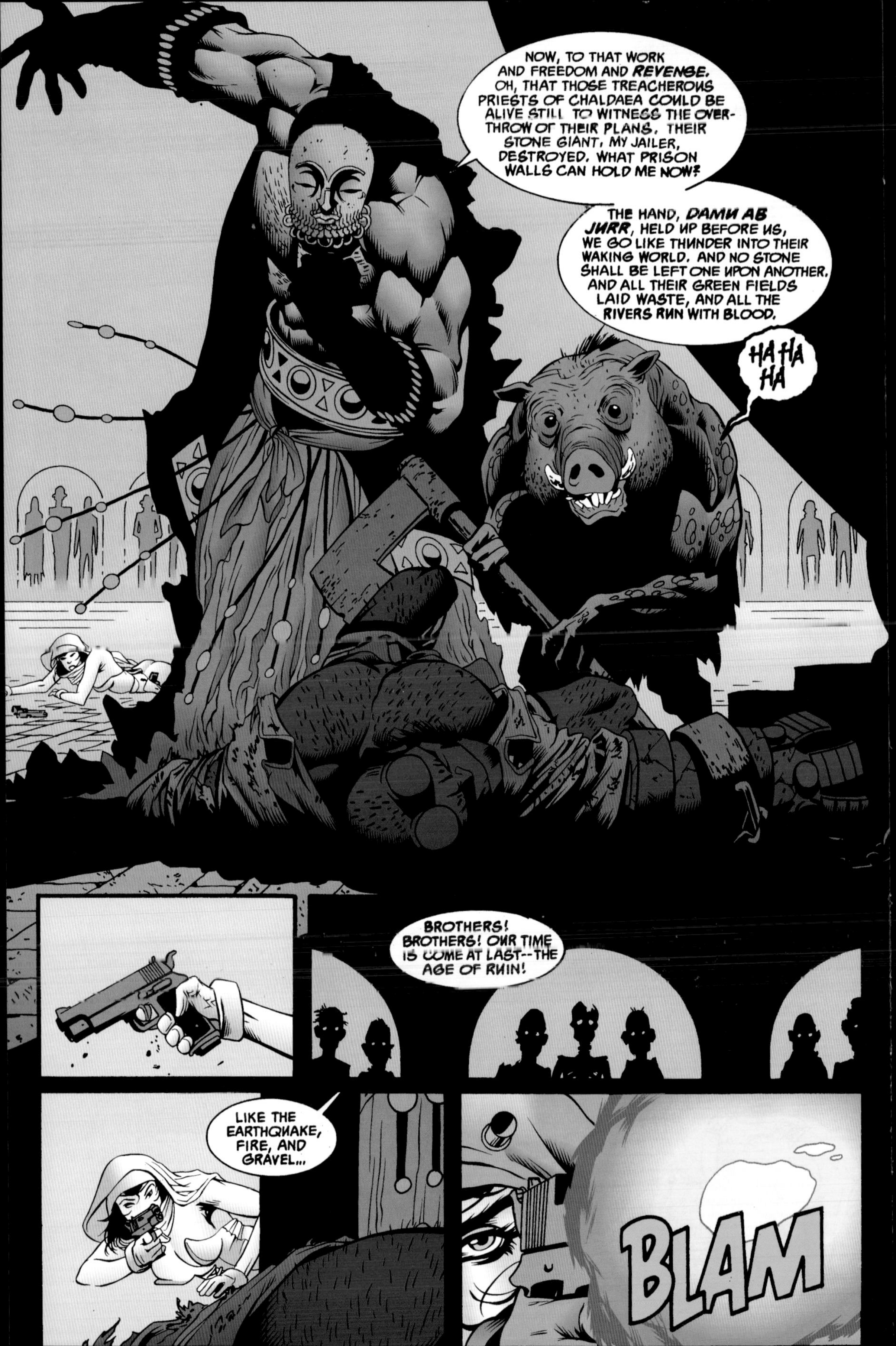
NOW, TO THAT WORK AND FREEDOM AND REVENGE. OH, THAT THOSE TREACHEROUS PRIESTS OF CHALDAEA COULD BE ALIVE STILL TO WITNESS THE OVERTHROW OF THEIR PLANS. THEIR STONE GIANT, MY JAILER, DESTROYED. WHAT PRISON WALLS CAN HOLD ME NOW?
THE HAND, DAMU AB JURR, HELD UP BEFORE US, WE GO LIKE THUNDER INTO THEIR WAKING WORLD. AND NO STONE SHALL BE LEFT ONE UPON ANOTHER. AND ALL THEIR GREEN FIELDS LAID WASTE, AND ALL THE RIVERS RUN WITH BLOOD.
HA HA HA
BROTHERS! BROTHERS! OUR TIME IS COME AT LAST--THE AGE OF RUIN!
LIKE THE EARTHQUAKE, FIRE, AND GRAVEL...
BLAM

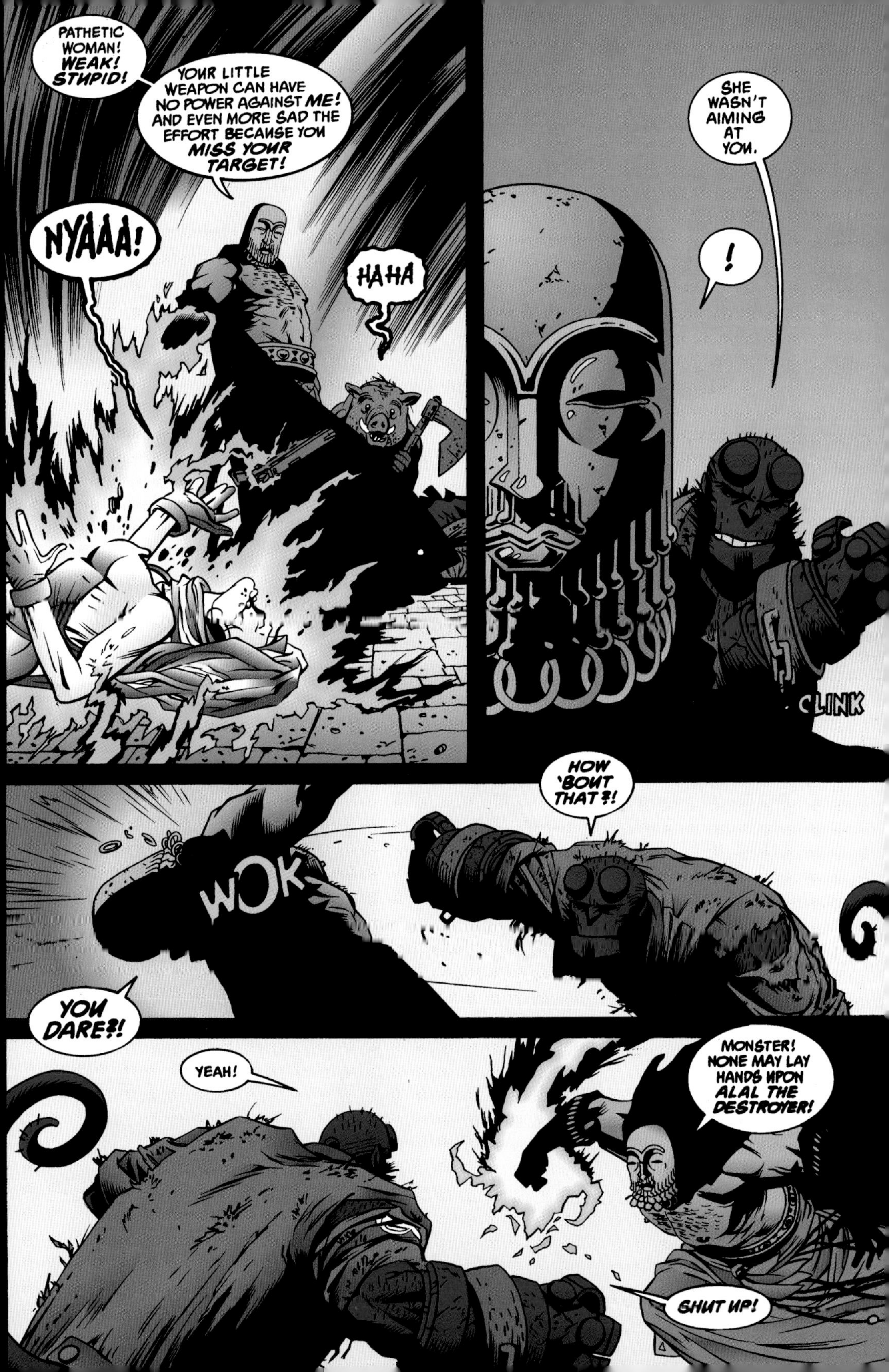
PATHETIC WOMAN! WEAK! STUPID!
YOUR LITTLE WEAPON CAN HAVE NO POWER AGAINST ME! AND EVEN MORE SAD THE EFFORT BECAUSE YOU MISS YOUR TARGET!
NYAAA!
HAHA
SHE WASN'T AIMING AT YOU.
!
CLINK
HOW 'BOUT THAT?!
WOK
YOU DARE?!
YEAH!
MONSTER! NONE MAY LAY HANDS UPON ALAL THE DESTROYER!
SHUT UP!

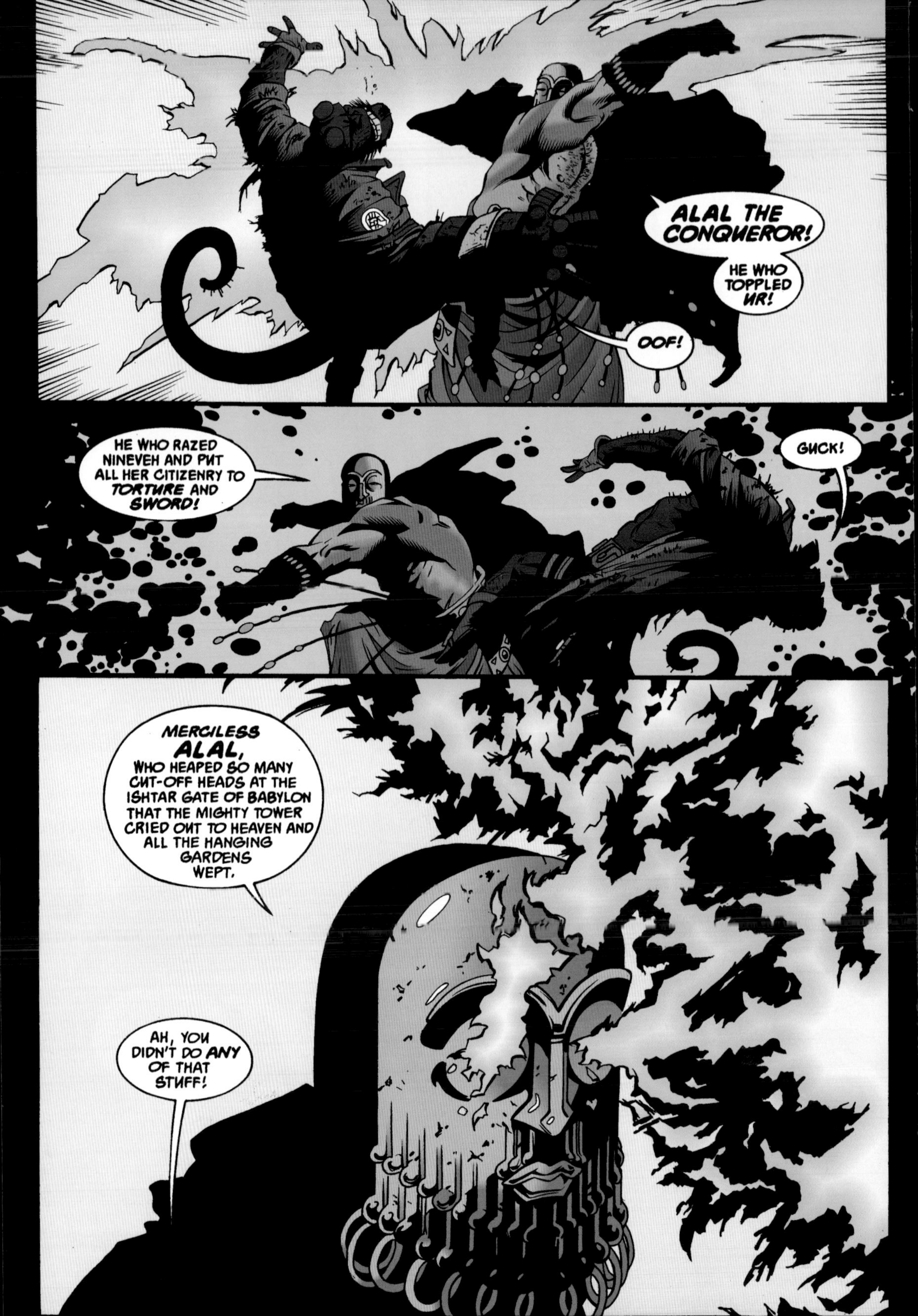
ALAL THE CONQUEROR!
HE WHO TOPPLED UR!
OOF!
HE WHO RAZED NINEVEH AND PUT ALL HER CITIZENRY TO TORTURE AND SWORD!
GUCK!
MERCILESS ALAL, WHO HEAPED SO MANY CUT-OFF HEADS AT THE ISHTAR GATE OF BABYLON THAT THE MIGHTY TOWER CRIED OUT TO HEAVEN AND ALL THE HANGING GARDENS WEPT.
AH, YOU DIDN'T DO ANY OF THAT STUFF!

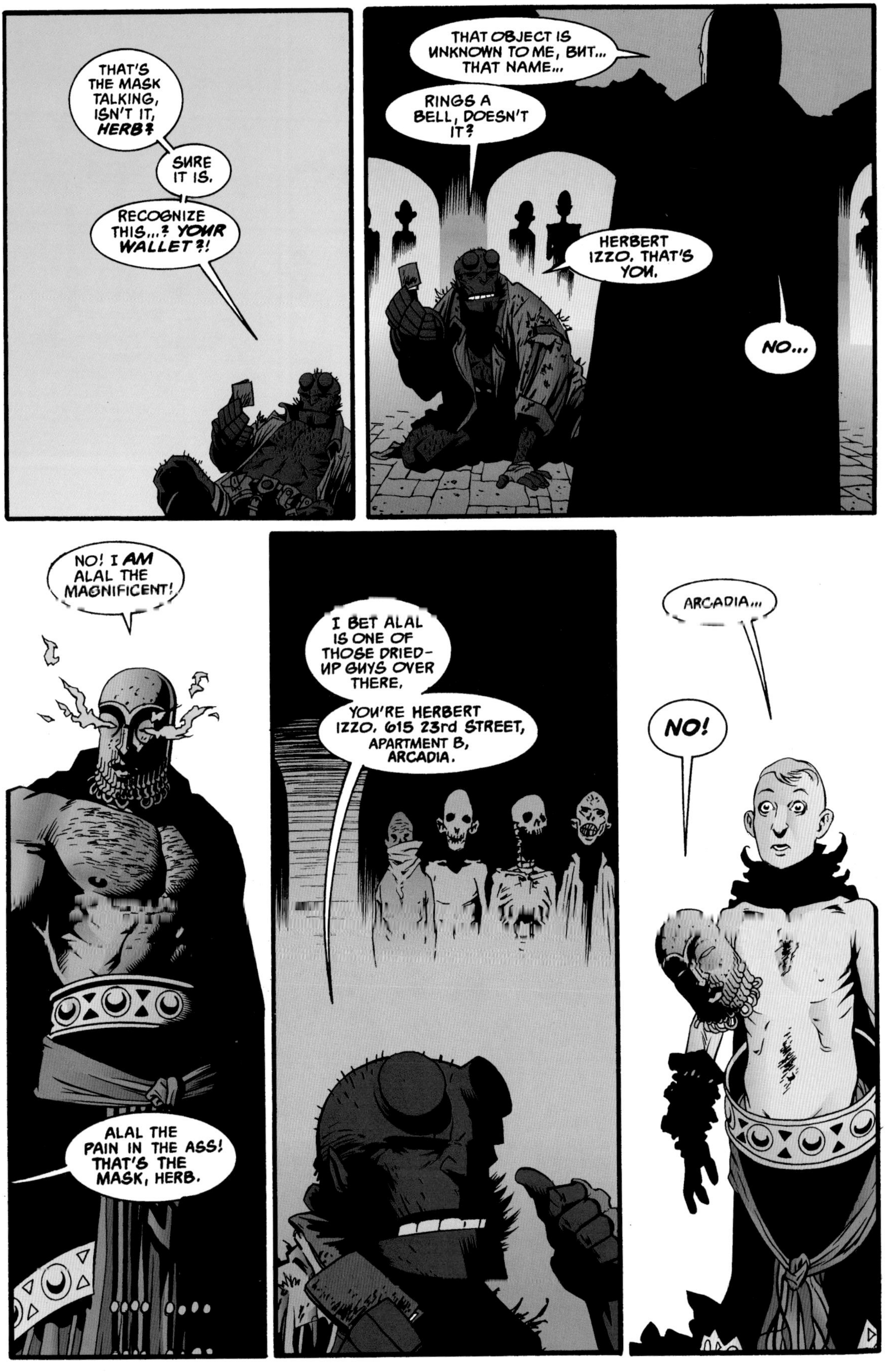
THAT'S THE MASK TALKING, ISN'T IT, HERB?
SURE IT IS.
RECOGNIZE THIS...? YOUR WALLET?!
THAT OBJECT IS UNKNOWN TO ME, BUT... THAT NAME...
RINGS A BELL, DOESN'T IT?
HERBERT IZZO, THAT'S YOU.
NO...
NO! I AM ALAL THE MAGNIFICENT!
ALAL THE PAIN IN THE ASS! THAT'S THE MASK, HERB.
I BET ALAL IS ONE OF THOSE DRIED-UP GUYS OVER THERE.
YOU'RE HERBERT IZZO, 615 23rd STREET, APARTMENT B, ARCADIA.
ARCADIA...
NO!

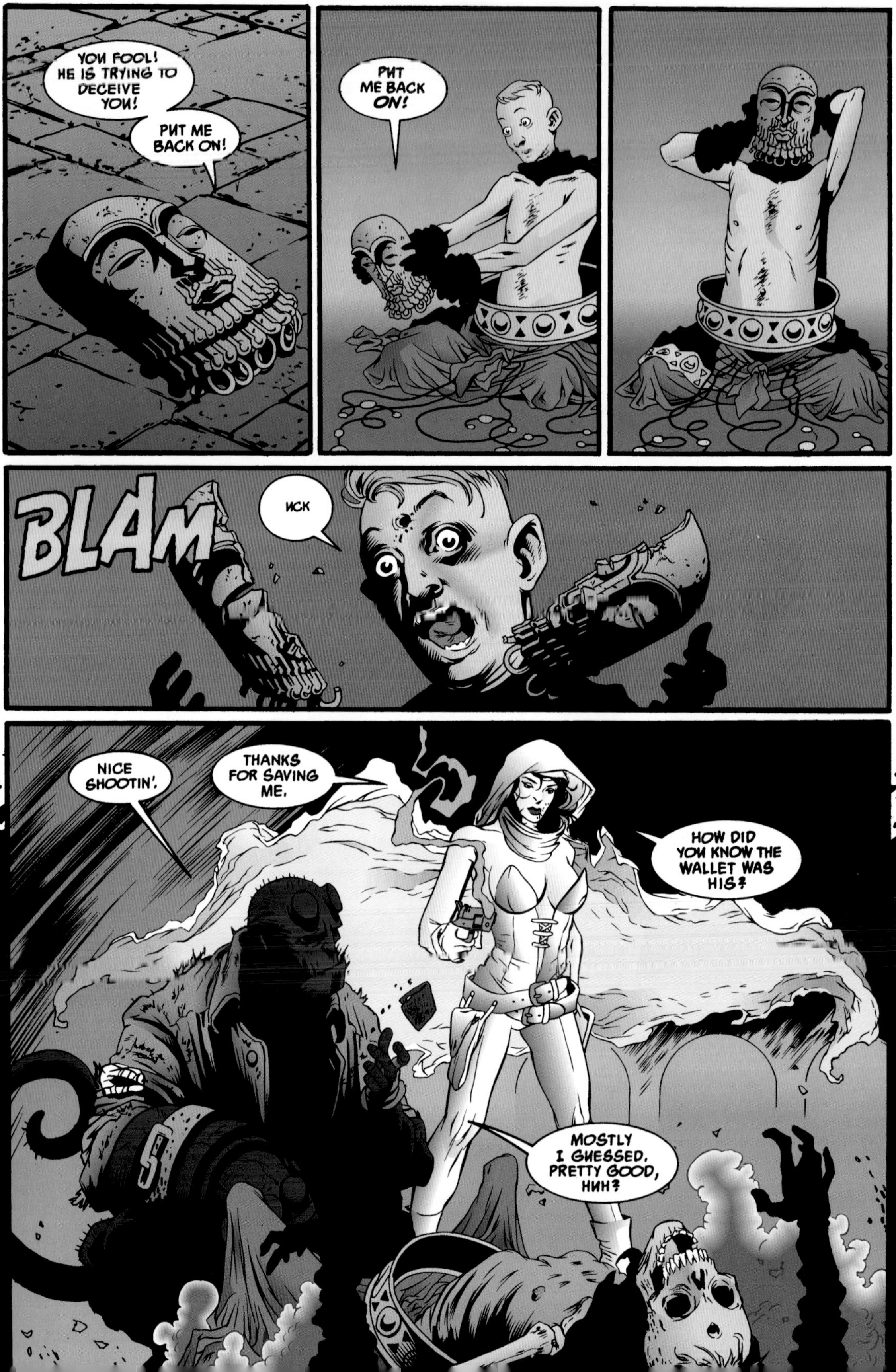
YOU FOOL! HE IS TRYING TO DECEIVE YOU!
PUT ME BACK ON!
PUT ME BACK ON!
BLAM
UCK
NICE SHOOTIN'.
THANKS FOR SAVING ME.
HOW DID YOU KNOW THE WALLET WAS HIS?
MOSTLY I GUESSED. PRETTY GOOD, HUH?

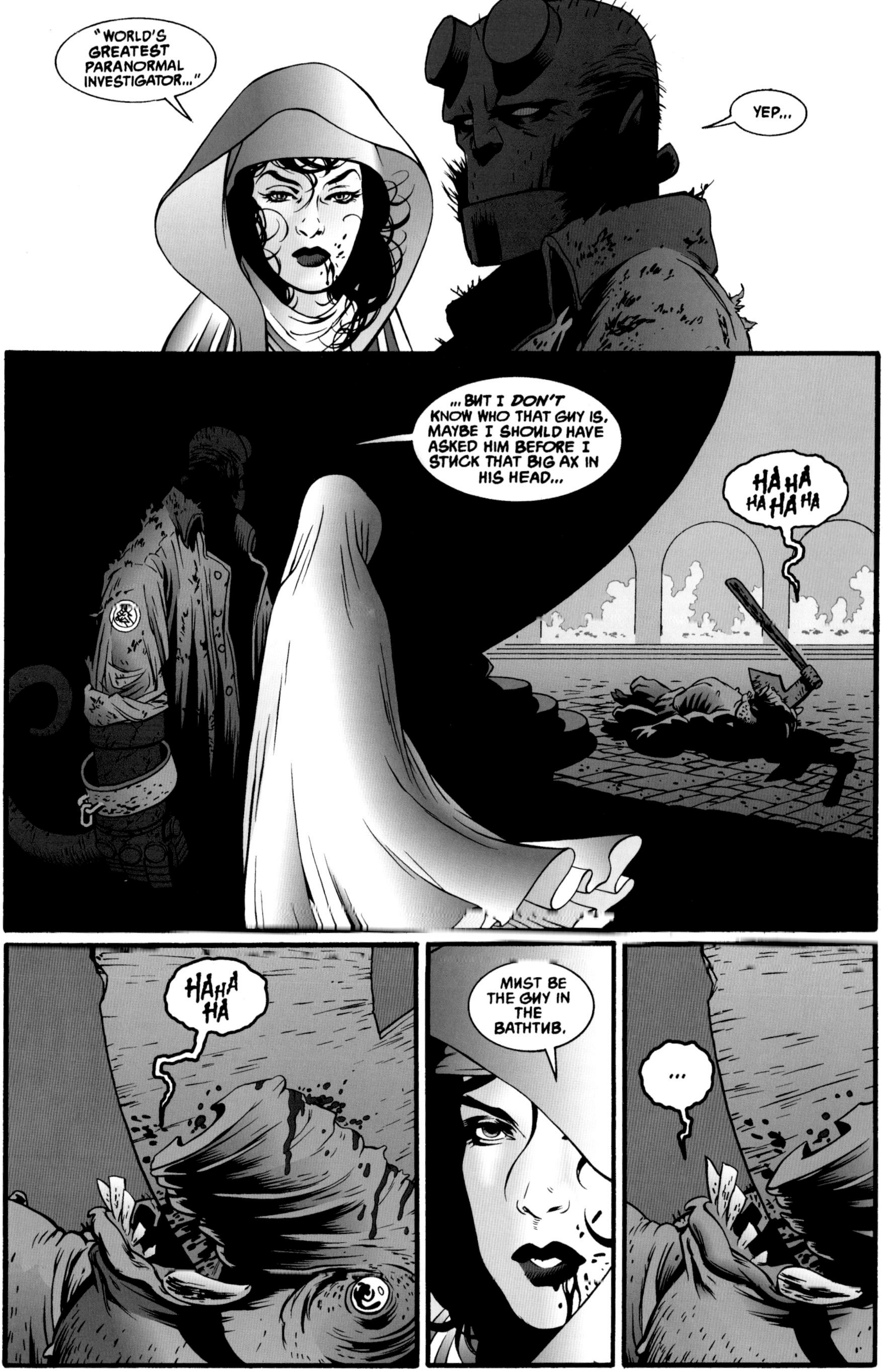
"WORLD'S GREATEST PARANORMAL INVESTIGATOR..."
YEP...
...BUT I *DON'T* KNOW WHO THAT GUY IS. MAYBE I SHOULD HAVE ASKED HIM BEFORE I STUCK THAT BIG AX IN HIS HEAD...
HA HA HA HA HA
HA HA HA
MUST BE THE GUY IN THE BATHTUB.
...

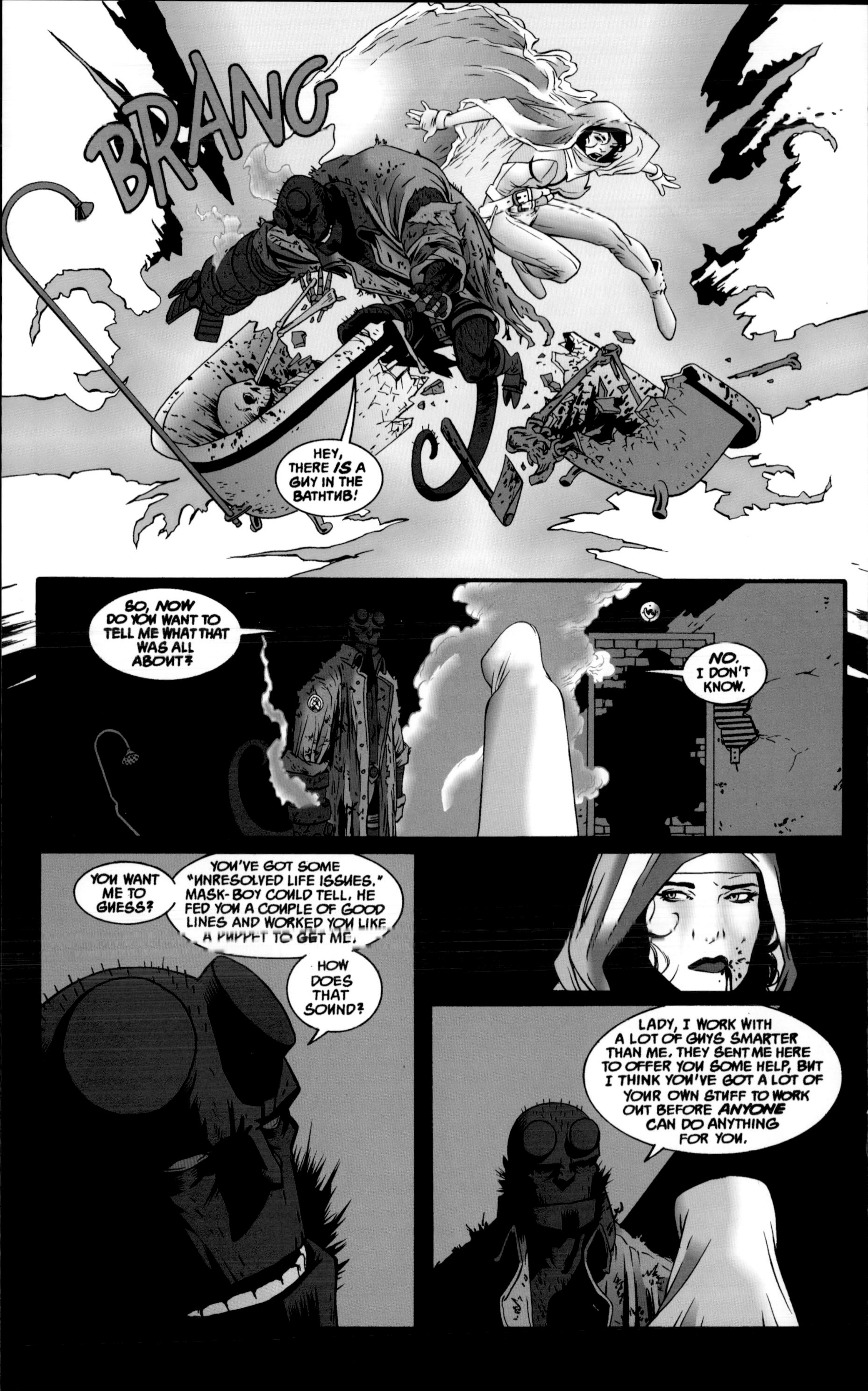
BRANG
HEY, THERE IS A GUY IN THE BATHTUB!
SO, NOW DO YOU WANT TO TELL ME WHAT THAT WAS ALL ABOUT?
NO. I DON'T KNOW.
YOU WANT ME TO GUESS?
"YOU'VE GOT SOME "UNRESOLVED LIFE ISSUES." MASK-BOY COULD TELL. HE FED YOU A COUPLE OF GOOD LINES AND WORKED YOU LIKE A PUPPET TO GET ME.
HOW DOES THAT SOUND?
LADY, I WORK WITH A LOT OF GUYS SMARTER THAN ME. THEY SENT ME HERE TO OFFER YOU SOME HELP, BUT I THINK YOU'VE GOT A LOT OF YOUR OWN STUFF TO WORK OUT BEFORE ANYONE CAN DO ANYTHING FOR YOU.

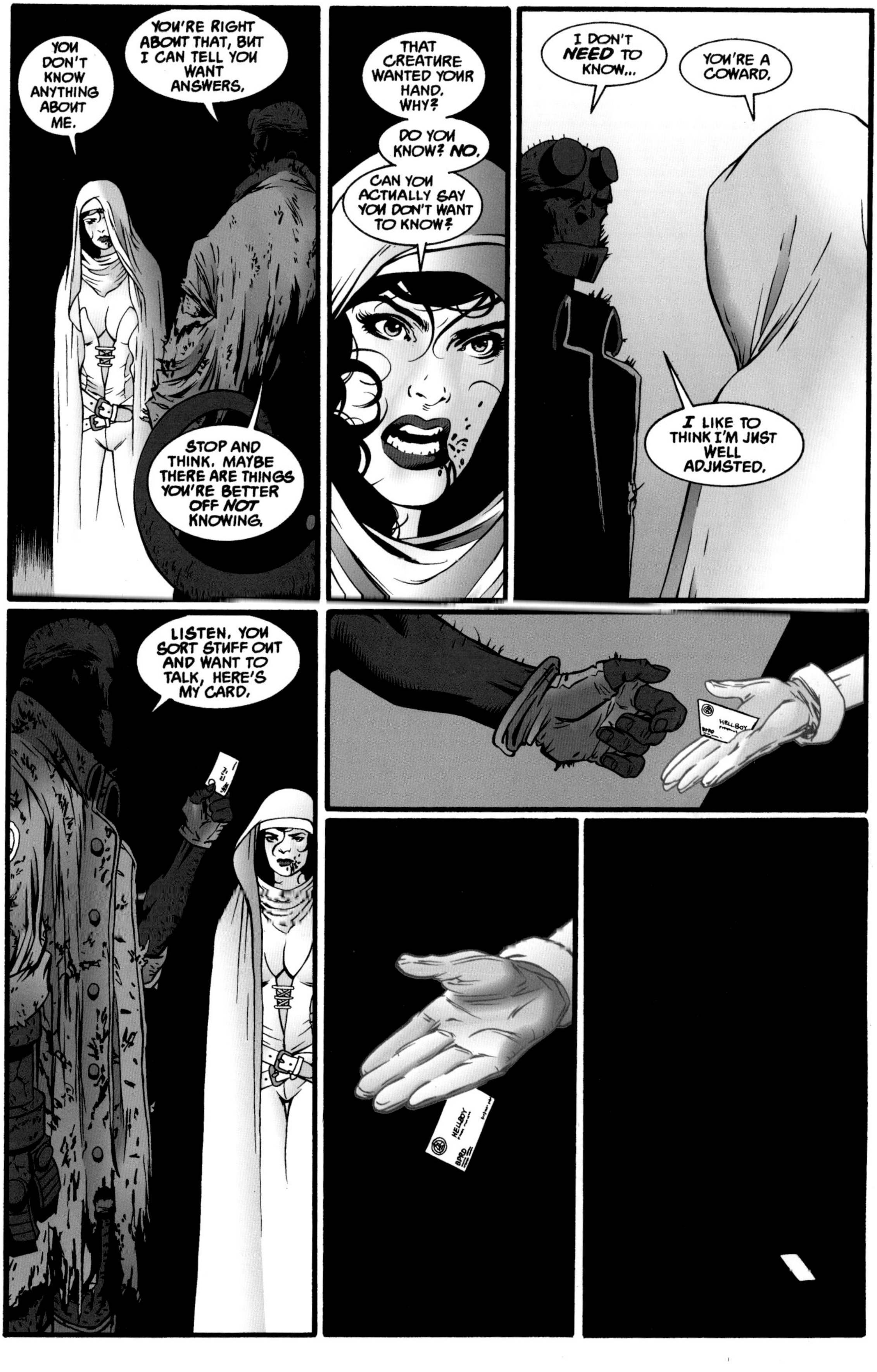
YOU DON'T KNOW ANYTHING ABOUT ME.
YOU'RE RIGHT ABOUT THAT, BUT I CAN TELL YOU WANT ANSWERS.
STOP AND THINK. MAYBE THERE ARE THINGS YOU'RE BETTER OFF NOT KNOWING.
THAT CREATURE WANTED YOUR HAND. WHY?
DO YOU KNOW? NO.
CAN YOU ACTUALLY SAY YOU DON'T WANT TO KNOW?
I DON'T NEED TO KNOW...
YOU'RE A COWARD.
I LIKE TO THINK I'M JUST WELL ADJUSTED.
LISTEN. YOU SORT STUFF OUT AND WANT TO TALK, HERE'S MY CARD.
HELLBOY
BPRD

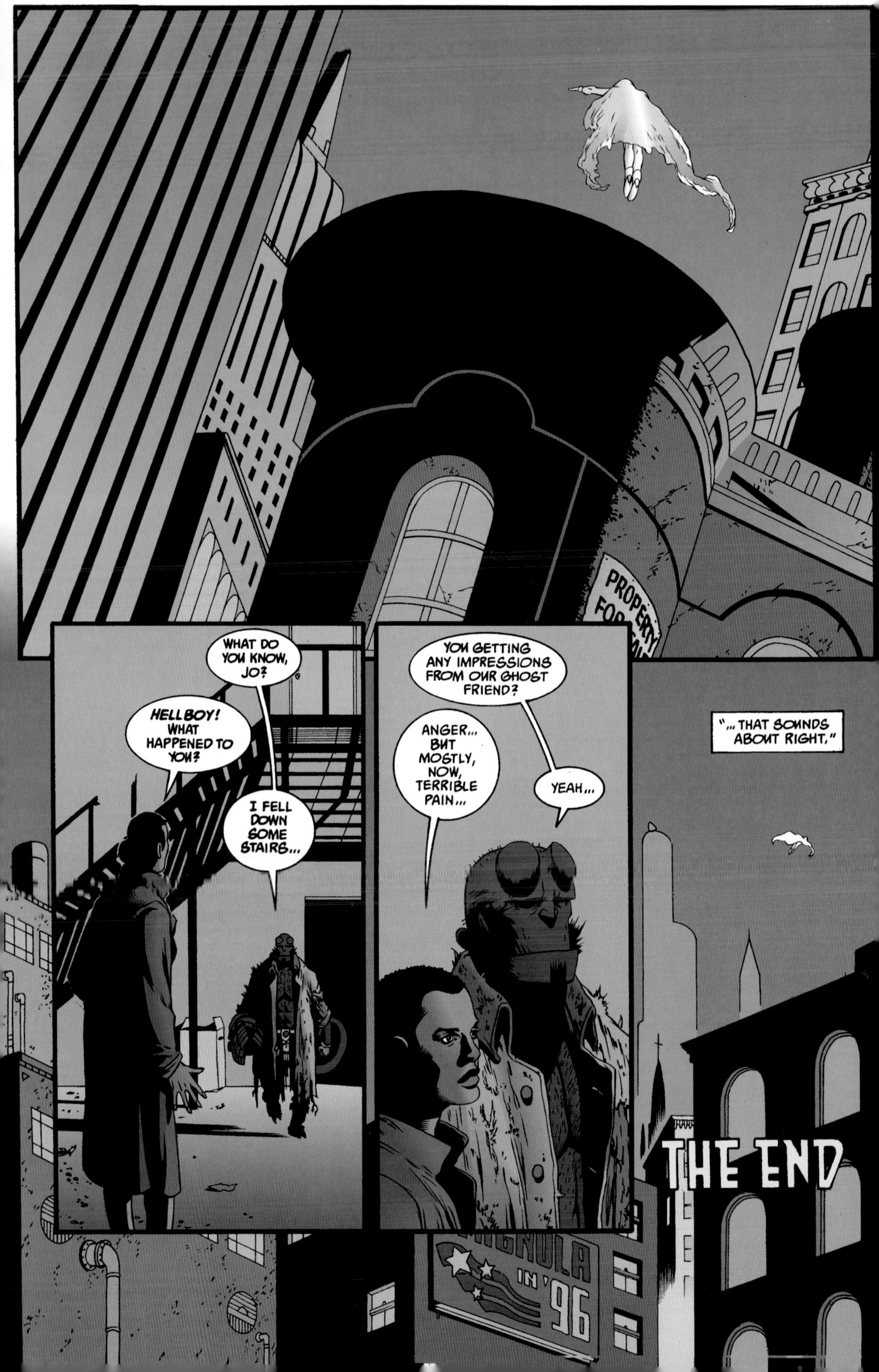
PROPERTY FOR SALE
WHAT DO YOU KNOW, JO?
HELLBOY! WHAT HAPPENED TO YOU?
I FELL DOWN SOME STAIRS...
YOU GETTING ANY IMPRESSIONS FROM OUR GHOST FRIEND?
ANGER... BUT MOSTLY, NOW, TERRIBLE PAIN...
YEAH...
"...THAT SOUNDS ABOUT RIGHT."
MIGNOLA IN '96
THE END

THE MAKING OF GHOST|HELLBOY

MODEL SHEET: At the time we did *Ghost / Hellboy*, no artist other than myself had drawn more than a pinup of Hellboy—and, given that when I draw him he is usually at least half in shadow, I felt I needed to take a stab at doing a model sheet for him.

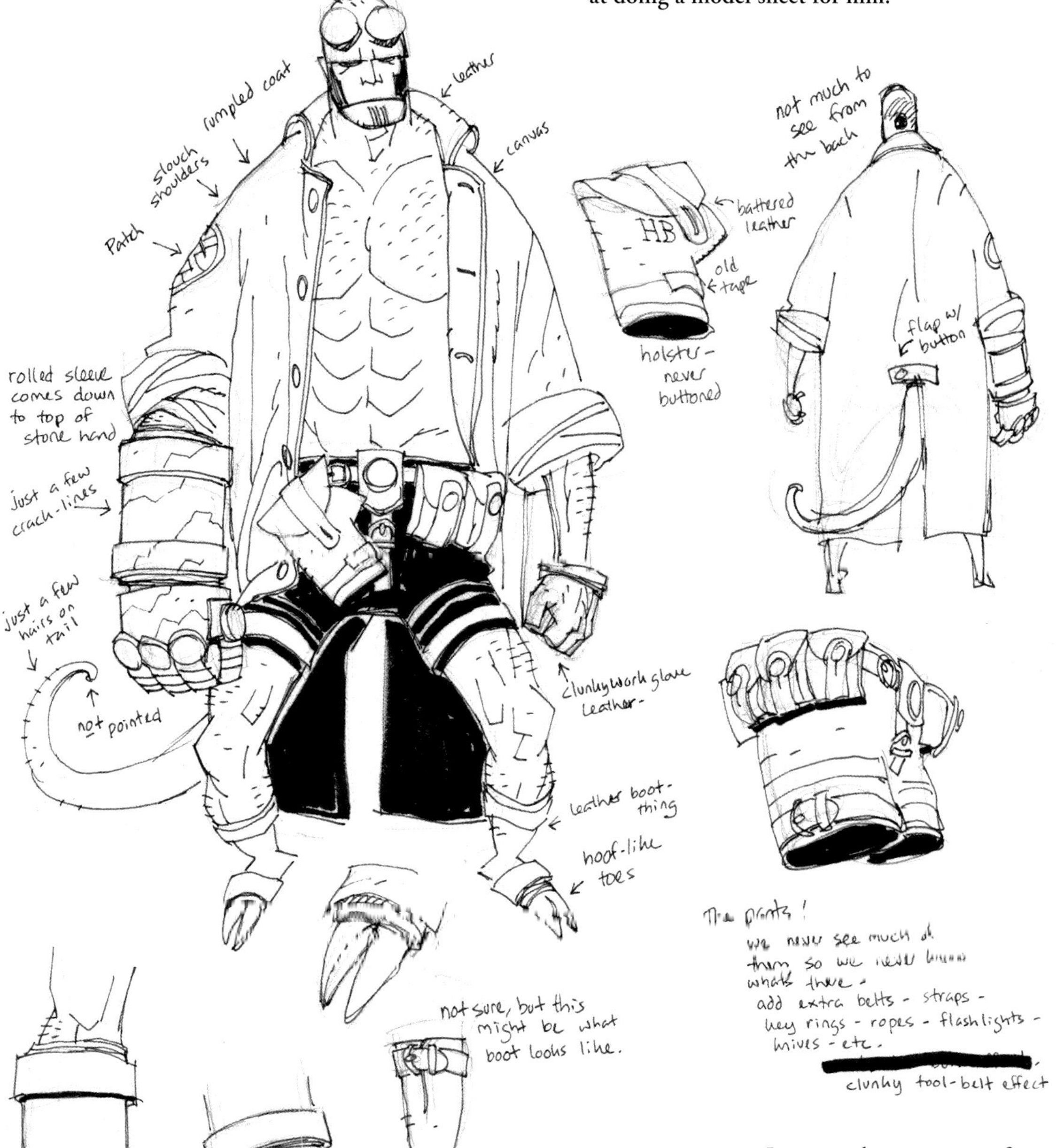

rumpled coat
leather
canvas
slouch shoulders
Patch
not much to see from the back
battered leather
HB
old tape
holster- never buttoned
flap w/ button
rolled sleeve comes down to top of stone hand
just a few crack-lines
just a few hairs on tail
not pointed
clunky work glove leather-
leather boot-thing
hoof-like toes
The pants! we never see much of them so we never know what's there. add extra belts - straps - key rings - ropes - flashlights - knives - etc.
[redacted]
clunky tool-belt effect

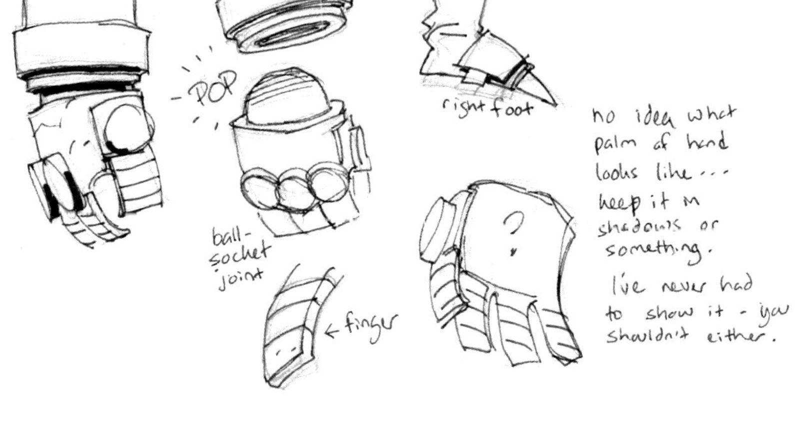

not sure, but this might be what boot looks like.
POP
right foot
ball-socket joint
finger
no idea what palm of hand looks like... keep it in shadows or something.
I've never had to show it - you shouldn't either.

I am not, however, one of those artists who knows exactly how tall his character is, how much he can lift, what's in all his pockets . . . and I STILL don't know what the palm of his right hand looks like.

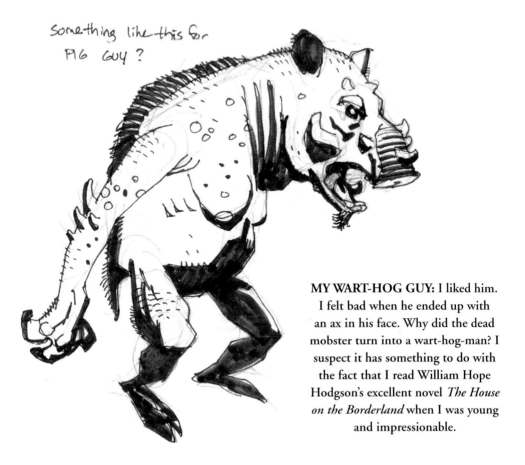

something like this for
PIG GUY ?

MY WART-HOG GUY: I liked him.
I felt bad when he ended up with
an ax in his face. Why did the dead
mobster turn into a wart-hog-man? I
suspect it has something to do with
the fact that I read William Hope
Hodgson's excellent novel *The House
on the Borderland* when I was young
and impressionable.

LAYOUTS: When writing my stories I never start with a detailed script. I usually have
a beginning and an end, some of the in-between bits, and a general idea how the whole
thing is going to go. A lot of the actual plotting of the stories has always happened as
I've done the thumbnail layouts for the pages. *Ghost / Hellboy* was the first story I wrote
for someone else to draw, and the only way I knew to do that was to lay it out just
as I do for myself. I then sent those layouts, along with just enough script to explain
what was going on in the layouts. It's no reflection on artist Scott Benefiel's storytelling
abilities—it's not that I didn't trust him—it was just the way I did things in those days.
It's still pretty much the way I work today when I write for other people—it's the only
way I know how to pace a story—but now my layouts are much rougher, and I rarely
send them on to the artist. Now I write a much more detailed plot based on my layouts.
It's not as much fun as what I did here on *Ghost / Hellboy*, but it frees up the artist a lot
more. Sorry, Scott—you were a victim of my inexperience. I hope you didn't suffer too
much, and if you did suffer I hope you are fully recovered now.

HB·Ghost #1 ②

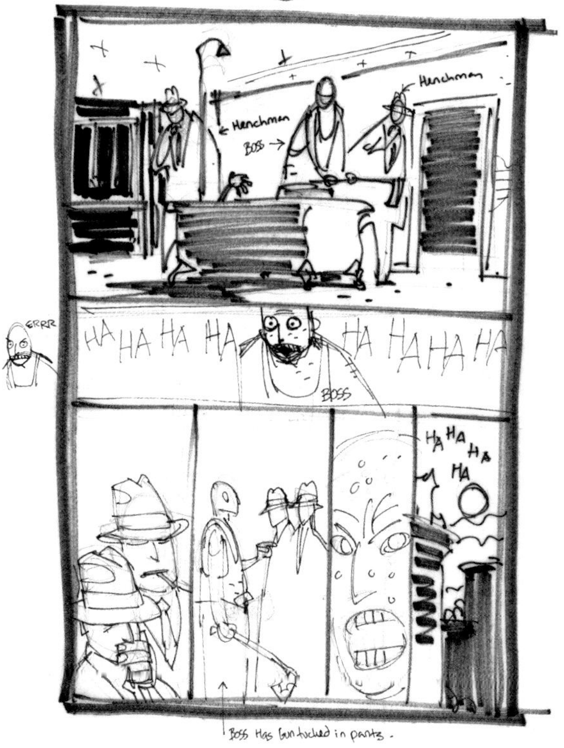

Henchman
Henchman
BOSS
ERRR
HA HA HA HA
HA HA HA HA HA
BOSS
HA HA HA HA HA
Boss Has Gun tucked in pants -

HB·GHOST #1 ③

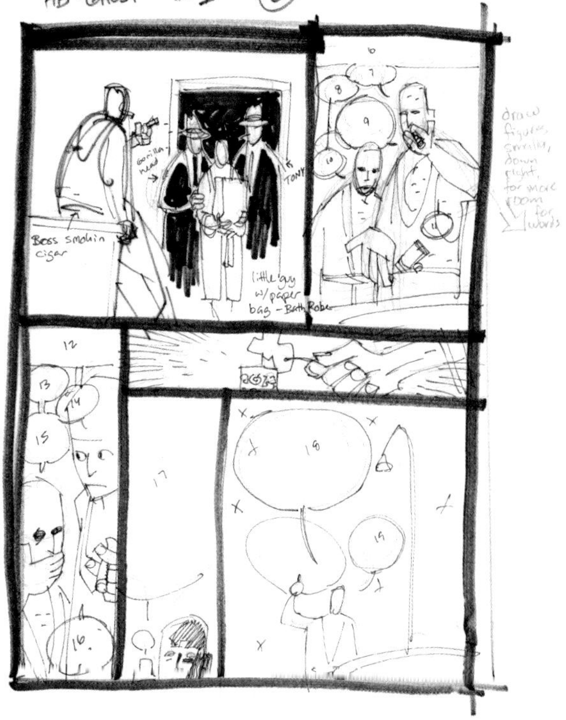

Boss smokin cigar
Gorilla head
TONY
little guy w/ paper bag - Bath Robe
draw figures smaller, down right, for more room for words

HB·GHOST #1 ④

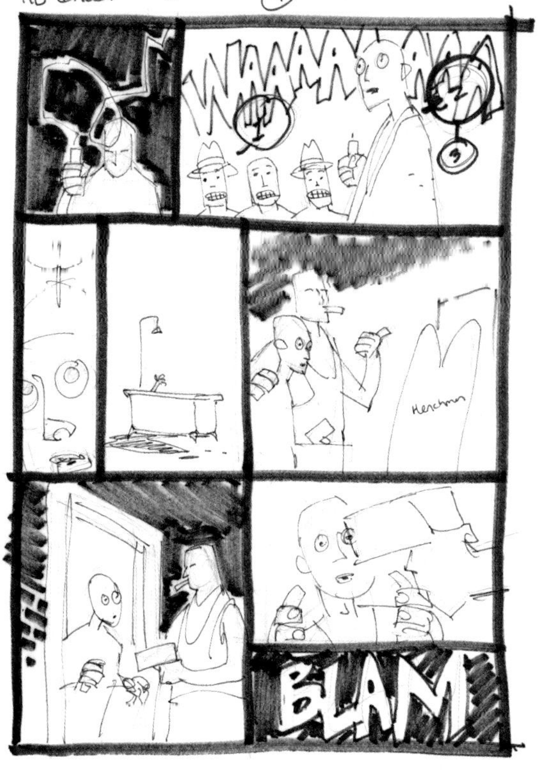

WAAAAAAA
Henchman
BLAM

HB·GHOST #1 ⑤

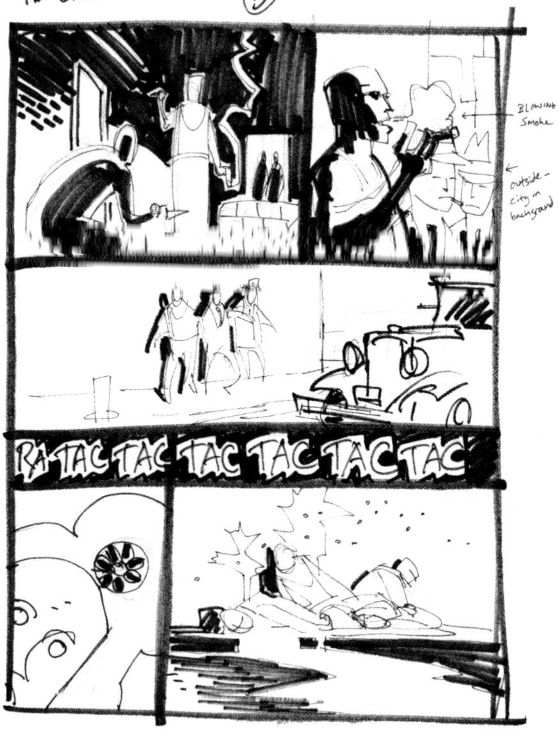

BLOWING Smoke
outside - city in background
RA TAC TAC TAC TAC TAC TAC

HB·GHOST #1 (17)

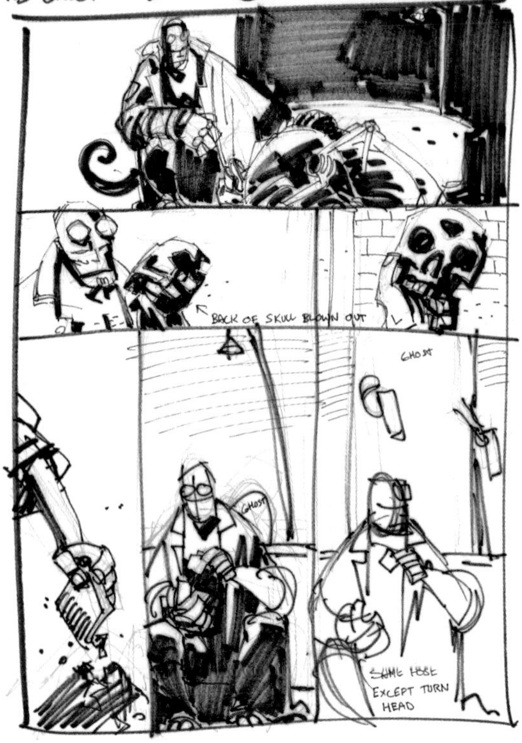
BACK OF SKULL BLOWN OUT
GHOST
GHOST
SAME POSE EXCEPT TURN HEAD

HB·GHOST #1 (18)

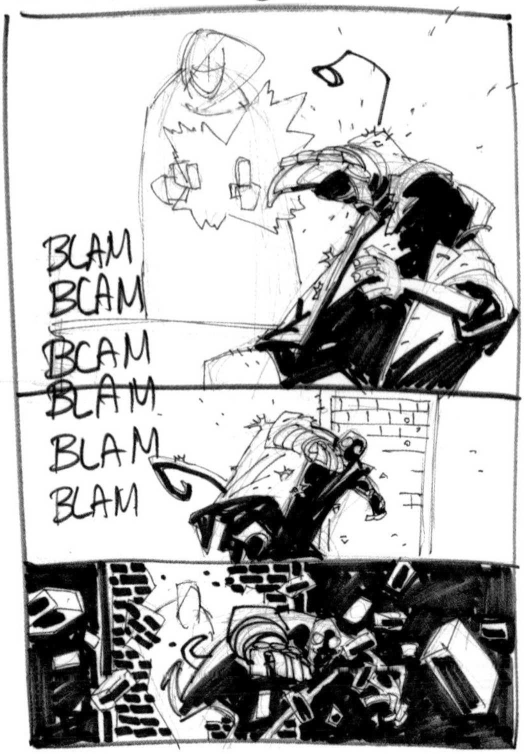
BLAM
BCAM
BCAM
BLAM
BLAM
BLAM

HB·GHOST #1 (19)

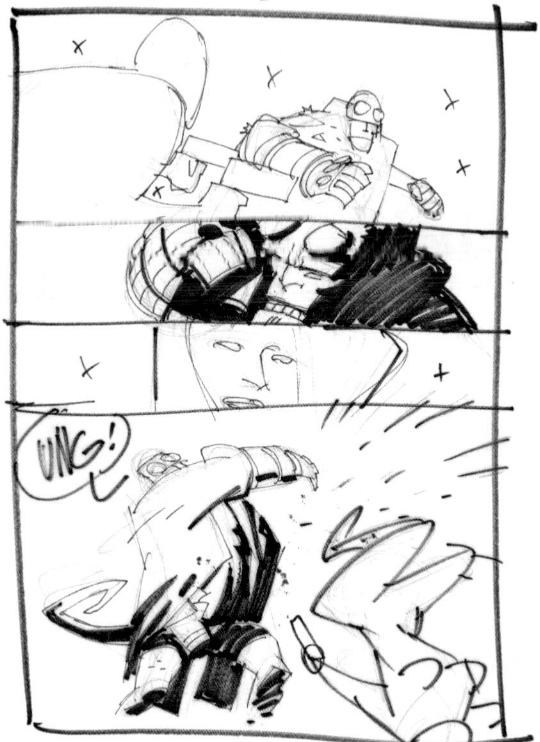
UNG!

HB·GHOST #1 (20)

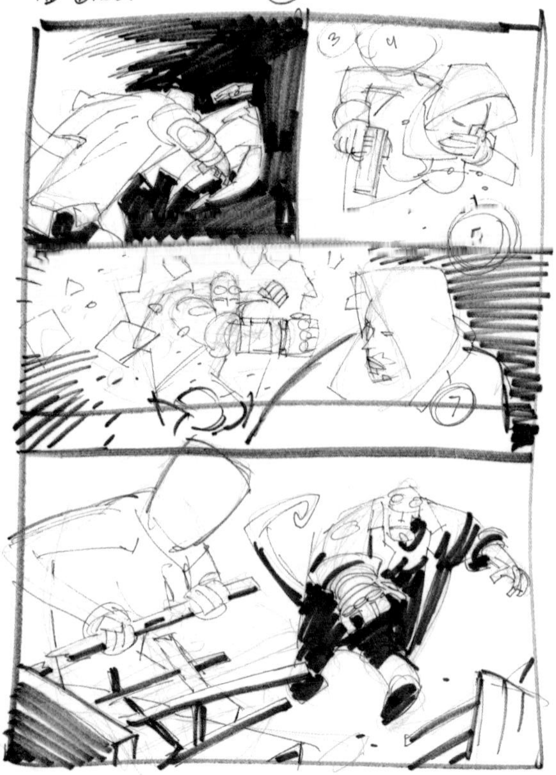

HELLBOY · GHOST #2
Page 2

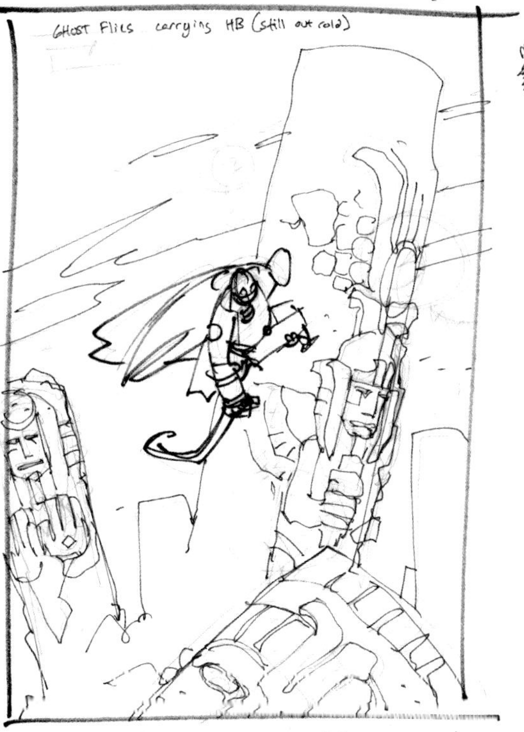

GHOST FLIES carrying HB (still out cold)

Features on statues should be very worn down - indistinct. weather beaten.

HELLBOY · GHOST #2
Page 3

MAKE Things in this panel smaller
more room between guys and mask

Ghost → should still be off ground.
HB is pushing himself away from her (w/right hand) and just touching down on ground.

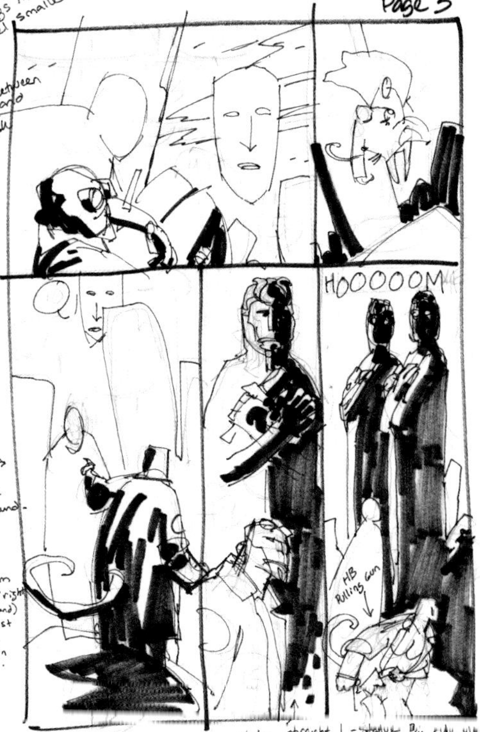

HOOOOOM
HB Pulling Gun

statue straight on.

- statue 3/4 side view, but heads have turned to face us.
- eyes light up.

HELLBOY · GHOST #2
PAGE 4

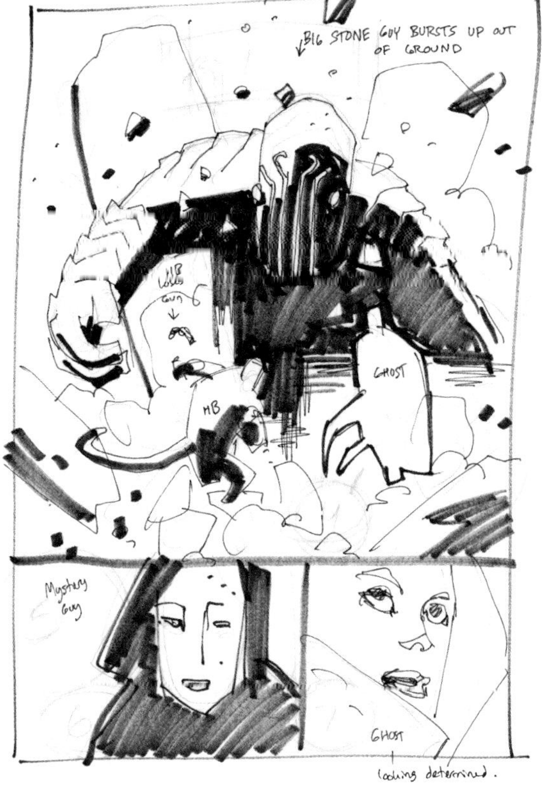

BIG STONE GUY BURSTS UP OUT OF GROUND
HB Loses Gun
GHOST
HB
Mystery Guy
GHOST

looking determined.

HELLBOY · GHOST #2
PAGE 5

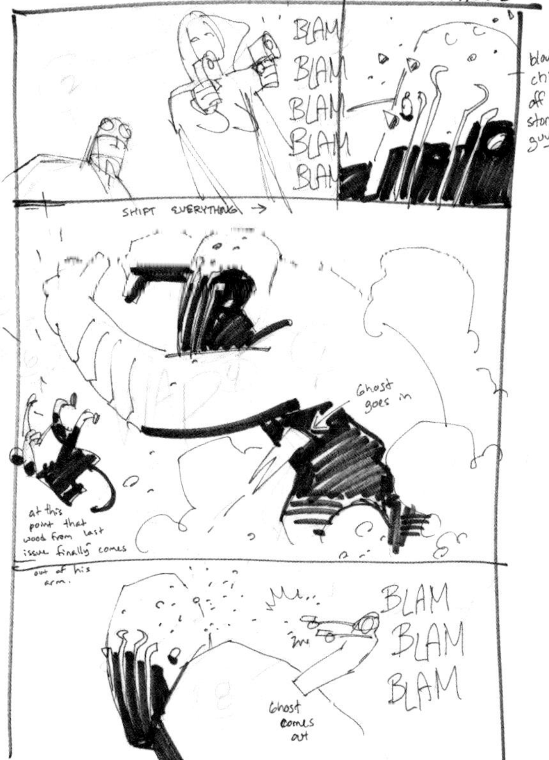

BLAM
BLAM
BLAM
BLAM
BLAM
SHIFT EVERYTHING →
Ghost goes in
at this point that wood from last issue finally comes out of his arm.
BLAM
BLAM
BLAM
Ghost comes out

blow chips off stone guy

HELLBOY · GHOST Issue 2 PAGE 17

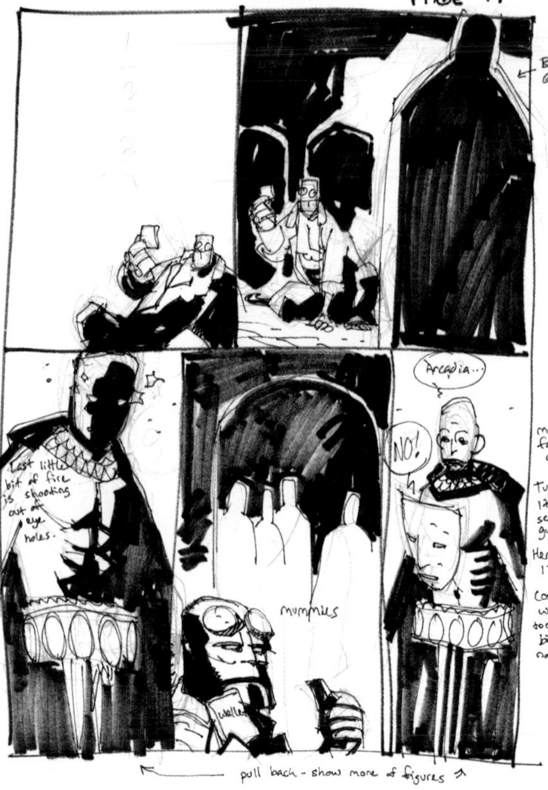
Bad Guy
Arcadia...
NO!
Last little bit of fire is shooting out of eye holes.
mummies
wallet
mask falls off.
Turn into little screaming guy
Herbert 1220
Costume way too big now.
pull back - show more of figures

HELLBOY · GHOST Issue 2 Page 18

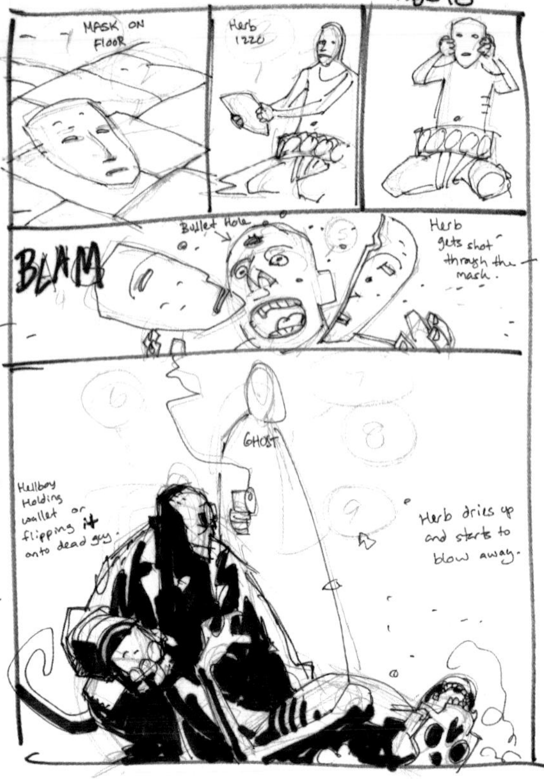
MASK ON FLOOR
Herb 1220
Bullet Hole
BLAM
Herb gets shot through the mask.
GHOST
Hellboy Holding wallet or flipping it onto dead guy.
Herb dries up and starts to blow away.

HELLBOY · GHOST Issue 2 Page 19

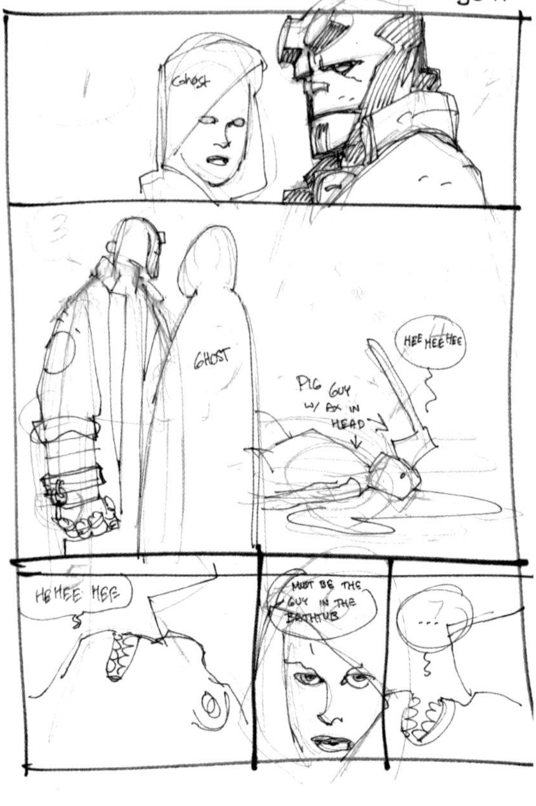
Ghost
GHOST
HEE HEE HEE
PIG GUY W/ AX IN HEAD
HE HEE HEE
MUST BE THE GUY IN THE BATHTUB
...?

HELLBOY · GHOST Issue 2 Page 20

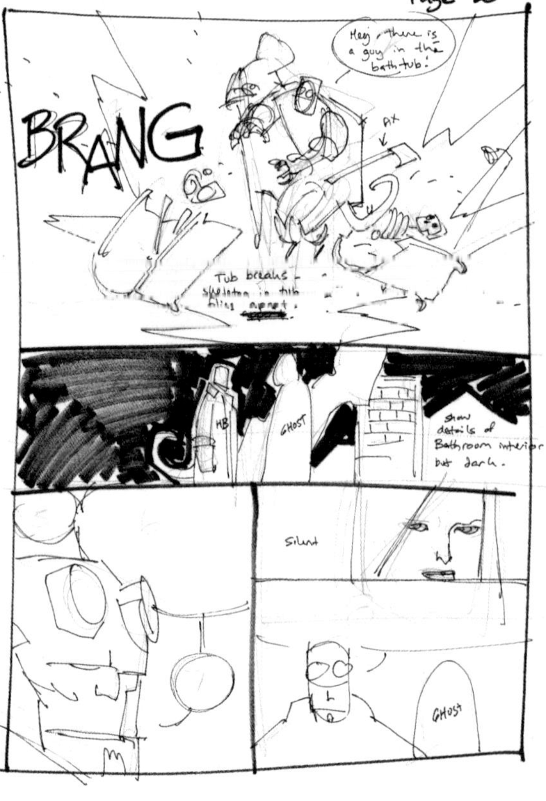
Hey, there is a guy in the bath tub!
AX
BRANG
Tub breaks -
HB
GHOST
show details of Bathroom interior but dark.
Silent
GHOST

HELLBOY

by MIKE MIGNOLA

To find a comics shop in your area,
call 1-888-266-4226
For more information or to order direct:
• On the web: darkhorse.com
• E-mail: mailorder@darkhorse.com
• Phone: 1-800-862-0052
Mon.–Fri. 9 AM to 5 PM Pacific Time

DARK HORSE COMICS *drawing on your nightmares*™
darkhorse.com

ALSO FROM DARK HORSE BOOKS

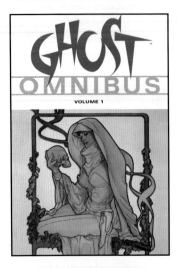

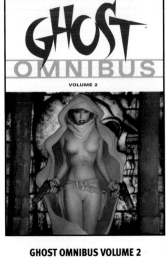

GHOST
OMNIBUS
VOLUME 1

GHOST OMNIBUS VOLUME 1
Written by Eric Luke
Art by Adam Hughes, Terry Dodson, Scott Benefiel, Matt Haley, and others

Someone brutally murdered reporter Elisa Cameron, but back from the grave as the spectral avenger Ghost, Elisa intends to find out who killed her and why . . . and grab a double dose of .45-caliber retribution. But Ghost's journey to the truth follows a dark, twisted path, and the revelations she unearths may lead not to redemption, but damnation.

ISBN 978-1-59307-992-5 | $24.99

GHOST
OMNIBUS
VOLUME 2

GHOST OMNIBUS VOLUME 2
Written by Eric Luke
Art by Ivan Reis, Doug Braithwaite, and John Bolton

Death is a lot less peaceful than it used to be, and infinitely more dangerous—at least for Elisa Cameron. Being a ghost is no protection from the dark forces that infest Arcadia, which are out to prove that even a ghost can be killed! *Ghost Omnibus* Volume 2 features over three hundred story pages of the spectral avenger, created by some of the top talents in comics.

ISBN 978-1-59582-213-0 | $24.99

ERIC POWELL & KYLE HOTZ
BILLY THE KID'S
OLD TIMEY ODDITIES

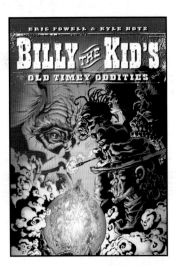

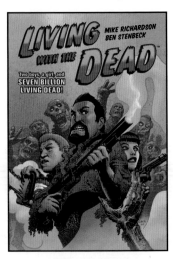

BILLY THE KID'S OLD TIMEY ODDITIES
Written by Eric Powell and Steve Niles
Art by Kyle Hotz

From the Eisner Award–winning creator of *The Goon* comes an over-the-big-top horror romp pitting outlaw legend Billy the Kid and a band of circus "freaks" against the evil machinations of the nefarious Dr. Frankenstein!

ISBN 978-1-59307-448-7 | $13.99

LIVING WITH THE DEAD
MIKE RICHARDSON
BEN STENBECK
Two boys, a girl, and
SEVEN BILLION
LIVING DEAD!

LIVING WITH THE DEAD
Written by Mike Richardson
Art by Ben Stenbeck and Richard Corben

From the mind of Mike Richardson, creator of *The Mask* and *The Secret*, comes this hilariously frightening tale of best buddies Straw and Whip, who have lived through a plague that's left the world with seven billion brain-hungry zombies.

ISBN 978-1-59307-906-2 | $9.99

AVAILABLE AT YOUR LOCAL COMICS SHOP OR BOOKSTORE! • To find a comics shop in your area, call 1-888-266-4226.
For more information or to order direct, visit darkhorse.com or call 1-800-862-0052 Mon.–Fri. 9 AM to 5 PM Pacific Time.

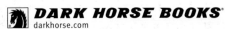

DARK HORSE BOOKS
darkhorse.com